Portland Rock Climbs

A Climber's Guide to Northwest Oregon

by Tim Olson

printed by
Book Crafters
Chelsea, MI

Cover Photo: Walter Anyan on E. Pluribus Pinhead (5.11D), by Dave Sowerby.

ISBN 0-9635660-0-8

Published and distributed by:
Tim Olson
Piton Press
Portland, Oregon

Printed by Book Crafters
Chelsea, Michigan

Warning

The sole purpose of this guide is to acquaint climbers with the local crags. Rock climbing does contain certain inherent dangers. Those who will venture onto the routes described herein should be thoroughly familiar with the use of modern rock equipment and techniques, and also be aware of the hazards of the sport. The author of this book makes no guarantees whatsoever about the condition of fixed bolts, pitons, slings, trails, etc. This guide is not a substitute for competent training and experience. The user of this book assumes full responsibility for their own safety.

Contents

Preface

Nearly a decade has passed since a comprehensive study of Portland's major climbing areas has been published. Since 1984, new and exciting cliffs such as The Madrone Wall have been discovered and thoroughly explored by climbers, bringing about a virtual explosion of route climbing activity.

Certain well-known crags like Broughton Bluff, have once again been catapulted forward into today's limelight through climber resurgence. This 'latest rage' of information continues to rapidly expand with each passing day.

The surge can surely be associated with today's generation of climber and their views (ethos). They bring new methods such as rappel-bolting, top-roping and are viable assets to the climbing community. I hope you will benefit from this long awaited and desperately needed testimony of information.

Certainly, there has been a tremendous influx of new climbers onto the local scene. This growth in our community can be directly attributed to several common factors.

First, there has been a trend towards outdoor sports activities (such as climbing, mountaineering and skiing) locally and nationally for health and fitness reasons.

Next, businesses such as the Portland Rock Gym, The Mazamas, CCC climbing program, and other outdoor organizations all have been good assets, in that the experience needed to climb can be learned there.

Third, through the successful marketing of guidebooks, magazines and other literature, many people have become readily attracted to the sport of climbing.

In a subtle way, easy access to all of our local crags has also helped to strengthen this community of climbers.

For those areas discussed in detail in the following chapters all are within 20 miles of Portland except Beacon Rock, which is but 29 miles distant.

The first Oregon guidebook to put forth a compilation of climbing history and route statistics was a series of publications (in the 1970's) called **"A Climbers Guide to Oregon"** by Nicholas Dodge. The book contains a wealth of interesting content from the earlier years of climbing and mountaineering. Even though the guide contained occasional misleading descriptions, it nonetheless described many fascinating areas in Oregon, from Beacon Rock to the Menagerie, some of which have yet to see another update.

In 1984, after years of prolific mountaineering and rock climbing, Jeff Thomas compiled and published the **"Oregon Rock"** guide. Chock full of excellent photos and descriptions, the broad scope of the guide allowed for good marketing success, while focusing needed attention on two of Portland's local crags, Broughton Bluff and Beacon Rock. A virtual avalanche of route climbing information from the 1980s quickly outpaced the guide since it was not updated. To this day the casual reader still finds humor in the appendix section describing the often 'unusual' styles of ascent by known local climbers.

Another book, the **"Rocky Butte Quarry Guide,"** published in 1987 by Robert McGown and Mike Pajunas, contributed equally toward bridging the gap in crag information. The book suffered from a narrow scope and inadequate topographs, yet has made a reasonable comeback via an updated edition in 1992.

In all, the previous guidebook authors have helped immensely to focus the necessary community interest toward our local crags.

The primary aim of **Portland Rock Climbs** is to focus on the logistics of five crags: **Broughton Bluff, Rocky Butte, The Madrone Wall, Carver Bridge Cliff** and **Beacon Rock**. Specifically encompassed are sections on the Seasons, Equipment, Ethics, Topograph Maps, Route Descriptions (i.e., ratings and quality) and photographs. Less emphasis will be placed on routes of minor quality or interest, or on crags that are obscure and dirty beyond the norm.

The author suggests that climbers take the time to read the chapter on ethical standards and practices in the Introduction. These principles are often encouraged with vigilance, and feigned ignorance is not suggested.

For that special breed, you (after years of waiting) will discover in the final chapters a comprehensive study of "Winter Ice Climbing" in the Columbia Gorge. To some of you, this may seem an incredibly trivial sport compared to rock climbing, yet the exponential increase of ice climbers as well as the presently available data has necessitated inclusion. This sport has gained interest as well due to the easy access afforded to many of the ice routes in the Gorge. Everyone, climber and hiker, should go see this staggering yet delicate wonder of the Columbia Gorge during winter ice conditions. It is spectacular, even though the season may be short! Read the chapter and grip those ice tools.

Last, but not least, you will find a helpful chapter showing enticing alternatives for your climbing destination. The section is a colorful and quality mix of crags offering rock climbing in pleasant, low-altitude wooded settings as well as pinnacle or cliff climbing at higher altitudes. Most of these places are within an approximately 100 mile radius of Portland, while many are located along the Mt. Hood scenic highway.

I'd like to thank the indispensible number of individuals who have helped toward the success of this guidebook. I am personally grateful and indebted to Nicholas Dodge, Jeff Thomas, Robert McGown and Mike Pajunas for having laid the groundwork upon which this guide is founded.

Thanks to Chuck Buzzard for the route information at the Madrone Wall, to Mark Cartier for his frankness about Beacon Rock, and to Nathan Charleton, Chad Franklin, Gary Rall, Scott Tracy, Dave Sowerby, Wayne Wallace, Greg Lyon, and Steve Mrazek for freely sharing their detailed first ascent particulars.

Terri Walker has worked with dedication and thoroughness throughout the editing, typesetting and graphics phase of this demanding project. Your ideas have certainly improved the quality of this guide.

The author would like to thank R. McGown, W. Wallace, D. Sowerby, G. Murray, M. Smelser, Keith Gover, and Jim Apilado for the inspiring climbing action photos.

Of the endless hours and late nights needed to complete this book, Cindy my Love, your patience and perseverence will forever shine through. This book is dedicated to You, Tweeder Deeder, and Murpharbian Dinard.

Remember, tradition and history are essential to all guidebooks and their success.

INTRODUCTION

City of Roses and city of rock. Portland is conveniently situated at the northern tip of the Willamette Valley, and is blessed with a fine mixture of sunshine and rain. Much is offered by way of excitement to the dedicated rock climber. With over 500 route climbing options, Portland may be the only large city in the Pacific Northwest that offers easily available rock climbing within 20 miles. This and a centralized location make it a great starting out point for well known destinations such as Smith Rock, Index, Squamish or City of Rocks.

The local favorite rock climbing crags are composed of dense grayish and often angular basalt, formed from the Boring Lava Flow formation (originating from Chamberlain Hill). The exception of course is Beacon Rock, which is columnar jointed basalt and formed from the core of an ancient volcano. The flows were deposited upon the Troutdale conglomerates (rounded gravels) during the Plio-Pliestocene age approximately 7 million years ago, then subsequently eroded to the present outcrops and crags. Many of the buttes near Gresham and Damascus as well as the numerous hills near Oregon City are made up of Boring Lavas. Rocky Butte (in east-central Portland) and Mt. Sylvania, Mt. Tabor and Mt. Scott contain ash-cinders and buried flows of this same series. The flows had insufficient time to cool and resulted in large, angular and well vegetated rock walls on which we climb.

Geology aside, it is worth noting that a staggering amount of gardening (route cleaning) has gone into the development of the local crags. Rappel-cleaning is often necessary to remove extensive amounts of dirt, moss and loose rock before a "clean" ascent can be made. Even the base of these cliffs were at one time choked with dense undergrowth that made passage difficult if not impossible. Years of increased climber presence and personal individual efforts have helped greatly to upgrade and maintain these crags. Through community involvement it is hoped that the future generation of climbers will learn to focus on the trail and route maintenance (such as wirebrushing). The Oregon rains do erode the narrow trails, invite rust corrosion on fixed gear and promote moss growth.

Climbing Season and Access Info

Though the winters, in recent years, thanks to continued efforts by the locals, virtual year-round climbing has gained a foothold. Two of the finest winter cragging areas are Broughton Bluff (near Troutdale) and the Madrone Wall (on the Clackamas River). Both face southwest to attract the winter sunshine and are also well protected from strong easterly winds; particularly at Broughtons where the notorious Gorge winds howl. Climatic conditions in Western Oregon are generally mild and temperate. Summer months will average in the 80's with short peaks of unusually hot weather (90-110°), while the winters may average in the 40's to 50's. Frequent heavy rains occur in November or March through April, sometimes leaving the crags saturated and dripping with moisture.

At **Broughton Bluff**, during the spring, summer and fall, poison oak and nettles must be contended with as well as the heat. True, these are a nuisance, but increased foot traffic has kept most of it pushed back, especially near the popular routes. Summers here are quite muggy, yet it's easy to find shaded routes or visit on cool overcast days. Or better still, focus your energy on other exciting areas like **Beacon Rock**, where the breezes of the Columbia Gorge prevail or **Carver Bridge Cliff**, where the shades of time dominate.

Along the lower Clackamas River basin, the **Madrone Wall** (a.k.a. Red Bluff) and **Carver Bridge Cliff** together have achieved the long sought after year-round climbing status. The Madrone Wall's southwest orientation allows easy reception to warm winter sunshine sometimes reaching 65-70° F in January or February. When the month of May arrives, the Madrone Wall

1

becomes downright stifling. Throughout the summer it's often best to climb here in the early morning hours 'til the heat builds up, then (after a stop at the Carver General Store for jo-jos and eggrolls) hike up to Carver Bridge Cliff for the afternoon. Other minor setbacks at the Madrone Wall are wasps, who love sunshine and warm ledges. They are much less active in the winter and usually congregate only on certain areas of sunny rock. Once you are aware of them, you tend to *almost* forget they're there.

Ah! Poison oak – the dirty word to local climbers. It's everywhere! It has been pulled out, cut down and even sprayed, but the stuff continues to proliferate. Fortunately, it is at its worst only from May to September (the hot months). Then there are the ants. A route has even been dedicated in their honor: "Ant Abuse." During the summer you can often see trails of these critters travelling out of one crack across the wall to another. They do attack and they do bite, but then again, during the long winter months (the best season) the ants are not active.

Aside from these minor environmental nuisances, the Madrone Wall is a tremendous crag with many beautiful trees, brilliant reddish-orange rock walls and a spectacular view of the Clackamas Valley. Well worth the visit. (Note: the reddish-orange color is due to the leaching of oxides and water that drip down and stain the rock.) As the shattered rock and rusting, twisted hulks of debris below the Shining Wall indicate, this used to be a gravel quarry. Originally called the Hardscrabble Rock Quarry, it is now under public domain and jurisdiction of Clackamas County. Due notice is hereby given: it is expected of all climbers who frequent this cliff to maintain a clean environment and respect the county laws.

Carver Bridge Cliff is a series of small cliffs of intricate beauty. The cool, perpetually shaded basalt walls have long "aged" beneath dense layers of dirt and moss. Together, the wirebrush and bolts have turned this once formidable obstacle into a challenging climbing area and dream come true. Seasonally speaking, mid-April through October is prime, with pleasant mornings and cool shade throughout the extended warm summer months.

The following guidelines apply to all visitors to Carver Bridge Cliff. It is privately owned. To gain access you must sign a liability release waiver, obtainable at the Portland Rock Gym or through the local Climbers Association. When visiting the crag you must carry picture I.D. and the Carver Club "button." Do not litter (cigarette butts included) or vandalize, no excessive noise, respect all rights of the owner, including right of privacy, and be vigilant concerning others who may trespass or cause problems. Please do nothing to jeopardize the privilege to climb here. This wonderful little crag in the woods initially began as the pride and joy of just a few, but now with increased climber presence it has become a favorite recreation spot for many.

The great basaltic monolith of the Columbia Gorge, **Beacon Rock** is situated among some of the most vivid scenery in the Pacific Northwest. Frequent harsh winds and cold temperature keep Beacon void of climber traffic in the winter, even though sporadic climbing days do exist. For example, the first ascent of Blownout was done on January 19-20, 1969 under adverse weather conditions. What a feat! The best months to climb here are mid-April through September. You're probably asking yourself, why do climbers come to Beacon Rock? Because it offers steep, highly sustained, full and multi-pitch, technically demanding climbs of almost unlimited styles and ratings. This *is* bold climbing! And for that very reason it is not a training ground for novices, but a place where competent leadership skills can be honed. Beacon's easiest route is 5.7 (and multi-pitch), while the majority of routes range from 5.10 to 5.11+. To date the most difficult climbs established are 5.12+ with virtually unlimited potential beyond that!

There are several objective dangers. Occasional accidents and countless close calls due to stonefall have occurred. The rockfall is often loosed from above and near the west side hikers' trail at a point above Dod's Jam. Irresponsible sightseers are usually at fault. While near the Southeast Face, the careless climber on Grassy Ledges, along with poor rope management (dragging through loose rocks) has continued to be a serious detriment to people near the base of the cliff. Because of this, hard hats are recommended for safety. When resting at the base of the cliff, sit under trees or close to the wall. And if other parties are known to be above you (on the Southeast Corner or Right Gull), take the precaution and move a safe distance away from their area of activity. The other problem is poison oak. Usually, long pants will suffice. Learn to recognize the three-leaf pattern and color. Several routes are virtually unclimbable because of the oak, such as Left Gull and a few climbs on the west face up left of the Arena of Terror.

Aside from these simple distractions, Beacon Rock has produced routes of the highest standard, easily taking first place (locally) in bold, technical natural protection climbs. Nearly all of the dihedral systems have been aided (pinned) in the 1960's and 70's. During the following decade these aid routes were free climbed at surprisingly moderate ratings, thus establishing some of the finest stemming and jamming problems in the region. In the mid to late 1980's extreme, partly-bolted routes became the rage of the active climbers. This proliferation of activity has given the local Portland climber better reason to visit this black stallion of the Columbia Gorge.

Rocky Butte Quarry is a unique crag located in Northeast Portland just off I-205. Easily accessible to the public, this has become a great place to top-rope or teach novices the sport. As the name implies, the place was a rock quarry prior to 1956, but the forests have now grown around this area, enveloping it in a natural, shaded environment, great for 3-season activity. Numerous persons have visited this north-facing crag during the 1960's and 70's to practice their free and aid climbing skills, and only a few known ascents remain from that period. It was not until mid to late 1980's when the crag was eventually explored and thoroughly tapped for climber use. Several areas, such as Video Bluff, Toothpick Wall and Breakfast Cracks have become traditional classics to all who visit. If you can overlook the trashy outer appearance, the broken glass, paint, and litter, then you will begin to see the inner beauty of this favorite haunt.

Ratings

The Yosemite Decimal System (YDS) is the standard method for rating the difficulty of climbs in Oregon as well as across the U.S. This system is subdivided into three sections: **Overall Difficulty** (Grade), **Free Climbing Difficulty** (Class), and **Aid Difficulty**.

For the longer routes an **Overall Difficulty** rating (Roman numerals I through VI) denotes how long it will take an average party. For example, a Grade I, virtually no time at all; Grade II, only a few hours; Grade III, half a day; Grade IV, most of a day; Grade V can be climbed in one long day if the climbers are experienced and fast; Grade VI requires multiple days to ascend. It is purely subjective, though. Some climbers may be able to climb very efficiently on two Grade V routes while others may barely manage a Grade III without bivouacking. Most of the climbs within this guide fall between the Grades I and III.

Free Climbing Difficulty, or technical free climbing, is rated on an ascending scale from 5.0 (the easiest climbs requiring ropes and belays) to 5.13, which is currently the most extreme climbing done to date in Portland. This scale is open-ended to allow for future routes of increasing difficulty. If a particular pitch contains a series of moves of the same difficulty, a higher rating is assigned (or should be!). Further "subgrading" is promoted to separate the "easiest" 5.10's and the "hardest" 5.10's by using the letters A,B,C and D. A recent trend in free-climbing at the local crags is the downrating of routes because of overfamiliarity. As a person repeats an ascent several times, he or she may feel it is easier than when first climbed. Thus to "wire" a climb through memorizing occurs, and it is often incorrectly downrated. The best solution, naturally, is to rate according to an on-sight or "flash" lead by a person unfamiliar with the route in question.

Aid Difficulty. The letter A followed by the numbers 0 through 6 indicate the aid difficulty.

A-0 pendulum, shoulder stand, tension rest or a quick move up by pulling on protection.

A-1 placements still hold charging rhinos.

A-2 is more difficult to place with good protection.

A-3 involves marginal placements and potential for a short fall.

A-4 has frequent marginal pro and it holds only body weight.

A-5 entails enough marginal pro to risk a good 50-60 foot fall.

A-6 involves full pitch leads of A-4 and groundfall "zipper" potential.

Aid ratings are unlike the free grades in that they reflect both technical placement difficulty and how a pitch is protected. It is a closed rating system that reflects difficulty only in terms of security and does not take into account modern advances in aid climbing. Should an aid climb subsequently be free climbed, the aid rating will be dropped and the free or "clean" rating will be given. And though aid climbing (the use of pitons, skyhooks, bashies and other rudiments) has diminished in recent years, there is still considerable respect for this historically time honored sport. Unless otherwise noted under route descriptions, the established free climbs do not require pitons or hammer. Do respect all of the permanently fixed pitons and bolts by leaving them in place for others who follow.

For those routes requiring a "seriousness" rating, they are as follows:

PG-13: specific protection required; otherwise, serious fall potential possible. This will include routes with minor runouts where little or no protection is possible for short distances.

R: Definite serious fall potential; may involve questionable or poor protection; serious injury likely.

X: Ground fall potential; very poor to no protection available; serious or fatal injury possible.

Be aware that the seriousness ratings in this guidebook are not the final gospel concerning a route's dangerous or extreme nature. Even routes without this rating may still qualify if there is a lack of information to verify the seriousness. Climbers need to be aware that any route may be inherently dangerous. A route may seem perfectly safe to one climber while unsafe to another. So please, proceed with caution and at your own risk.

The "star" or quality rating used throughout this book is designed to allow visiting climbers to selectively choose the interesting or more aesthetic climbs. This is a highly subjective system, for many of the lesser or unstarred routes may certainly be worthy of attention. There will also be redundant routes, some of which deserve nothing short of dust and obscurity.

No Stars: Average quality route.

One Star (*): Good quality route, recommended.

Two Stars (**): Excellent route, good position, quality climbing, sound rock, highly recommended.

Three Stars (***): Highest quality, should not be missed in a lifetime!

A wider variety of enjoyable climbs will be starred and some of these will probably deflate the egos of bolt-loving gymnastic climbers. Of these starred routes not all will be bolted face climbs: a good selection will be crack climbs, several will be short but worthy, a few will be two routes connected together to create a finer quality climb. The routes are unique to climb as well as interesting to the eye and they vary in rating from 5.6 to 5.14 (if such a rating exists in Portland). Remember that there are superb multi-pitch 5.9 crack climbs.

To bring the quality rating closer to home, the author will *not* be comparing the "star" routes of one crag to another. Specifically, the quality climbs at Madrone Wall will vary considerably from the quality routes at Beacon Rock or Smith Rock. Thus,

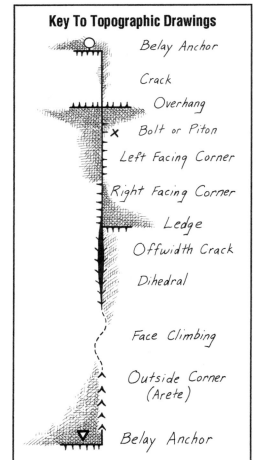

Key To Topographic Drawings

Belay Anchor

Crack

Overhang

Bolt or Piton

Left Facing Corner

Right Facing Corner

Ledge

Offwidth Crack

Dihedral

Face Climbing

Outside Corner (Arete)

Belay Anchor

when visiting a particular crag the "starred" route will represent the more favorable, interesting routes at that cliff only! The following chart shows the relative relationship between four other international ratings most often used.

INTERNATIONAL GRADE SCALE

Decimal	UIAA	Numerical	Australian	French
5.0	III		4	
5.1	III+		5	
5.2	IV-	3a	6	
5.3	IV	3b	7	
5.4	IV+	3c	8, 9	
5.5	V-	4a	10, 11	
5.6	V	4b	12, 13	4c
5.7	V+	4c	14, 15	5a
5.8	VI-		16	5b
5.9	VI	5a	17	5c
5.10a	VI+	5b	18	6a
5.10b	VII-		19	
5.10c	VII	5c	20	6b
5.10d			21	
5.11a	VI+	6a	22	6c
5.11b	VIII-		23	
5.11c	VIII	6b	24	7a
5.11d	VIII+		25	
5.12a	IX-	6c	26	7b
5.12b	IX		27	
5.12c	IX+	7a	28	
5.12d			29	7c
5.13a			30	
5.13b	X-		31	8a
5.13c				
5.13d			32	
5.14				8b

Equipment

Climbing equipment has improved dramatically over the last ten years. The advent of Friends, RP's, Curved Stoppers and Dolomite rock shoes have had a dramatic effect on the feasibility of both new and existing routes. For the climber visiting the crags, many of the routes up to 5.11 take excellent natural protection (outside the occasional fixed pin or bolt). Only when the rating exceeds 5.11 have numerous bolts and pins become necessary. At Broughton's you would be at an advantage to bring a selection of the following: QD's, small to large wired stoppers (1/4" to 1 1/2"), Friends (1"-3"), (or Hexcentrics), TCU's, runners and a few loose carabiners. Specialized pro such as RP's or Steel Nuts may also be necessary on some climbs. This average rack of gear if there is such a thing would also apply at the Madrone Wall and Beacon Rock. Although at Beacon, duplicates or triplets in specific sizes may be necessary for safe passage. At Carver Bridge Cliff a large number of routes are bolted, so a lean rack of gear should suffice.

For the climbing enthusiast who is uninformed of the latest in pro, several stores are available in Portland that offer competitive prices: REI at 1798 Jantzen Beach Center (283-1300) or at 7410 SW Bridgeport, Tigard (624-8600) and Oregon Mountain Community located at 60 NW Davis (227-1038). They offer the greatest selection of gear and are open 7 days a week. There are other sources available locally though limited where new and/or used equipment can be purchased.

Ethics

A clarification of local opinions and standards must be put forth. The following consists of generally accepted climbing views and practices. The author would like to ask climbers to be responsible in preserving this valuable resource or should consider finding another activity to occupy themselves. The rock is all we have.

Contemporary climbing views consist of two forces: style and ethics. Style is how you climb on the rock while ethics are what you do to the rock. In retrospect, present trends such as hangdogging, rappel inspection, rehearsing, top-roping, pre-protection and free-soloing are styles. Bolting, chiseling holds, gardening or scarring the rock is an ethic. Poor style, at worse, erodes a climber's personal integrity; bad ethics brutally violate the rock and as a result undermines the foundation and the essence of climbing.

Gardening and pre-inspection are standard accepted ethics on much of Western Oregon's lowland crags. Liberal amounts of foliage and soil hamper true efforts for ground-up leading. The debris is thoroughly gardened before a "clean" ascent can be done. Two of our local crags, Broughton's and Beacon Rock, yield a richer and more exciting earlier history of on-sight ground up ascents such as aid climbing or easier free routes.

Though not a serious problem in the past, as several of the local crags receive further limited development, the cramming of new, meaningless, contrived routes will certainly escalate. Keep routes unique, and try not to lose the true identity of those original climbs. Refrain from the use of modular holds. Do not place new rappel anchors or more fixed gear (bolts) on established routes without prior permission. If old 1/4" bolts or rusty pitons need replacing for safety reasons, either consult the original ascentionists if feasible or the inner community of climbers. Many of the old aid routes are now free climbs and should be ascended in "clean" style in the future without the use of pitons or bolts. Creative route crafting (chiseling) is definitely not accepted. Chopping holds to "improve" on nature is arrogant and in poor taste. People will certainly continue to climb at increasingly higher standards in the years to come.

Small groups of active climbers often have new routes under development. Respect these "projects in progress." It is their personal tightrope on which they walk and when others jump to "steal" a project it creates ripples of agitation within the community.

Considered a godsend to some and to others a curse, the roto-powered drill (Bosch, Hilti, Ryobi, etc.) has most certainly transformed the sport of route development. This new generation of "route pioneers" with their roto-power in hand, literally take it to heart and mercilessly bolt without restraint. The turn of this magical roto-hammer has reduced time and effort needed into a small cloud of rock dust and electrons. Therefore, some restraint should be exercised in bolting. Not every route needs to be bolted or climbed. Basalt rock is nearly as hard as granite, and can require 20-30 minutes to hand-drill a 2 1/2" deep 3/8" bolt hole. The power drill is the weapon of this era, but may be the scourge of future generations. Ask yourself what impact this has on the environment. Enjoy the sport of climbing for its social and outdoor benefits by respecting others as well as the rock.

"Ethical rules protect the best efforts of the climbers who have gone before us, and protect the rock for the climbers who will come after us." (*Yosemite Climbs*, Meyers & Reid.)

Wayne Wallace leading Crash of the Titans (5.10C)

Broughton Bluff

Historically speaking, Broughton Bluff is the all-time original Portland crag. Approached by a few sturdy climbers in the late '50s and frequented throughout the '70s, this dark, moss-covered basalt bluff has yielded many time-honored classics which the modern climber can still enjoy.

Located along the eastern outskirts of Portland, afforded by simple access and tall, vertical walls, Broughton has made a natural and excellent year-round climbers park. Even today, individuals of all walks of life come here to learn the ropes of climbing, to build courage, as well as to test their limits.

The early ascents were often done via ground-up mixed aid and free climbing on the Hanging Gardens Wall or the North Face. One of the first to become established was the **Hanging Gardens** (5.10 A) route ascended by Bob Waring, John Wells, and Bruce Holcomb in 1965. Today it is considered a trade route classic. This climb stands as an honorable testament to those early days of exploratory aid climbing.

Perhaps the finest achievement at Broughtons took place in 1968 when Steve Strauch and John Haek ascended the North Face via the super classic and ever popular **Gandalf's Grip** (5.9+). Accurately described, this route is one of the best crack climbs of this rating at Broughton Bluff.

The 1970's heralded forth a small but active core of climbers who succeeded to establish many more routes. Jim Mayers, Gail Van Hoorn, Alan Campbell, Dave Jensen, Talbot Bielefeldt, Dean Fry and others opened the doors by aid climbing routes like **Peach Cling** (5.11 B), **Mr. Potato** (5. 11 B) and **Sesame Street** (5.9+), all of which were ascended in 1972; **Peer Pressure** (5.10 D) in 1973, **Face Not Friction** (5.11 D) in 1975 as well as **Classic Crack** (early 1970's). Pitons and pages of history still ring true through these climbers and their accomplishments.

The mid-1970's brought a subtle change as rock climbers pushed beyond the known standards, firmly establishing a whole new dimension of free climbing. Many of the older routes were ascended free without the use of direct aid. Even the new climbs were pushed beyond the 5.9 norm of yesteryear.

Red Eye (5.10 C) and **Sheer Stress** (5.10 A) were done in 1976; **Sandy's Direct** (5.10 C) and **Physical Graffiti** (5.10 D), a short, nasty roof problem, were put up in 1977. South from the Red Wall stands the superb cliff known as the Bat Wall, where **Superstition** (5.11 A) and **Hanging Tree** (5.10 D) broke new barriers here in 1977 as well. It was this massive and secluded wall that became the key to the next generation.

The climbers who were instrumental in the 1970's are Doug Bower, Monty Mayko, Bruce Casey, Robert McGown, Mike Smelser, Jeff Thomas, Ken Currens, Mark Cartier, Jay Kerr, Dan Foote and others. They put much effort forth to free climb the untapped routes of their time.

Afterwards nearly ten silent years descended upon Broughton Bluff with hardly the sound of a hammer ringing true. The summer of 1990, brought another breed of lycra clad climbers noticed a realm of blank space still to be touched and bolted. The powered roto-gun quickly unraveled the final mysteries of Broughton, bringing with it the life and song of 5.12.

The **Unnamed Aid Route** on the Bat Wall, after numerous free climbing attempts, was finally overcome. A name with *real* bite stood out: **Dracula** (5.12 A). A virtually endless series of climbs soon followed, some more precious than the richest diamond mines of Africa. **Bela Lugosi** (5.12 C), **Bad Omen (Got the Horse for My Saddle)** (5.12 B), and **Kashmir** (5.12 B) were all established in 1990. In 1991, **Heart of Darkness** (5.12 B) brought renewed interest to the Jungle Cliff, while **Bloodline** (5.12 B) continued the legacy in 1992 at the Bat Wall.

Gary Rall, Tim Olson, Wayne Wallace, Dave Sowerby, Jay Green and many others have continued to push the standards of the nineties. This decade has been a realization of their destiny.

Broughton Bluff is composed of 13 major and distinct walls, with six minor subcliffs scattered in between. Of the 13 larger cliffs, only nine will be detailed with topo maps. For these are the ones which contain the vast majority of established and accessible climbs. The others (such as Aerie Wall, Perihelion and Eclipse Wall) are located on or adjacent to private land and are less frequented. The nine are as follows, from left to right: the North Face, Hanging Gardens Wall, Red Wall, Bridge Cliff, Spring Rock, Bat Wall, Trinity Wall, Berlin Wall (originally known as Trident), Jungle Cliff and New Frontier Cliff.

Broughton Bluff is located off I-84 at the Lewis & Clark State Park exit east of Troutdale. Turn south at the T-intersection, drive beneath the railroad tracks and park in the State Park day use area. Walk south along the roadway to the steep hillside and follow the path that leads upward. Either take the path straight up to where it meets rock or follow the newer gentle grade path that angles up right to the Hanging Gardens Wall. The general line of descent for the North Face and Hanging Gardens Wall is down the third class ridge between these two walls.

Broughton Bluff

North Face

1. **Traffic Court** 5.9 ★
   60' Thin Pro to 2" TCU's suggested
   Start as for Gandalf's left variation and climb past a bolt to a stance. Ascend a vertical corner (piton) til it eases to a slab. Muscle over a final bulge directly above then step right to rejoin with Gandalf's Grip at the belay.

2. **Variation** 5.9+
   Pro to 1 1/2"
   Start up left from the cave past a bolt to a small ledge. Continue up the right leaning dihedral to rejoin the regular route.

3. **Gandalf's Grip** II 5.9+ ★★★
   Multi-pitch Pro to 3 1/2" TCU's or small wires suggested
   One of Broughton Bluff's super classic routes. Commence up steep ground to the right of the alcove past a fixed pin. Interesting crack climbing leads to small ledges then move up left (bolts) via sloping insecure smears (5.9+) to the Gollum's Hang fixed with a piton. Surmount the crux and belay. The second pitch continues up cracks through two small overhangs (5.8) then angles up right to a belay on a ledge. Above is an obvious offwidth. Climb this to the top and walk off or rappel from here to previous anchor.

4. **New Wave** III 5.11C
   30' 1st Pitch Pro to 3/4"
   A thin seam to the right of Gandalf's Grip start. The second pitch is A2 and ascends the upper cliff via a thin crack.

5. **Peach Cling** II 5.11 B (PG-13) ★★
   Multi-pitch Pro to 2", mostly small wires
   Excellent route. Starts 15 ft. right of Gandalf's. Layback up a desperate thin left-leaning tips flake until it ends in a shallow corner. Continue up to a poor belay on a ledge. Move up left via strenuous and off-balance moves (bolts) ending on a ledge and bolt belay (2nd anchor on Gandalfs). Continue up leftward on downsloping (pitons) smears (5.10) to the top. Walk off.

6. **Project** 5.12 ★★
   30' QD's and pro to 1 1/2"
   Excellent quality route ascending the center bulge on the North Face between Gandalf's Grip and Peach Cling. Joins with Risky Business. Either rappel from Gandalf's second belay anchor with two ropes or climb up and then walk off.

North Face Wall

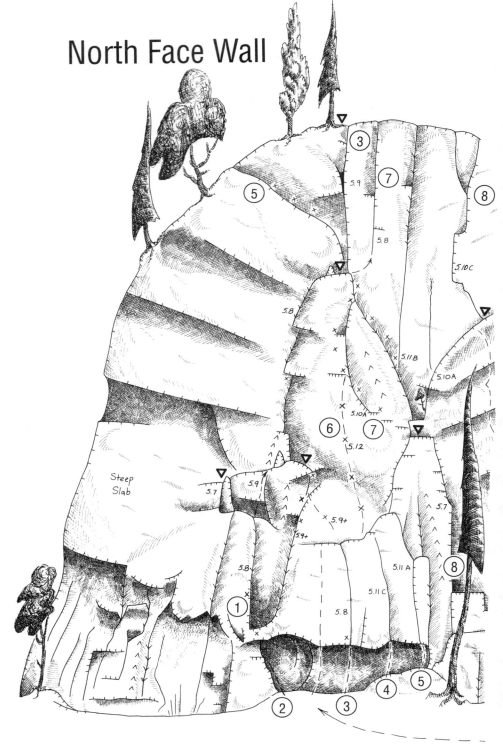

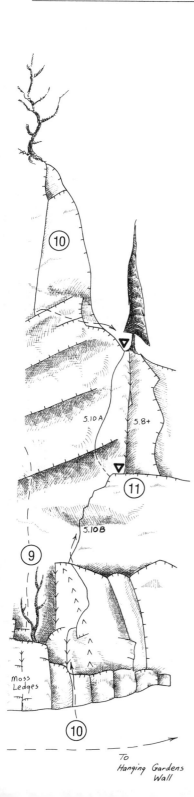

Moss
Ledges

To
Hanging Gardens
Wall

7. **Risky Business** 5.10 A (R) ★
40' QD's and pro to 1" Cams recommended.
Start at the first belay on Peach Cling. Step left
onto a sloping series of ledges (crux) passing
several bolts. Continue up good holds until able
to join with Peach Cling then to the belay anchor
on Gandalf's Grip. A surprisingly quality climb
of only moderate difficulty. The final pitch turns
right and around a spectacular corner to a
hidden jug, then ascends a crack dihedral
leading to the summit.

8. **Reckless Driver** II 5.10 C ★
Multi-Pitch Pro to 3" Cams or TCU's helpful
A good climb with variety and little traffic. Start
5' right of Peach Cling. Move up an easy corner
to a ledge then up a right-facing corner (5.6)
then leftward to the Peach Cling belay. Up to
the right is a bush. Thrash over the bush past a
crux (5.10 A) up an easy right angling ramp
system. Exit off down right to a large fir tree
(rappel) or from the top of the ramp, step left
then climb up a thin crack system (5.10 C) to
the summit.

9.

10. **Sweet Emotion** II 5.10 B (PG-13)
165' Pro to 2 1/2" Needs bolts on 2nd pitch
Unusual route on tricky pro. A little hard to
locate.

11. **American Graffiti** 5.8+
30' Pro to 2"
Climb the crack just below the large fir tree on
the west edge of the North Face.

Hanging Gardens Wall - Left Half

1. **Giant's Staircase** 5.6

2. **Edges and Ledges** 5.8 ★
30' 4 QD's

3. **The Sickle** 5.8 ★★★
60' Pro to 4"
This popular climb is the obvious curving
offwidth 30 ft. up the wall. Note: this area of
blocky ledges and numerous cracks makes an
excellent top-rope area for beginners who are
learning the ropes.

4. **The Hammer** 5.7 ★
60' Pro to 3"

5. **Prometheus Slab** 5.4
60' Pro to 3"
An original 1960's climb. Ascend an easy
corner near a tree to a ledge then up right via a
wide groove.

11

Hanging Gardens Wall
-Left Half

6. **Spud** 5.9
   60' Pro to 3"

7. **Tip City** 5.10 A ★★
   40' Pro to 1 1/2"
   An excellent thin crack. Locate two parallel cracks that join with Chockstone Chimney at a ledge. The left route is Tip City.

8. **Lean Years** 5.10 C ★
   40' Pro to 1 1/2"
   The right parallel crack. Both routes make excellent options to practice thin crack climbing.

9. **Hangover** 5.11
   40' (TR)
10. **Chockstone Chimney** 5.9
    80' Pro to 4"
    An original 1960's climb.
11. **Milestone** 5.7
    80' Pro to 3"

Hanging Gardens Wall - Right Half

12. **Loose Block Overhang** 5.9 ★★★
    165' Pro to 2 1/2"
    This very popular climb offers three optional starting points. You may climb easy steps to an offwidth (5.9) 25 ft. to the top of a large block. Bolt anchor. Or climb on the left via easy steps (5.7) and an offwidth move to the same anchor. Or, on the right ascend steep columns to a ledge then step up left via a short jam crack and left to the anchor. On the 2nd pitch, jam up a slightly overhung crack (crux) until it eases onto a ledge and bolt belay. Maneuver up a 5.8 left-facing corner, swing right onto a slab (piton) then up an easy blocky section and walk off left. Or exit up a left slanting crack (20') on steep rock and thin holds.

13. **Grace and Danger** 5.11 B (R)
    15' Pro to 1 1/2" Cams recommended
    Ascend the outside arete next to the 1st pitch of Loose Block.

14. **Slapfest** 5.12 B ★★
    40' 6 QD's and minor pro to 1"
    Climb the superb bolted face immediately right of Loose Block. A rather stiff, unusual route. Joins with Least Resistance.

15. **Least Resistance** 5.10 A
    30' Pro to 1"
    Start as for Hanging Gardens but step up left of the maple tree to ascend the left-leaning seam (fixed gear). Turn an outside corner and up to the bolt anchor on Loose Block.

16. **Dynamic Resistance** 5.10 D ★
    80' Pro to 1 1/2" Needs bolts
    Climb a strenuous dihedral between Least Resistance and Sandy's Direct. A good climb.

17. **Sandy's Direct** 5.10 C (PG-13) ★★
    165' Pro to 2" including small wires
    An exciting route and a must for everyone. Start as for Hanging Gardens route (stay left of the maple tree belay) but go straight up the vertical corner system 60 ft. (bolts) to blocky ledges then exit left to walk off.

18. **Face Not Friction** 5.11 D ★★
    60' QD's and minor pro to start
    Quality climbing, worth the effort. Up and left of the maple tree belay is a partially fixed face-seam problem on vertical rock. Climb this to a bolt anchor at a small ledge. Rappel or continue up left via steep, bushy cracks to an upper ledge, then exit left to hike down.

19. **Hanging Gardens** II 5.10 A or 5.6 A1 ★★
    Multi-pitch Pro to 1 1/2"
    One of the original Broughton favorites put up in 1965. Begins via numerous starts which lead up to the maple tree belay chain. From the tree move right 10 ft. across a slab, pull over a bulge, then right to an anchor for Mr. Potato. Traverse rightward along ledges then up a short corner and bolt belay on the left. Move back right and around a blind corner. Free (5.10 A) or aid (fixed pitons) diagonally right 20 ft. along the "bicycle path" to grassy ledges and an oak tree belay. Walk off.

20. **B.F.D.** 5.9 ★
    30' Pro to 1"

21. **Mr. Potato** 5.11 A
    40' Pro to 3/4"
    Unusual yet interesting climb. Start next to a tree stump and continue directly up a right facing vertical corner. Pull over several bulges (pins and bolts) to join with Hanging Gardens. Rappel.

22. **From Something to Nothing** 5.10 C
    40' Pro to 1" TCU's recommended

A good corner problem immediately right of Mr. Potato. Stem up corner until you can exit up right to join Hanging Gardens. Needs fixed gear.

23. **Fun in the Mud** 5.10 C
    40' Pro to 1"

24. **Circus Act** 5.10 C
    40' Pro to 1" including TCU's

25. **Shining Star** II 5.10 C ★
    140' Pro to 2"
    A great first pitch but the second pitch needs bolts. Located on the right side of Hanging Gardens Wall. Climb a crack on a mossy slab immediately right of a maple tree. Pull through the bulge (5.10 A) and continue up to an easy stance on sloping ledges. Step left to join Hanging Gardens route or step right and climb a broken crack system (5.10 C) via edges and corners (needs bolts). Cross over the "bicycle path" and ascend up a dark dihedral above. Walk off.

26. **Hung Jury** 5.10 D
    130' Pro to 2 1/2" including pitons

27. **Hang 'Em High** 5.10 B
    130' Pro to 2" Needs bolts

The following seven routes are located in a small amphitheatre above the second pitch of the Hanging Gardens route.

28. **Main Vein** 5.11 A   30'
    Pro to 2"
    This is the obvious prow right of Face Not Friction and above the maple tree belay. Follow the standard Hanging Gardens route past the tree, but at the old bees nest move up left around the corner by way of a crack. Once on the steep slab angle left then right and finish up a bolted arete until it joins with Sesame Street. Bolt belay.

29. **Sesame Street** 5.9+ ★★
    Pro to 3"
    Excellent but short. Climb the first pitch of Hanging Gardens. At the piton anchor for Mr. Potato step up left on easy ledges to a bolt belay. To your left is a slightly overhung zigzag jam crack. Climb this 15 ft. to another belay. Rappel with two ropes or traverse left along ledges to the descent trail.

30. **Demian** 5.10 D (PG-13) ★★★
    30' Pro to 3" TCU's optional
    Superb, strenuous route ascending a desperate overhanging crack.

31. **Endless Sleep** 5.11 A (R)
    30' Pro to 2"

32. **Peer Pressure** 5.10 C (R)
    30' Pro to 2'
    Poorly protected at the start but exciting stemming above. From the bolt anchor at the base of Scorpion Seams angle up left on slabs then ascend the overhung corner (pitons) to the top.

33. **Scorpion Seams** 5.12 D ★
    30' 6 QD's
    On the right face of the overhanging alcove is a bolted series of seams. Two separate starts lead to an extreme lunge move to a jug. A desperate but quality route.

34. **Black Prow** 5.11 B A-O
    30' Pro to 3" including pitons

Hanging Gardens Wall
- Right Half

Blocky and Loose
No Routes

5.8

5.8

(12)

5.10 C

5.11 A

(28)

5.11 D

(11)

5.7

5.9

(16)

5.10 C

5.10 C

(18)

5.10 A

(15)

(17)

Poison
Oak

Steep
Slab

5.7

5.9

(13)

5.8

(14)

5.11 B

5.12 B

5.9

5.9

5.6

5.6

(12)

(19)

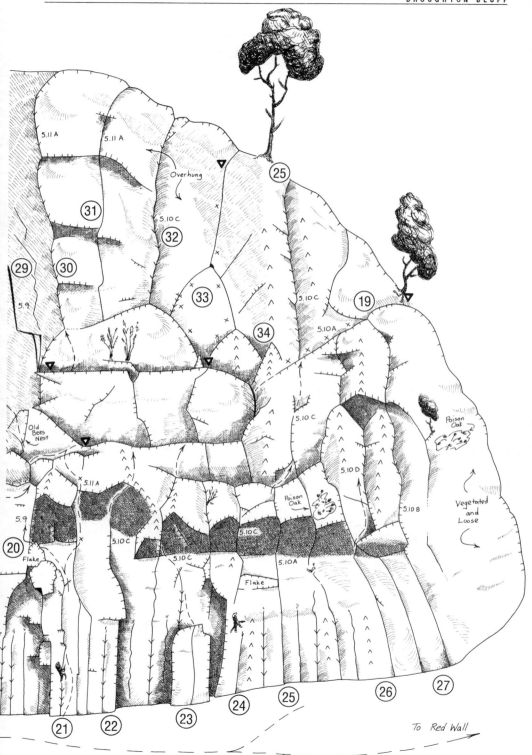

5.11 A

5.11 A

Overhung

(25)

(31)

5.10 C

(32)

(29)

(30)

5.9

(33)

5.10 C

(19)

(34)

5.10 A

Old
Bees
Nest

5.10 C

Poison
Oak

5.11 A

5.10 D

Poison
Oak

5.9

5.10 B

Vegetated
and
Loose

(20)

Flake

5.10 C

Poison
Oak

5.10 C

5.10 C

5.10 A

Flake

(26)

(27)

(24)

(25)

(21)

(22)

(23)

To Red Wall

Red Wall

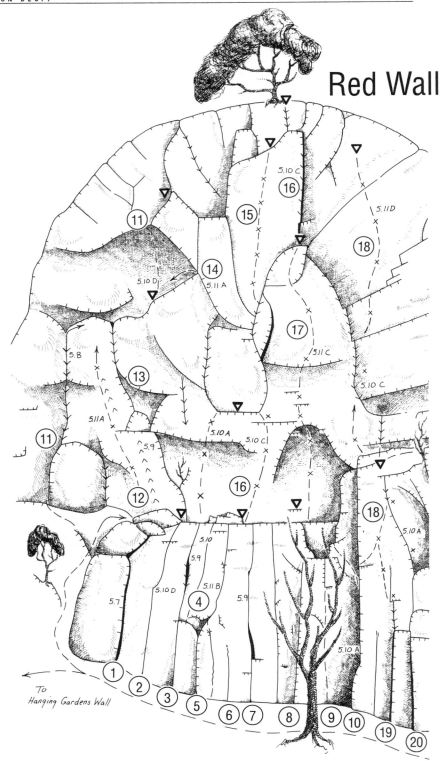

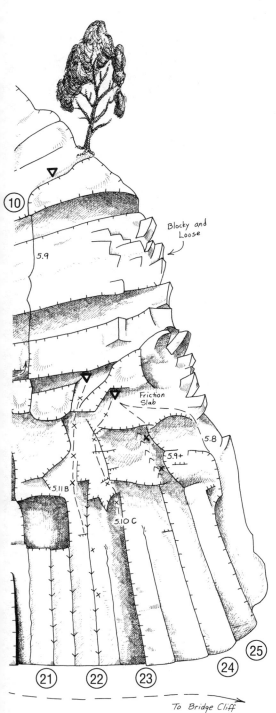

Blocky and Loose

5.9

Friction Slab

5.8

5.9+

5.11 B

5.10 C

⑩

㉑ ㉒ ㉓ ㉔ ㉕

Red Wall

1. **Arch de Triumph** 5.7
   20' Pro to 4"

2. **Arcturus** 5.10 D
   20' (TR)

3. **Anastasia** 5.9
   25' (TR)
   Climb a thin crack to a flared crux problem.

4. **Dead Bones** 5.10+
   25' (TR)

5. **On the Loose** 5.11 A ★★
   30' (TR)
   An excellent top-rope problem left of Classic Crack

6. _____ 5.13
   30' (TR)

7. **Classic Crack** 5.9+ ★★★
   30' Pro to 2"
   That's exactly what it is. A beautiful hand/finger crack that splits a smooth wall. Can be top-roped by scrambling up an access trail to the left.

8. **Thai Stick** 5.10 D ★★
   30' (TR)
   Two variations exist, one a little harder than the other. A rather poor name for a unique problem.

9. **Mr. Bentley** 5.11+ ★★
   30' (TR)
   Remarkable route; physically exciting.

10. **Sheer Stress** II 5.10 A (PG-13) ★★★
    Multi-pitch Pro to 2 1/2"
    Very popular, quality route. One of the ten super classics. Commence up the shallow left-facing corner (crux) 15 ft. right of Classic Crack. Climb up until it eases then turn an odd corner right to an anchor. Belay. Move right to a semi-detached block (maple tree) then climb straight up the hand crack (5.9+) until possible to exit right on good holds to a ledge and bolt anchor. Rappel with 2 ropes.

    The following routes are located generally above Classic Crack or Sheer Stress and can be accessed by most of the previous routes on the Red Wall.

11. **Physical Graffiti** II 5.10 D ★★★
    Multi-pitch Pro to 2"

A fascinating route highlighted by a hand jam roof problem. Move up an easy dihedral (5.7) on the left corner of Red Wall and above Arch De Triumph. Upon reaching a roof traverse right (bushes) to a ledge and bolt belay. Jam the overhang! The climb eases onto a steep crack and an anchor. Rappel or finish up one of the upper variations (5.10 A and dirty).

12. **Habitual Ritual** 5.11 A
    30' 4 QD's and minor pro to 2"

13. **Physical Direct** 5.9
    30' Pro to 2" TCU's recommended

14. **Hit the Highway** 5.11 A ★
    30' Pro to 1 1/2"
    Good yet surprisingly harsh lead. Begin on the ledges next to the maple tree. Ascend directly up a steep bolted face (5.10 A) then move right to the Red Eye belay. Step right and up (5.10 A) a few moves until possible to move left to an ominous looking steep

Debi Applebaum following on E. Pluribus Pinhead (5.11 D)

corner. Climb this and exit left to join with Physical Graffiti or jam directly up a vertical crack to a ledge. Angle up left to a bolt belay. Rappel.

15. **Kashmir** 5.12 B ★★
    40' 5 QD's and minor pro to 2 1/2" (#5 Rock and 2 1/2" Friend)
    This superb line is located on the brilliant orange face in the upper amphitheatre. The route's quality is boosted tremendously when connected with Red Eye and Classic Crack. Ascend Red Eye approximately 30 ft. until possible to enter onto a steep bolted face on the left. Rappel from bolt anchors with 2 ropes unless you rappel to the Red Eye anchor.

16. **Red Eye** II 5.10 C ★★
    Multi-Pitch   Pro to 2 1/2" (1st pitch is 4 QD's)
    A very popular route, especially the first pitch. Lead Classic Crack or start at the ledge above Classic, and climb a bolted face past a round red "eye" to a bolt anchor on a ledge to your left. Belay, then step right and up a crack system to easier ground. Belay at stance. Finish up a wide offwidth corner (5.10 C) with numerous edges. Exit left then up to the tree. Rappel with 2 ropes or walk off.

17. **Critical Mass** 5.11 C ★★★
    80' 8 QD's and optional pro to 1 1/2"
    Impressive bolted climb on a vertical orange wall. Retrobolting in 1991 focused the route from a 5.11 A problem to a 5.11 C face. Ascend Sheer Stress for 30', step left and then up

the steep wall above. The bulge is the crux. Joins with Red Eye at a bolt anchor below the prominent offwidth. Rappel.

18. **E. Pluribus Pinhead** (a.k.a. Pinhead) 5.11 D ★★★
    100' 8 QD's and minor pro to 1 1/2"
    A fabulous route ascending the beautiful upper orange face of the Red Wall. Commence up approximately 18 ft. of Sheer Stress, step right via jugs and a shaky mantle then up to a bolt anchor. Move up left (bolts) then up an easy corner and finally up right onto a desperate vertical face to a bolt anchor. Rappel with 2 ropes unless descending to a nearby anchor.

19. **Opus** (Direct Start) 5.11+ (R)
    25' 3 QD's to 1st anchor

    The next several routes lay just to the right of Sheer Stress on a darker shaded section of wall.

20. **Sheer Energy** 5.10 A
    45' Pro to 1 1/2"
    Step to the top of several free-standing columns of basalt, then climb a crack up a short face (bolts) to a belay anchor.

21. _____

22. **Hard Body** 5.11 B ★★
    50' 6 QD's
    Very popular route. Received its name from a female body builder / rock climber. Unusual crux. Commence up a shallow corner to a strenuous move then pull through a bulge and up steep rock to an anchor capped by a roof. Rappel.

23. **Shoot from the Hip** 5.10 C ★
    45' Pro to 1" and QD's
    Fun climb with big holds and a crack to start.

24. **Balls Not Friction** 5.9+
    45' Pro unknown

25. **That's the Way** 5.8
    45' Pro unknown

Robert McGown leading the roof on Physical Graffiti (5.10D)

Bridge Cliff

② ④

③

⑤ 5.10 B

① 5.10 B

⑥

59

5.11 A

59

⑦ 5.8

Dirty

5.11 D

5.9+

⑤

Blocky

Brushy Hillside

Approach

①

③

To Spring Rock

To Red Wall

22

Bridge Cliff

1. **Under Your Belt** 5.9+ (R)
   165' Pro to 2"
   A little known climb ascending the blocky 5th class section on the lower left. From a belay ledge 2/3 up the wall, step left and finish up a clean dihedral to the top. Rappel or walk off.

2. **Walk on the Wild Side** 5.10 B (PG-13) ★★
   45' Pro to 2"
   The standard approach to this classic begins via the first pitch of Fruit Bat. Belay on the halfway ledge, then traverse left roughly 15 ft. past a central corner (Spidermonkey) to a second left-leaning corner. Ascend this to the top. Rappel or walk off.

3. **Edge of Eternity** II 5.11 D ★
   Multi-pitch Pro to 2"
   A long climb that begins on the lower section of wall. Climb the dihedral and move right around a difficult corner (5.11) to dirty ledges. Above an easy wide corner is a clean angular face with bolts. Climb this (crux) to a big ledge. Belay. Step right and climb (bolts and pitons) the right face of an arete (5.11 A) to a tiny ledge, then a short face to the tree belay. Rappel or walk off.

4. **Spidermonkey** 5.9 ★
   40' Pro to 3"
   This is the large, dark dihedral on the upper face above the belay ledge.

5. **Fruit Bat** II 5.10 B ★
   Multi-pitch Pro to 2"
   This is the best option for approaching all the upper tier routes. Start past a bolt into a sloping corner. Exit up left via grassy ledges and corners to a ledge. Belay here. On the right face of the deep dihedral is a thin finger crack. Ascend this and top out. Note: several of the previous routes have original start points but are heavily vegetated and dirty.

6. **Seventh Sojourn** 5.9
   Pro unknown

7. **Shandor** 5.9
   Pro to 3"

Spring Rock

1. **Toe Cleavage** 5.8+
   30' Pro to 1" Needs pitons

2. **Velcro Fly** 5.10 D (PG-13)
   30' Minor pro to 1" Needs bolts and pitons.

Heather Macdonald on Sheer Stress (5.10 A)

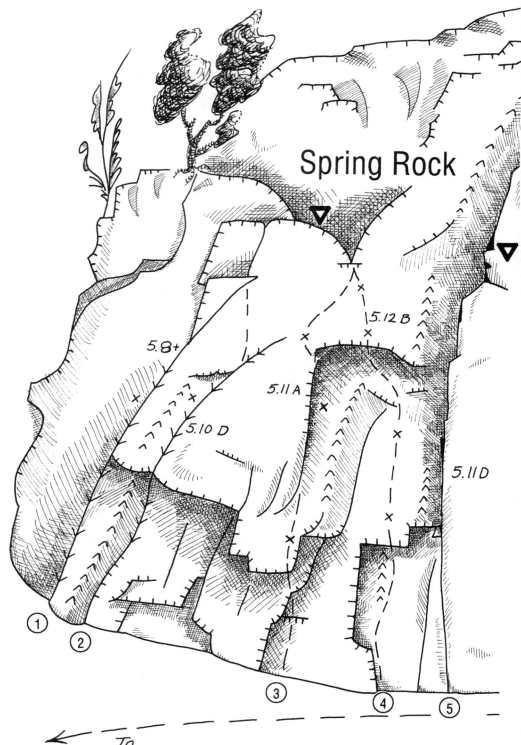

Spring Rock

5.8+

5.10 D

5.11 A

5.12 B

5.11 D

① ② ③ ④ ⑤

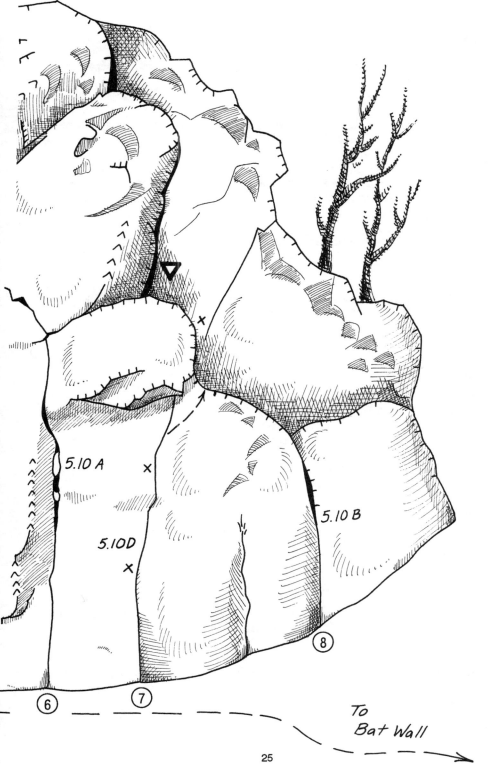

5.10 A

5.10 D

5.10 B

To
Bat Wall

⑥   ⑦   ⑧

Located on the left side. The route is highlighted by a thin crux move in a shallow corner at a bulge. Wander up easier slabs to a bolt belay.

3. **Free Bird** 5.11 A ★★
40' Minor pro to 1"
Excellent route. Step up to a small corner, reach left, then climb a second corner to a roof. Exit left onto slabs that lead up left to a bolt anchor.

4. **Ground Effects** 5.12 B ★★
40' 4 QD's
Probably the most unusual and fascinating route on Spring Rock. The climb involves two roof moves using very unorthodox technique. Solve the puzzle.

5. **Jumping Jack Thrash** 5.11 D (R) ★★
40' Pro to 1" TCU's and RP's recommended
A great classic climb, as a lead or on top-rope. Ascend a thin crack in the center of the face to a bolt anchor under an overhang. Rappel.

6. **The Spring** 5.10A ★
40' Pro to 2"
This interesting flared crack with several chockstones wedged in it joins at the Jumping Jack Thrash anchor. Rappel.

7. **Short Fuse** 5.10 D ★
35' 3 QD's
Yes, it is quite short, but it is still a worthy climb. Ascend the blank face and exit right to a ledge, step up left to a bolt anchor. Rappel.

8. **Dyno-mite** 5.10 B
35' Pro to 1 1/2"

Bat Wall

1. **Hanging Tree** III 5.10 D (R) ★
Multi-pitch Pro to 3" including KB, LA, Rurps
Notoriously loose and dirty in places, yet the upper portion of the climb offers excellent quality stemming and face climbing. Ascend sloping ledges and vertical cracks just left of a huge leaning tree. When possible friction down a ramp to the right 15 ft. to a belay. Then ascend a stiff (5.10 D) dihedral to a ledge. Step left and up, then up a smooth bolted face leading to a hanging belay just below the summit. Rappel with 2 ropes for 160 ft. Note: the original line varies slightly from the present finish. For reference see previous guidebooks.

2. **Go Back to the Gym** II 5.7 A4
40' Pro to 3" includes cams and TCU's, KB, LA, Leepers, Hangers, Bathooks
Desperate, merciless aid problem.

3. **Dracula** 5.12 A ★★★
65' 10 QD's
One of Broughton's premiere classics. Originally called the Unnamed Aid Route. Commence up a right-facing corner immediately right of the leaning tree. From a small ledge embark up a diagonal right leaning hand ramp, then up left, then right to a seam. Balance up the seam and surmount the final obstacle, a flared pea-pod corner. Rappel from bolt anchor.

4. **Bela Lugosi** 5.12 C ★★
65' 10 QD's
Fascinating route worthy of attention. Ascend a shallow corner gracefully to a thin stance. Pull through a desperately thin crux then up left via a zigzag seam (crux) until it joins with Dracula to the pea-pod finish.
Note: All of the routes from Dracula to Well Hung offer virtually endless variations, none of which are mentioned here out of necessity as well as originality.

5. **Frightnight** 5.13 C (PG-13)
65' 8 QD's
A serious and committing climb. Presently the most difficult route at Broughton Bluff.

6. **The Haunting** 5.12 B ★
65' 6 QD's and pro to 2"
Originally called Snap, Crackle, Pop (aid climb), this fascinating vertical seam has yielded a sequential and difficult free climb of modern standards. Ascend the seam 25 ft., then angle right across Bad Omen and enter a fist jam that eases to a hand crack (5.9) corner ending at the Superstition belay anchor.

7. **Bad Omen (Got the Horse for My Saddle)** 5.12 B ★★★
65' 10 QD's
Superb! Has gained immediate appreciation as a super classic face climb. Begin up a steep face via sidepulls to a thin stance, move over the bulge (crux) and up small edges to an unorthodox high step (crux). Carefully work up a left leaning flared slot until a protruding roof forces you left and up to a sloping ledge and bolt belay. Rappel.

8. **Danse Macabre** 5.12 A (?)
40' 3 QD's

9. **Bloodsucker** 5.11 D
40' 3 QD's

10. **Bloodline** 5.12 B ★★★
65' 7 QD's
Originally called Beeline, this "go for it" gusto climb offers the local rockjock a wicked start and a fantastic roof to exit through. One of the most exciting and interesting routes on the Bat Wall. Layback up an overhung face to several natural pockets then crank up to a stance. Balance up a smooth section then up a thin crack to a stance below a large roof. Start on the right and ape your way up left then over the lip and finally to the ledge and bolt belay for Superstition.

11. **Project** 5.12+
60' (TR)

12. **Superstition**
III 5.11 A ★★
Multi-pitch Pro to 2" (1st pitch = QD's and minor pro to 1")
A great route and quite popular, particularly the first pitch. Step up onto an outside corner and ascend

Mark Hudon at the roof on Bloodline (5.12B)

27

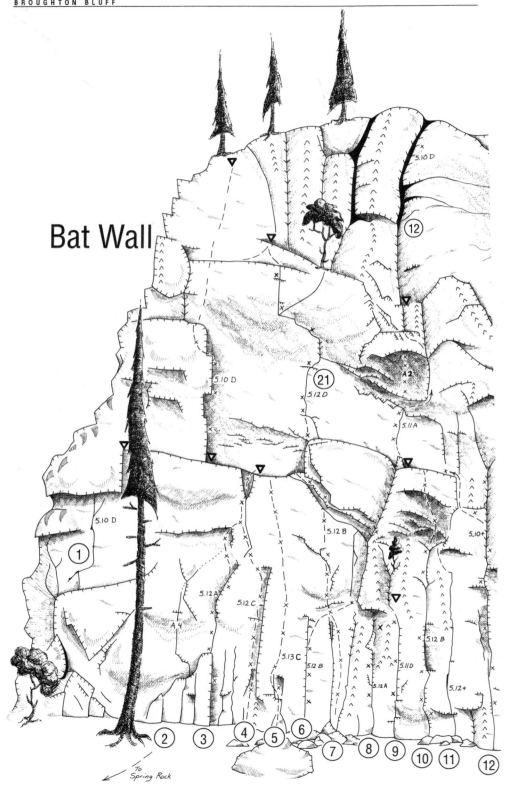

Bat Wall

5.10 D

12

A 2

5.12 D

21

5.11 A

5.10 D

5.10 D

5.10+

5.12 B

1

5.12 B

5.12 A

5.12 C

5.11 D

5.13 C

5.12 B

5.12 A

5.12+

2

3

4

5

6

7

8

9

10

11

12

A 4

To
Spring Rock

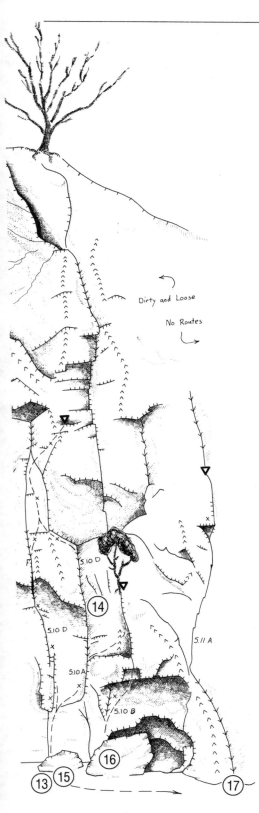

Dirty and Loose

No Routes

a shallow groove corner system until possible to smear left via underclings (5.10+). Move up a thin crack then left along on a narrow ledge to a bolt anchor. Rappel or continue up the vertical face above to the roof (the 1/4" bolt line out the roof is "Snap, Crackle, Pop") then fight (5.11 A) rightward around a corner and up to a belay ledge. Continue up the dihedral above to a steep, brushy and surprisingly strenuous offwidth problem (5.10 D). Rappel with 2 ropes to the ground.

13. **Lost Boys** 5.10 D ★★
70' 8 QD's
A fun climb and an excellent warm-up. On the right side of the Bat Wall are several large boulders in front of a cave. Begin behind the left one, face climb up to an overhang (crux) with a slot. Move up, then right, mantle, then up until you can exit right via an undercling and reach (crux) around a corner to a bolt anchor on a ledge. Rappel.

14. **Mystic Pizza** (a.k.a. Mystic Direct) 5.10 D
70' QD's and pro to 1 1/2"
An interesting variation with good pro. Start as for Mystic Void; instead of traversing to the right to join Well Hung, continue up the obvious corner system then exit up left (crux) to join Lost Boys.

15. **Mystic Void** 5.10 A
45' Pro to 1"
Ascends the face left of, then joins with Well Hung just above the large roof. Rappel from bolts at the maple tree.

16. **Well Hung** 5.10 B ★★
45' Pro to 1"
An original Bat Wall favorite, even if it is a bit dirty. Step directly off the large boulders onto the face under the large roof (piton). Traverse right then swing onto the roof via jug holds to a stance. Move up the corner to the bolt anchor at the maple tree. Rappel.

17. **Gold Arch** 5.11 A
70' Pro to 3"
At one time a fantastic line, but getting dirtier every year due to soil erosion from the field above the cliff. Start 30' right of Well Hung and ascend a slab then a strenuous barn door lieback on a gold-streaked wall. Belay. The second pitch leads to easier ground above.

18. **The Hunger** 5.11 D
55' Pro to 1 1/2" Cams suggested
Physically difficult route, but a little dirty.

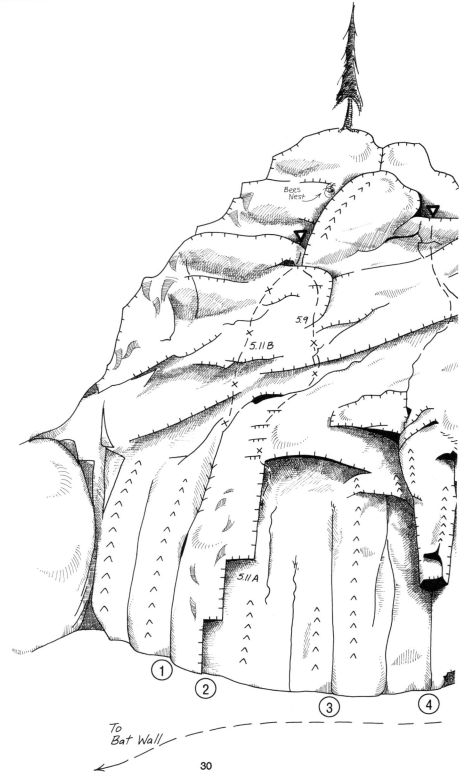

Bees Nest

5.9

5.11 B

5.11 A

① ② ③ ④

To Bat Wall

19. **Dark Shadows** 5.11 A ★
    40' Pro to 1 1/2" TCU's recommended
    Originally called Shadow Dancing (5.8 A-2), this climb was easily freed to produce a unique problem. Ascend a face to a left facing corner capped by a large roof. Step left, then up, then left (crux) past fixed pitons and up to a belay anchor on a small ledge. Rappel.

The following routes are located on the upper headwall of the Bat Wall.

20.

21. **Manson Family Reunion** 5.12 D ★★
    60' 7 QD's

22.

23.

24.

25.

Immediately south of the Bat Wall are several outcrops of rock with some route potential. The frequently wet slabs (up right of Dark Shadows) are referred to as Vampire Slab. Further along is a blocky short vertical chunk known as Broken Rock. Follow the trail beyond these outcrops to a better selection of rock at the "end of the world." Welcome to the great hidden walls of Broughton Bluff, steeped in mystery and tall tales.

Trinity Wall

Trinity Wall

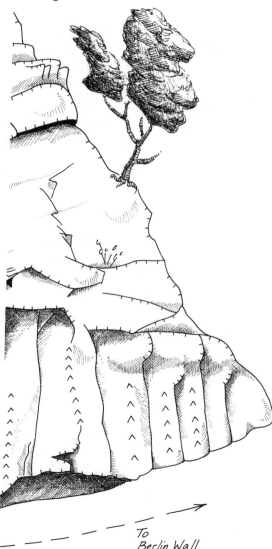

To
Berlin Wall

1. **Bust A Move** 5.11 B ★
   40' 4 QD's and optional pro to 1"
   Terrific climb with a surprising crux. Commence up a shallow corner then over a minor bulge. Angle rightward via thin holds and underclings (crux), then up an easy corner to a bolt anchor. Rappel.

2. **Father** 5.11 A ★
   40' Pro to 1 1/2" Needs pitons Quality climb. Ascend the strenuous right-facing corner until possible to exit up left onto a slab. Move up right on easy ground then up left (bolt) in the center of the face, and left to the bolt anchor in a corner. Rappel.

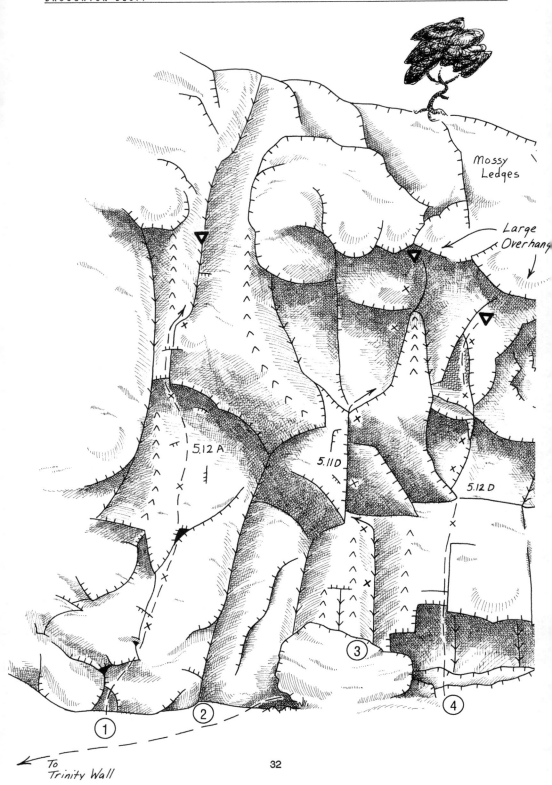

Mossy
Ledges

Large
Overhang

5.12 A

5.11 D

5.12 D

① ② ③ ④

To
Trinity Wall

Berlin Wall

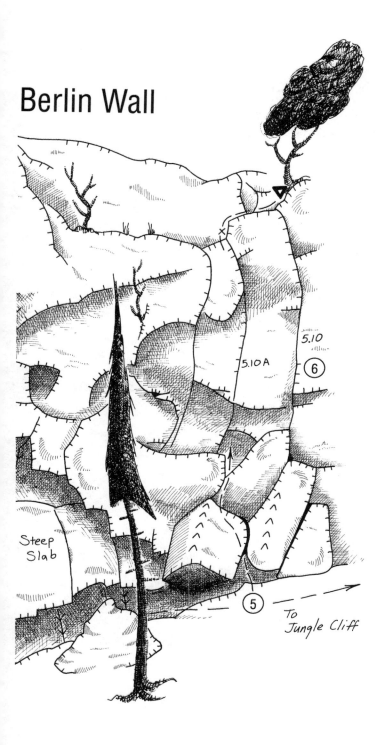

5.10

5.10A

⑥

Steep
Slab

⑤

To
Jungle Cliff

3. _____
   40' (TR)
4. _____
   40' (TR)

Berlin Wall (Originally known as Trident)

1. **Closet Nazi** 5.12 A ★★
   45' 5 QD's
   This remarkable route deserves attention. It's a challenge to all who ascend. Climb the bolt line on the left side of the wall up overhung, but very clean rock. Can be a virtual stream of water during the winter months.

2. _____

3. **Twist and Crawl** 5.11 D
   40' 5 QD's
   Located in the center of the wall directly under the huge roof. Unusual yet quite good. Move up a dihedral around a crux corner then up and out the overhang to the anchor. Rappel.

4. **Unknown** 5.13 A
   40' 5 QD's
   To the right of Twist and Crawl is another route on this virtually upside down wall. Start up a crack on a slab then up via physically articulate moves out the overhang to a bolt anchor.

5. **Pride and Joy** 5.10 A
   40' Pro to 1" Small wires recommended
   On the far right side of Berlin Wall is a smooth vertical section of rock broken with several thin cracks. The left is a 5.10 A, the right is a top-rope. Takes good pro. Rappel from the tree anchor directly above the top-rope problem.

6. _____ 5.10
   40' (TR)

Jungle Cliff

The next two crags are located on private land.

1. **Zimbabwe** II 5.10 A
   Multi-pitch Pro to 3" Cams recommended
   Ascends the steep face on the far left corner of Jungle Cliff via numerous ledges. Route description begs for mercy.

2. **Slash and Burn** 5.11 D
   60' QD's and minor pro to 2"
   A good route on fantastic steep rock. Begin at the cave, pull up (5.9), move up the slab to the right, then up the face to an anchor. Continue up the overhanging corner above, move left at difficult section and finish up a vertical dihedral to a final crux move. Rappel from bolt anchor.

3. **Under the Yum Yum Tree** 5.10 D
   40' Pro to 2" Needs bolts
   Fun climb with an appropriate name. Start to the right of the cave and ascend a slightly dusty slab via a thin crack and corner system to a bolt anchor. Rappel.

4. **Tarzan** 5.12 C
   50' 7 QD's
   The obvious and impressive arete. Tarzan is definitely one of the most unusual routes of this kind at Broughton Bluff. Worth the blast.

5. **Crime Wave** 5.10 C
(PG-13)
50' QD's, TCU's, #2
Friend required
A slightly awkward
variation next to Gorilla
Love Affair.

6. **Gorilla Love Affair**
5.10 D ★★
50' 6 QD's, optional
TCU's
An instant popular
favorite. Well protected
yet exhilarating to climb.
Stem up to a small roof,
move left, then up to
another roof. Step right
and up a smooth dihedral
(crux) until possible to
step left to finish up a
crack leading to the bolt
belay for Under the Yum
Yum Tree. Rappel.

7. **Out of Africa** II 5.9 A3

8. **Heart of Darkness**
5.12 B ★
50' 6 QD's
A beautiful route that
leads up an overhung
arete in the heart of
Jungle Cliff country.
Desperately struggle out
the overhung start to a
stance, then up and left
along a hand ramp. Pull

Dave Sowerby climbing Heart of Darkness (5.12B)

through the crux (thin) then up the right side of the arete to a stance. Make a quick move up
a smooth face to a bolt anchor. Proceed up left out the fiercely overhung headwall (5 bolts)
via face and jug holds. Rappel with 2 ropes unless descending to a nearby anchor.

9. **Mowgli's Revenge**
5.11 B
40' 4 QD's
Underneath a large roof to the right of Heart of Darkness, you will find two bolt routes. The
left one is Mowgli's Revenge. An interesting climb that exits the roof on the left side. Rappel
from bolt anchor.

10. **Amazon Woman** 5.10 D
40' 4 QD's and minor pro to 1 1/2" Cams recommended
Commence up a vertical stem problem via small edges to a stance. Reach up right under the
roof, then traverse right and exit to a good stance. Step up a wide crack to a huge ledge and
bolt belay. Rappel.

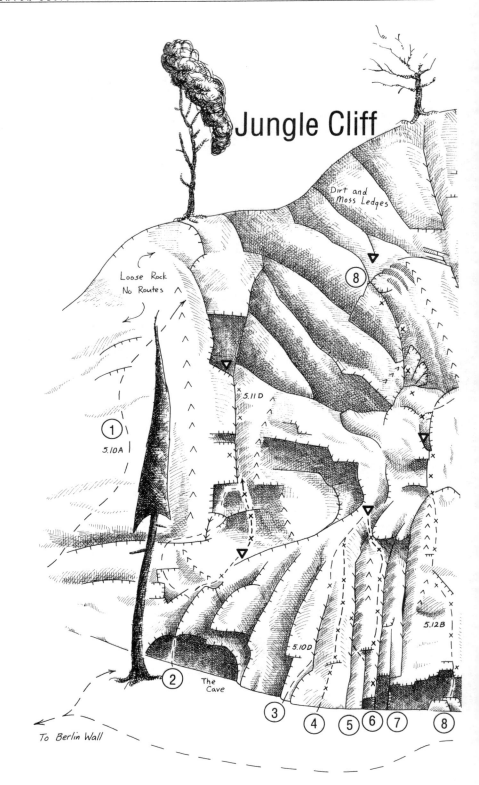

Jungle Cliff

Dirt and
Moss Ledges

Loose Rock
No Routes

5.11 D

① 5.10A

② The Cave

5.10 D

5.12 B

③ ④ ⑤ ⑥ ⑦ ⑧

⑧

To Berlin Wall

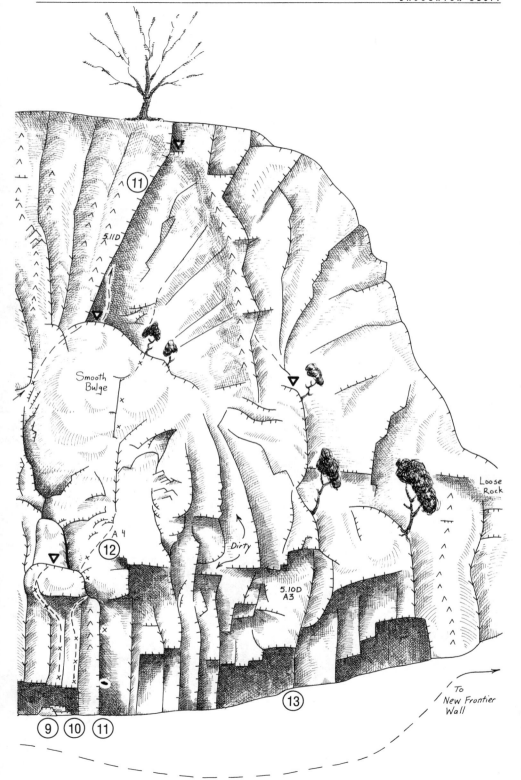

New Frontier Cliff

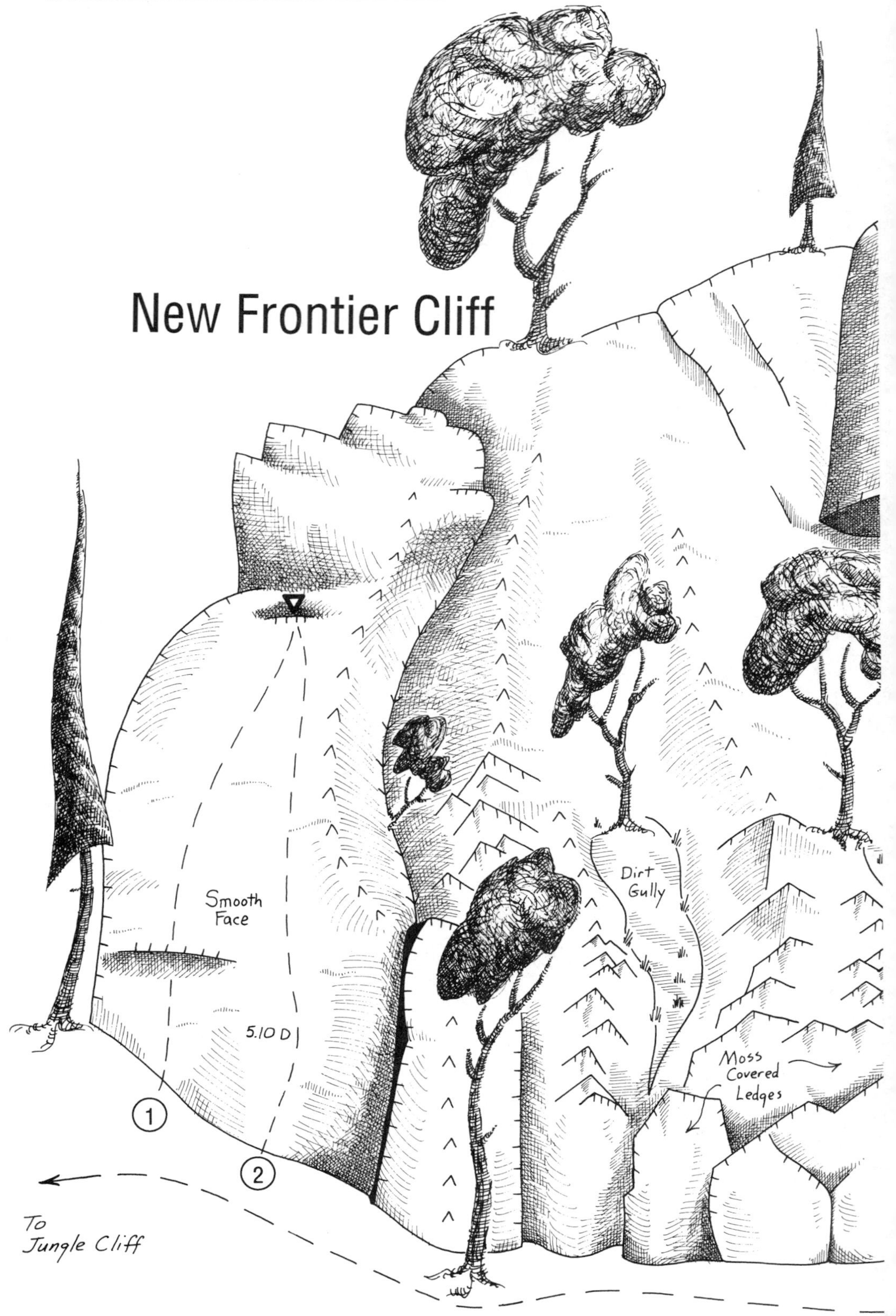

Smooth
Face

5.10 D

①

②

Dirt
Gully

Moss
Covered
Ledges

To
Jungle Cliff

5.10C

5.11C

Clean
Face

④

Gully

5.10A

5.11B

Poison
Oak

⑦

⑤

⑥

③

39

11. **Amazon Man** III 5.11 A3 (or 5.11D) ★
    Multi-pitch Pro to 3" Need KB, LA, and bolts
    This staggering and original achievement, put up in 1979, penetrates through the heart of
    Jungle Cliff. Begin up a corner (immediately right of Amazon Woman) past a fixed piton to a
    stance, then up a wide crack to a big ledge with a good anchor. Mowgli's Revenge joins
    here. Continue up by one of two cracks to a stance, then delicately traverse left via sloping
    ledges (bolts) to the Heart of Darkness belay. Ascend directly above you (5.10+) to another
    belay then move right around the sweet headwall and up a difficult section. Belay at bolts on
    Skull Ledge. Storm the dihedral (5.11 D) directly above that leads to the summit. Rappel
    with 2 ropes.

12. **Killer Pygmy** III 5.10+ A4 ★
    Multi-pitch Pro to 4" Cams, TCU's, KB, LA, Angles and bolts
    Outrageous aid line that boldly pushes up the smooth center face to Skull Ledge. The final
    pitch angles up right via two optional cracks (A-2).

13. **Mujahideen** II 5.10 D A-3
    20' Pro to 4" including KB, LA, and Angles

New Frontier Cliff

1. _____
   80' (TR)

2. **Alma Mater** 5.10 D (X) ★★
   80' Needs bolts
   Beautiful steep slab on the left side of New Frontier Cliff. Commence up an odd balance start
   (5.10 D) until it eases to a continuous, fun 5.8 ending on a ledge and belay anchor. Rappel.
   (Note: the route was soloed.)

3. **Happy Trails** II 5.10 A
   Multi-pitch Pro to 3"
   Interesting climb with some grungy, loose sections. Walk to the right side of the wall (trail's
   end). Above is a short clean jam crack that pulls through a slot to a left-facing slab corner.
   Climb this and enter into a loose chimney then belay at the oak tree. Continue up right a few
   moves until you can undercling left then up a broken slab above to top out. Rappel or walk
   off.

4. **Wild, Wild West** 5.10 C
   60' Pro to 3" Cams suggested
   Ascend the first pitch of Happy Trails. From the oak tree, step left to a crack then up to a
   large roof. Undercling out right (crux) and around corner (rope jams easily) then up easy
   cracks to the top. Rappel or walk off.

5. **Pioneer Spirit** 5.11 B ★
   45' 4 QD's and minor pro to 1"
   Climb the short, clean jam crack of Happy Trails. Step right and then up this tantalizing face
   climb. The crux is a blind lunge. Rappel from bolt anchor.

6. **Promised Land** 5.11 C (R) ★★
   80' Pro to 3" Cams and small wires (RP's) recommended
   Superb climb on beautiful rock, yet located virtually "at the end of the world." Start to the
   right of Happy Trails and behind several trees. Pull up an easy bulge, move up left on a slab
   to a vertical step. From a ledge, climb the exciting and steep crack system to a huge block.
   Lean out right (bolt) and layback up the arete to a bolt anchor. Rappel.

7. _____ 5.10+
   65' (TR)
   A thin seam on a short face just to the right of Promised Land.

Rocky Butte Quarry

Urban rock describes the Butte very well. Centrally located with easy access in NE Portland adjacent to I-205, the Butte in recent years has become a very popular afternoon crag. Numerous individuals and organizations visit the crag each year to teach classes and to top-rope the more than 100 climbs.

Extensive and secluded, this north facing crag is comfortably hidden amongst a tall, green canopied forest. Used infrequently during the 1960's, it was the 1970's that heralded a new era. Several established climbs received recognition, such as **Blackberry Jam** (5.10 A) in 1974 by Jim Davis and T. Crossman, located on the White Rabbit Buttress. **Expresso** (5.9) and, **White Rabbit** (5.10) in 1977, **Birds of Paradise** (5.10 C) in 1979, **Toothpick** (5.11 C), **Close to the Edge** (5.12), and **Blueberry Jam** (5.10 A) were soon to follow. Those young people who proved instrumental during the 70's phase were key to the future of climbing here. Doug Bower, Bill Coe, Jay Kerr, Robert McGown, Mike Smelsar, John Sprecher, Scott Woolums and others developed rock climbing as a traditional sport at the Butte. Though the crag fell quiet from 1979 to 1984, these same persons and others such as Mike Pajunas, Tim Olson, Wayne Wallace, Joe Parsley and Gary Rall eventually tamed the Rocky Butte "frontier" in the late 1980's.

Scores of urban classics were produced. **Bite the Bullet** (5.11 A), **Fandango** (5.10 C), **Live Wire** (5.11 A), **Edge of Might** (5.11 B), **Stranger than Friction** (5.10 A) **Ziva's Book** (5.10 B), **Phylynx** (5.11 B), **Wizard** (5.11 A), **Crack Warrior** (5.11 B), **Emotional Rescue** (5.10 B), **Vertical Therapy** (5.9), **Red Zinger** (5.11 C) to name a few.

The Quarry is generally a top-rope area. Virtually all of the routes have been led at one time, but now, since much of the original fixed gear has been removed, top-roping is the name of the game. Those few routes that are still leadable are well worth it, such as **Emotional Rescue**, **Phylynx**, or **Wizard**. Do bring extra slings to use as extensions from the nearest tree anchor.

The Quarry environment does have several drawbacks. Poison oak, spray paint, litter and freeway noise from I-205 are the most obvious. Yet this crag is very accessible to the public, especially for the local rock jock tired of the office blues.

Thanks to the tiny sparks cast from the **"Rocky Butte Quarry Guide"** (1987) by Robert McGown and Mike Pajunas, climber interest at this crag has increased rapidly. Trails have improved with use, the climbs are cleaner and the general image of Rocky Butte has changed for the better.

There are 16 sections of wall at the Butte. The following are described left to right as if facing the crag: Poodle Pinnacle, Trivial Pinnacle, Silver Bullet Bluff, Video Bluff, New Era Cliff, Dream Weaver Wall, Wizard Wall, Far East Wall, Warrior Wall, Freeway Wall, Mean Street, Easy Street, Toothpick Wall, Breakfast Cracks, Wall of Shadows and the Grotto area.

To reach the cliffs, take the 82nd Ave. exit (eastbound) from I-84 and drive north to the intersection of Freemont and 82nd. Turn right (east), drive approximately 1/2 mile. The road curves north to become 91st street, (eventually to loop clockwise around to the top of Rocky Butte). The cliffs are located on the north side of the road near the Bible Temple Church "domes." There are several obvious dirt pullouts available. The top of Rocky Butte offers several fun boulder traverse problems to entice the fingertips of those seeking to try their luck. If not, the views are fantastic, both of the City of Roses and the surrounding mountains.

Poodle Pinnacle

1. **Poodle with a Mohawk** 5.11 A
   Pro to 2 1/2"
   A neat climb located by itself along the eastern perimeter trail. Hike approximately 300 ft. along the trail. Above the trail is a face with an easy start, a crack and an outside arete. Lead this to a tree. Rappel.

ilver Bullet Bluff

Approach Trail

5.9+

5.10A

③

⑤

④

5.9

5.7

No Routes

5.11A

5.9+

5.10

5.9

5.8

⑧

⑨

⑥

⑦

⑩ ⑪

Trivial Pinnacle

Hike east on a perimeter trail to the tunnel under the road. Angle north toward the cliff.

1. **Harlequin** 5.10 B ★
   Pro to 1 1/2"
   A good climb. Commence up an easy start then angle right up the curved crack (25 ft.) until it eases near the top. Belay at tree.

2. **Trivial Pursuit** 5.10 B
   Pro to 1 1/2"
   A minor face climb just to the right.

3. **The Joker** 5.8

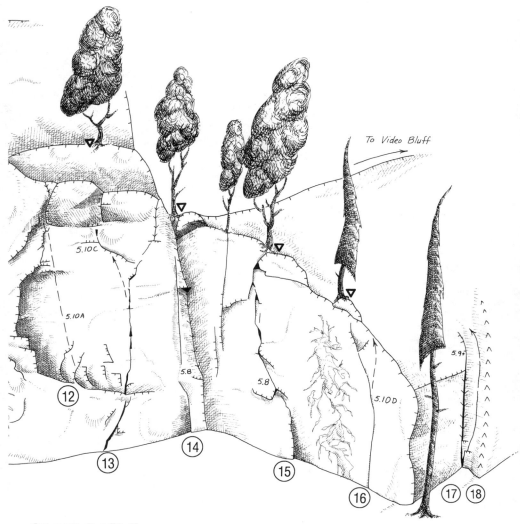

Silver Bullet Bluff

Named because of all the bullet scars dotting the face of this elusive crag. Approach by hiking east along the perimeter trail to the tunnel under the roadway. Aim north to the crag and down, step 20 ft. to a large ledge. Belay here for the routes in the main wall below. Height approximately 35 to 40 ft.

1. _____ 5.10+ (TR)

2. **Captain She's Breaking Up** 5.8 (R)
   Pro to 2"

3. _____

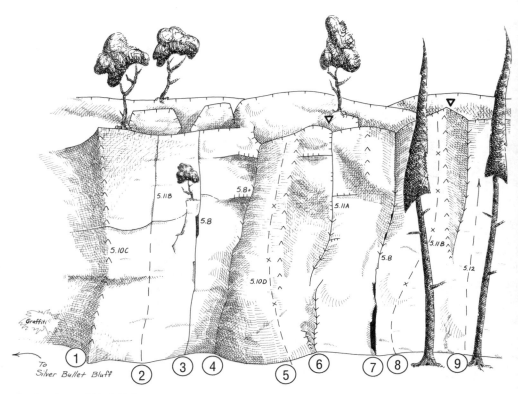

4. **Sundance Kid** 5.10 A
   Neat shallow corner climb on upper left corner of Silver Bullet Bluff.

5. **Panama Red** 5.9+
   Climb the smooth face broken with small edges and cracks immediately right of Sundance Kid.

6. **Miss Kitty** 5.7

7. **Gunsmoke** 5.9 ★★
   An excellent easy face climb just left of Bite the Bullet.

8. **Bite the Bullet** 5.11 A (R) ★★★
   One of the best routes on Silver Bullet Bluff. Start up left of a tree and on a face with good but angled edges. From a good stance 15 ft. up angle left onto a bullet-scarred face and climb desperately to a sloping ledge, then more up right to join with the last move on Jack of Hearts.

9. **Jack of Heart** 5.9+ ★
   Pro to 1"
   An exciting thin crack climb. Start up a short right facing corner to a stance. Then up a thin crack to a sloping ledge. Finish up a last vertical step to the belay ledge.

10. **Silver Bullet** 5.9 (R) ★
    A good route that starts up the face, then enters a dihedral that is lacking a crack. Smear up the corner to join with Jack of Hearts.

11. **Urban Cowboy** 5.8 (R) ★★

12. **Last Tango** 5.10 A

13. **Fandango** 5.10 C (R) ★★★
    A superb route of only moderate difficulty. Start up a crack on a slab left of a main corner.

Video Bluff

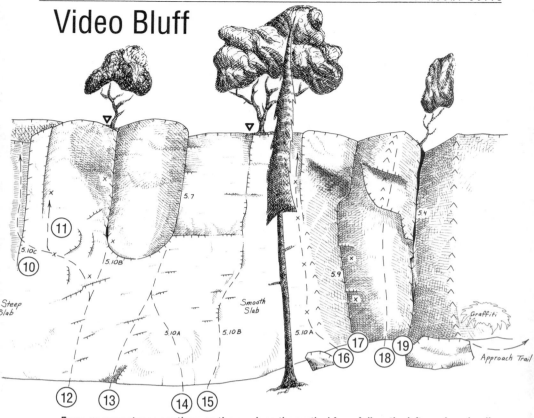

From an easy stance continue up the crack on the vertical face, follow the left crack and pull a mantle (crux). Move up further via a corner to a ledge. Belay from the large tree above.

14. **Midnight Warrior** 5.8
    Pro to 2"
    The main corner on this side of the wall.

15. **Superman Crack** 5.8 (R) ★
    Pro to 1"
    A fun problem on good edges and sloping smears.

16. **Centurion** 5.10 D ★★
    A unique short vertical crack problem on the lower right corner of this wall. Climb the crack until you can reach over right (crux) and up to easy steps and tree belay.

17. **Invisible Man** 5.9+

18. **Temporary Arete** 5.10 A

Video Bluff

One of the two most popular walls frequented at Rocky Butte. Excellent place to top-rope and learn technique. Approach Video Bluff by parking at the easternmost pullout (just before the **stone** guardrail) and aim north to the crag. A well beaten trail starts here and loops along the crag west to emerge at the guardrail descent trail. Height approximately 35 ft.

1. **Body Language** 5.10 C (R)
   The overhanging arete with a horizontal crack halfway up.

45

2. **Body Bionics** 5.11 B (R)

3. **AC / DC** 5.8

4. **Eve of Destruction** 5.8+
    A slabby dihedral problem. A good practice climb.

5. **Live Wire** 5.10 D ★★
    4 QD's
    Excellent difficult face problem on the round outside corner right of Eve of Destruction. A must for everyone.

6. **Damaged Circuit** 5.11 A ★★
    Challenging stem problem up a shallow scoop. Begin up a shattered start, pull a thin move to an awkward stance, then smear, stem up a face using strange finger holds in the seam.

7. **Robotics** 5.8

8. **Edge of Might** 5.11 B ★★
    Fantastic climb. Begin up the face immediately right of Robotics and angle up onto the arete. Thin holds and pinches on the arete are the crux.

9. **Hard Contact** 5.12 C

10. **Lever or Leaver** 5.10 C

11. **Persistence of Time** 5.11 C
    3 QD's

12. **Ziva's Book** 5.10 B ★★
    3 QD's
    A popular climb with a narrow dihedral crux section. Climb up the slabby face on good holds to a large hold below the corner. Reach and stem up the corner to the top. Fun route.

13. **Flakey Old Man** 5.7 ★★
    The flake has long since fallen away but the popularity of this and the routes nearby make it a favorite.

14. **MTV** 5.10 A
    Boulder problem variation.

15. **Stranger Than Friction** 5.10 B ★★★
    In the center of the slab is a pocketed boulder start and slap move leading upward to a seam. The local classic favorite on this wall and certainly worth it.

16. **Panes of Reality** 5.10 A ★
    4 QD's
    Step left and up onto the face immediately left of Stained Glass. A neat problem on a rounded bulge.

17. **Stained Glass** 5.9 ★
    QD's and pro to 2"
    Obvious fun dihedral corner.

18. **Toxic Waltz** 5.11D
    4 QD's
    Vertical face to the right of the dihedral.

19. **E-Z Corner** 5.4

New Era Cliff

An obscure wall located below and parallel to Video Bluff. An easy 3rd class descent trail splits the cliff on the west. Possible top-rope, yet the climbs are becoming overgrown and dirty except for the more prominent lines. The longest route is 35 ft.

1. **Point of No Return** 5.11 C (TR) ★
    An exciting face climb on beautiful rock just left of Simba.

2. **Simba** 5.8 ★
   Pro to 2"
   Prominent dihedral in center.

3. **Love on the Rocks** 5.11+ (TR)
   A difficult top-rope problem just to the right of Simba.

4. **Fiddler on the Roof** 5.8
   Pro to 2"
   A short neat problem that climbs a dihedral just above a large cave.

5. **Cuts Like a Knife** 5.10 A (R)

Dream Weaver Wall

This is a narrow section of wall located between Video Bluff and Wizard Wall. These climbs are good though infrequently ascended. Height is approximately 65 ft.

1. **Dream Weaver** 5.9 ★
   Pro to 2"

2. **Head Bangers Ball** 5.10 A
   Pro to 1 1/2"

3. **Tiger's Pause** 5.9 ★
   Pro to 2"

4. **Kleen Korner** 5.9

Wizard Wall

One of the finest long vertical sections of rock at the Butte. All of the routes are located on the upper half of the wall. Either top-rope from trees at the top of the cliff or rappel down approximately 60 to 80 ft. to bolt anchors or ledges and then lead back up. This wall is of superb quality, yielding some of the finest high angle face climbs at Rocky Butte.

1. **Kleen Korner** 5.9

2. **Naked Savage** 5.10 A

3. **Lord of the Jungle** 5.9+ (variation)

4. **Slavemaker** 5.10 B

5. **God Monster** 5.10 C
   Pro to 3" Cams suggested
   Flared, overhanging, awkward offwidth roof problem.

6. **Eye in the Sky** 5.10 C (R) ★
   Pro to 1"
   Start at the Phylynx belay, but stay just to the left of the route on an outside corner after the bulge crux.

7. **Phylynx** 5.11 B ★★★
   Pro to 1 1/2"
   One of the finest routes at Rocky Butte. Rappel to a hidden anchor 80 ft. down on the left, then lead up right (bolts), pull through bulge (crux) then directly up the crack on the face.

8. **Walk on Water** 5.11 D ★
   QD's and pro to 1"
   An impressive and extreme face route to the right of Phylynx.

9. **Mind Games** 5.10 A
   Offwidth Chimney.

10. **Wizard** 5.11 A ★★★
    QD's and pro to 1"
    Excellent climb on a beautiful rock. Dynamic and unusual.

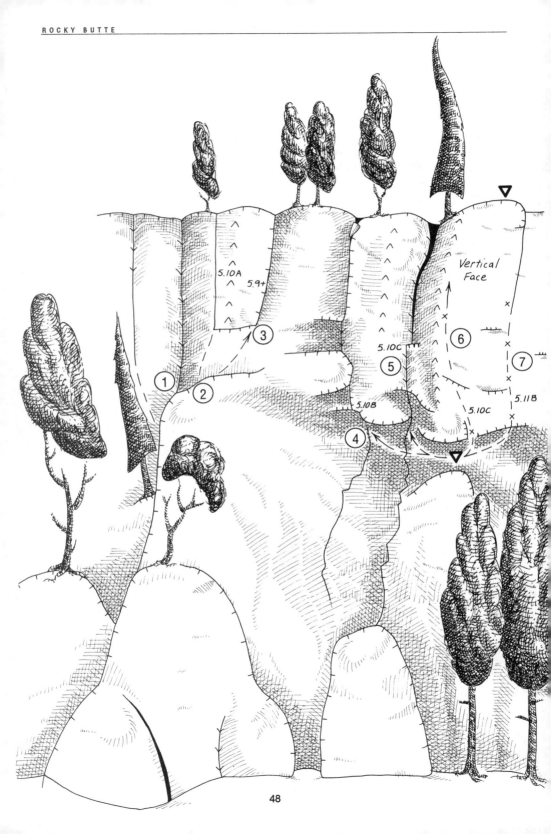

Vertical Face

5.10A
5.9+
5.10C
5.10B
5.10C
5.11B

① ② ③ ④ ⑤ ⑥ ⑦

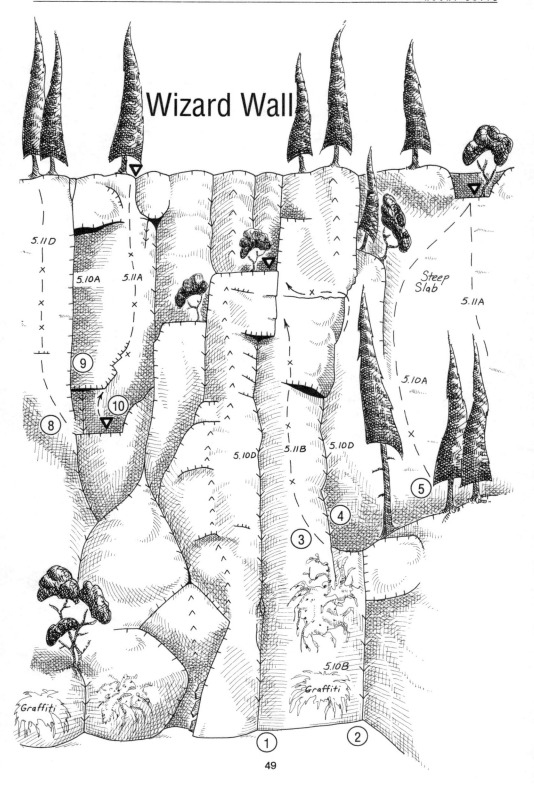

Wizard Wall

5.11D

5.10A 5.11A

Steep Slab

5.11A

⑨

⑩

⑧

5.10A

5.10D 5.11B 5.10D

⑤

④

③

5.10B

Graffiti

Graffiti

①

②

Far East Wall

5.8

5.11A

5.10D

5.11B

5.10D

5.10A

5.11B

Steep
Slab

5.10B

5.10B

Graffiti

① ③ ④ ② ⑤ ⑥ ⑦ ⑧ ⑨

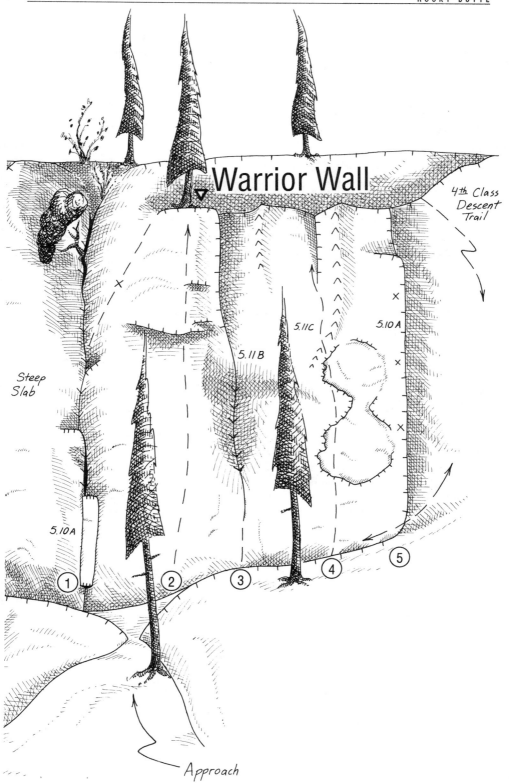

Warrior Wall

4th Class
Descent
Trail

5.11C

5.11B

5.10A

Steep
Slab

5.10A

① ② ③ ④ ⑤

Approach

Far East Wall

This hidden corner of wall is the westerly extension of the Wizard Wall. Approach by rappeling in from the tree at the top of Seventh Moon or scramble up a 3rd class trail from the bottom. Forty ft. to halfway terrace, 100 ft. approximate total height.

1. **The Wanderer** 5.10 D ★
2. **Great Wall of China** 5.10 B ★
3. **High Road to China** 5.11 B
4. **Chinese Finger Torture** 5.10 D ★
5. **Ghost Rider** 5.10 A
6. **(Flight of the) Seventh Moon** 5.11 A ★★
   A neat, challenging face climb that goes up just left of the Orient Express dihedral and ends at the tree belay.
7. **Orient Express** 5.8 ★
   Dihedral located at the center of the face.
8. **Secret Maze** 5.11 B ★
   A difficult face climb. Start to the right of the dihedral and climb up (crux) to a stance, then meander up the face using holds that seem to be in all the wrong places. Captain Granite said so.
9. **Tigers Eye** 5.10 B
   Fun direct start leading to the terraced ledges below Orient Express.

Warrior Wall

An extension of the Far East Wall, it was coined because of the favorite difficult corner problem here. Casually referred to as the "Bug Wall." One can descend via the standard guardrail descent trail next to the chainlink fence. Approximate height ranges from 45 to 100 ft.

1. **Smears for Fears** 5.10 A
   Pro to 2"
   A good crack climb further right of Secret Maze. Ends at the large fir tree on a ledge.
2. _____ 5.13 TR
   The extreme face climb just left of Crack Warrior.
3. **Crack Warrior** 5.11 B (R) ★★★
   Pro to 1 1/2"
   A great climb with a nasty crux. Silverfish frequent here. Climb the corner stem problem up to a bulge (crux). Pull through and move up an easier right facing corner to the large fir tree. Belay.
4. **You'll Dance to Anything** 5.11 C (TR) ★★
   Beautiful face climb that makes use of a broken section of smooth rock. The exit is the crux due to numerous sloping finger edges.
5. **Sheer Madness** 5.10 A 3 QD's
6. **Quarry Cracker** 5.6
7. **Lathe of Heaven** 5.11 A
8. **Arch Nemesis** 5.11 A H
   Pro to 1 1/2" including pitons
   A major dihedral on this face. Climb up the vertical corner until possible to step out right and up a flake that leads to a large fir tree.
9. **Boy Sage** 5.10+ (variation)
   Pro to 1 1/2" including pitons
   Take the direct up a crack to the tree.

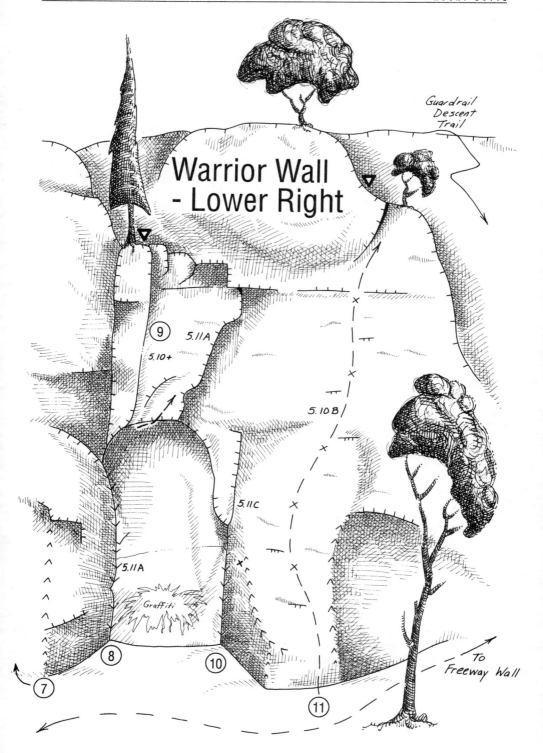

Warrior Wall
- Lower Right

Guardrail
Descent
Trail

9 5.11A

5.10+

5.10 B

5.11C

5.11A

Graffiti

7

8

10

11

To
Freeway Wall

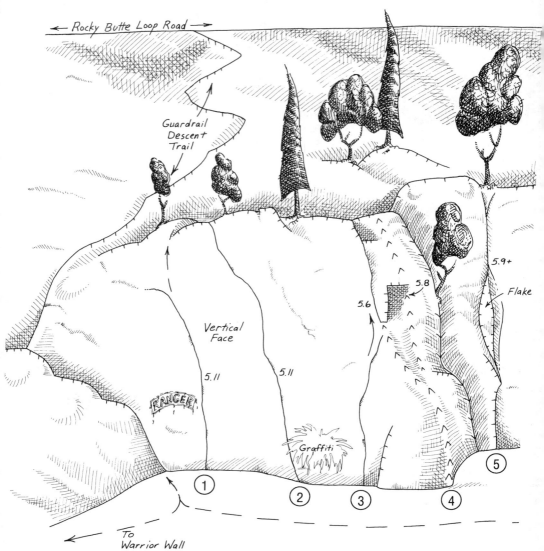

10. **Jealous Rage** 5.11 C (R)
Pro to 1"
Leads up an indistinct face (bolts) left to join with Arch Nemesis.

11. **Emotional Rescue** 5.10 B ★★★
QD's and pro to 2"
One of the finest classics at the Butte. Very popular. Climb the steep bolt and pin protected face to exit up a crack and a bolt anchor hidden around corner. Rappel.

Freeway Wall

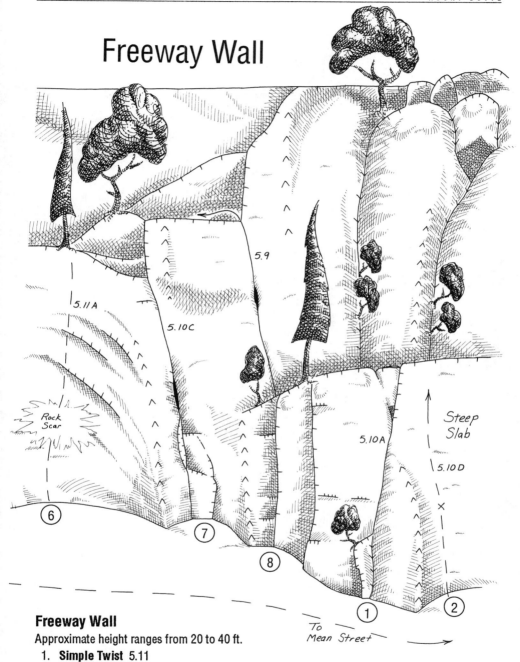

5.9

5.11 A

5.10 C

Rock
Scar

Steep
Slab

5.10 A

5.10 D

⑥

⑦

⑧

①

②

To
Mean Street

Freeway Wall

Approximate height ranges from 20 to 40 ft.

1. **Simple Twist** 5.11
2. **Hyper Twist** 5.11
3. **Passing Lane** 5.6
4. **Speeding Down South** 5.8
5. **Ranger Danger** 5.9+
6. **Telegraph Road** 5.11 A (TR)

Mean Street

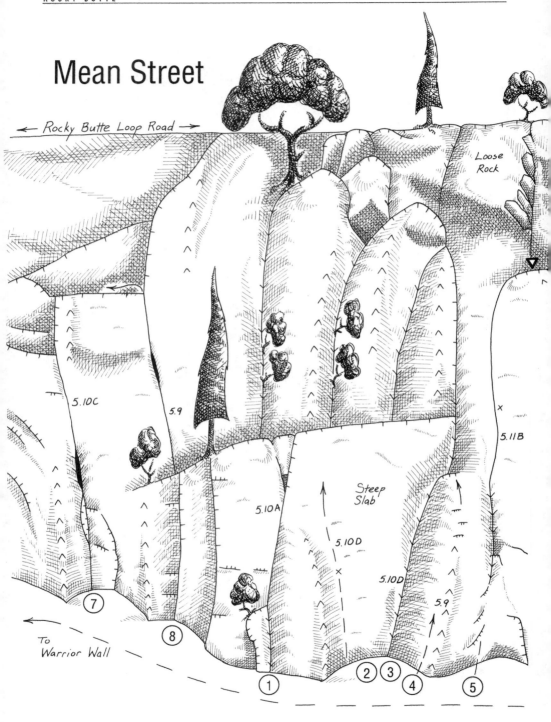

← Rocky Butte Loop Road →

Loose Rock

5.10C

5.9

5.11B

Steep Slab

5.10A

5.10D

5.10D

5.9

⑦

⑧

To Warrior Wall

①

② ③

④

⑤

56

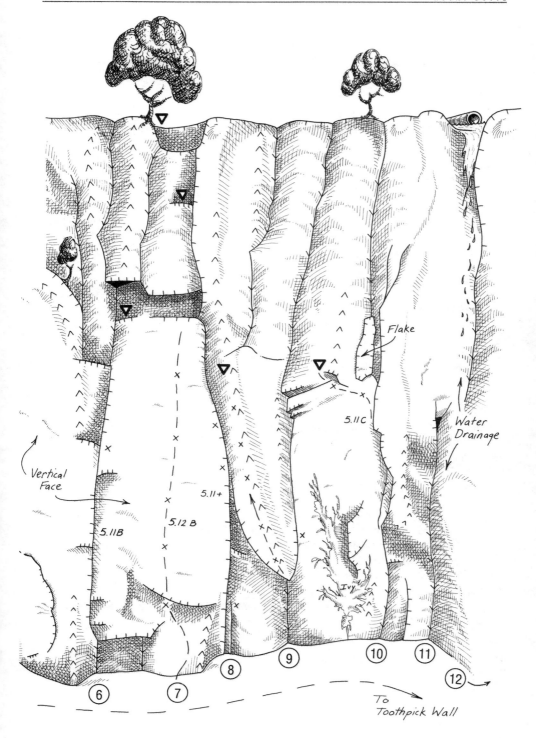

Flake

Water
Drainage

Vertical
Face

5.11C

5.11+

5.12 B

5.11B

Ivy

6

7

8

9

10

11

12

To
Toothpick Wall

7. **Highway Star** 5.10 C ★
   Pro to 1 1/2"
   A good crack climb with a strenuous exit move.

8. **Dead Man's Curve** 5.9

Mean Street

This steep wall is situated directly below the guardrail adjacent to the road. The routes are characterized by difficult, hard to protect and usually dust-covered rock. Height approximately 100 ft.

1. **Thunder Road** 5.10 A

2. **Lethal Ethics** 5.10 D (R)
   Poorly protected face climb intersected by a ledge halfway up.

3. **Spiritual Journey** 5.10 D
   Ascend the face just left of a minor arete and continue up an inside corner leading to the top.

4. **Little Arete** 5.9 (R)

5. **Seamingly Endless** 5.11 B ★
   Pro to 1"
   Start on the right side of the arete and zig zag up discontinuous cracks and corners to the top.

6. **Holy Bubbles** 5.11 B ★
   Start to the right of the arete, ascend up and over a roof, then up an inside corner to a belay anchor. Rappel.

7. **Pluto** 5.12 B
   A bolted face left of the "nose." A bit runout, strenuous, a little dusty. Has yet to see a free ascent.

8. **Stump the Jock** 5.11+
   The crack and inside corner just left of the prominent "nose" of rock. Begin up and angle left up an overhang corner until possible to turn the crux and continue up a steep wall above. Pull another small roof and rappel from trees just above. Dirty.

9. **Unknown**
   Pro = QD's
   The prominent "nose" of rock.

10. **No Leverage** 5.11 C
    Could be a good climb, but the new drainage ditch pours down immediately to the right. Begin up a bolt and pin protected face to a corner and traverse directly left just below a large detached flake of rock to a bolt belay. Rappel.

11. **Be Bold or Not to Be** 5.11 C
    A true blue water course now.

12. **Claymation** 5.10 C
    A crack corner system to the right of the water course. May be dusty, but still feasible to climb.

Easy Street

A good practice wall to teach rappelling and top-roping to novices. Approximately 35 ft. high.

A. **Hand Crack** 5.7

B. **Face** 5th Class

C. **Chimney** 5th Class

D. **Face / Finger** 5.9

E. **Chimney** 5.2 Descent trail approach for this area.

Tim J Olson 12-92

Toothpick Wall

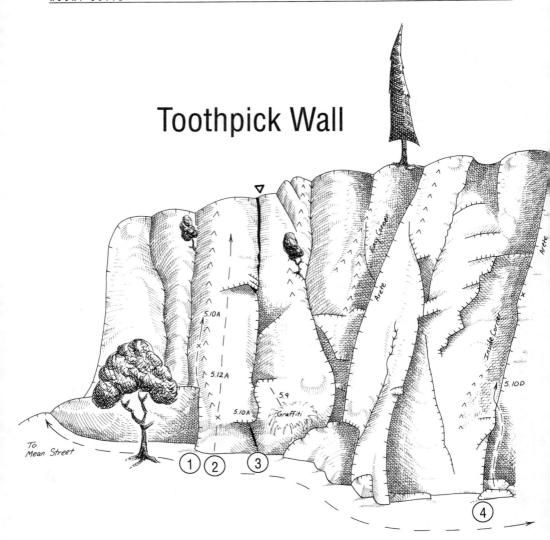

Toothpick Wall

A beautiful, colorful wall. Characterized by clean, steep rock and several incredible thin crack routes. Approximate height 50 ft.

1. **Reach for the Sky** 5.10 A ★
   Pro to 2"
   A fun climb. Ascend via a crack start then an outside corner until possible to move to the right side of the arete and top out. (1 pin - 1 bolt)

2. **Zenith** 5.12 A (TR)

3. **Blueberry Jam** 5.9 (5.10 A boulder start) ★★★
   Pro to 3"
   A very popular practice climb. Start to the right or do the direct boulder start, then ascend to the top via a broken crack system and large holds.

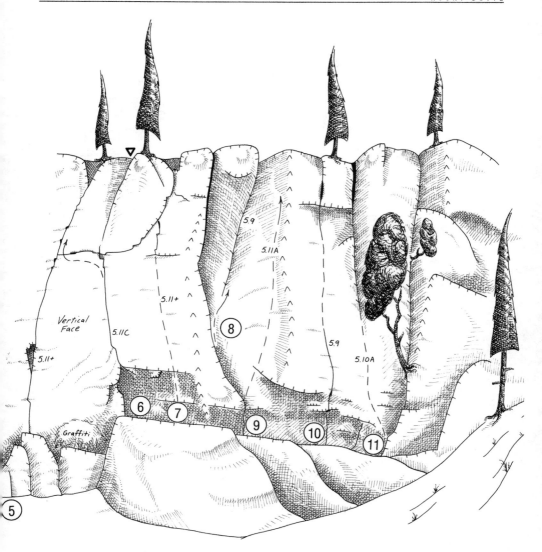

4. **Leading Edge** 5.10 D
   A corner to face arete system to the left of Close to the Edge.

5. **Close to the Edge** 5.11+ ★★★
   Excellent climb, superb rock, involving strenuous technique. Climb a thin crack that diagonals up rightward.

6. **Toothpick** 5.11 C ★★★
   The local classic, one of Rocky Butte's finest. Start on a ledge, step up left onto the vertical face via awkward holds. Either traverse left on a horizontal crack to finish up via Close to the Edge (the standard method) or climb straight up a crack-seam to the top (harder).

7. **Far from the Edge** 5.11+ (TR) ★

8. **Rob's Ravine** 5.9
   Pro to 3"
   A deep dihedral to the right of Toothpick.

Breakfast Cracks

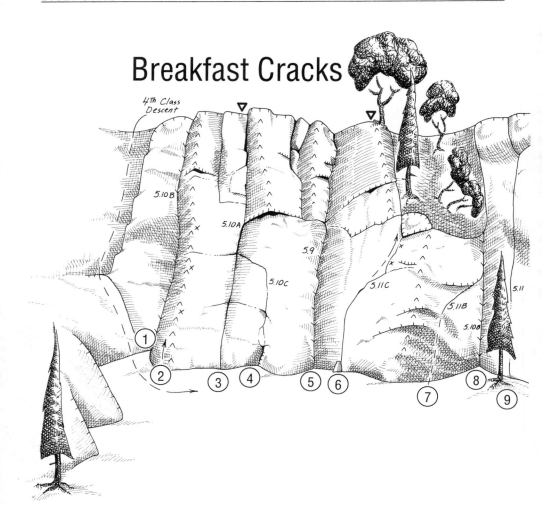

9. **Competitive Edge** 5.11 A
   Kind of interesting, not quite so easy to follow the arete.
10. **Vertical Therapy** 5.9 ★★
    Pro to 3"
    Ascend via a crack leading to a face, then finish up a crack near the top. An excellent climb and a must for everyone.
11. **Power Surge** 5.10 A
12. **Stiff Fingers** 5.9
    Obscure route 30 ft. right of the above climb.

Boulders in the Woods

1. **The T. Tube** 5.9
2. **Burgerville** 5.10 C
3. **Kindergarten Snack** 5.2

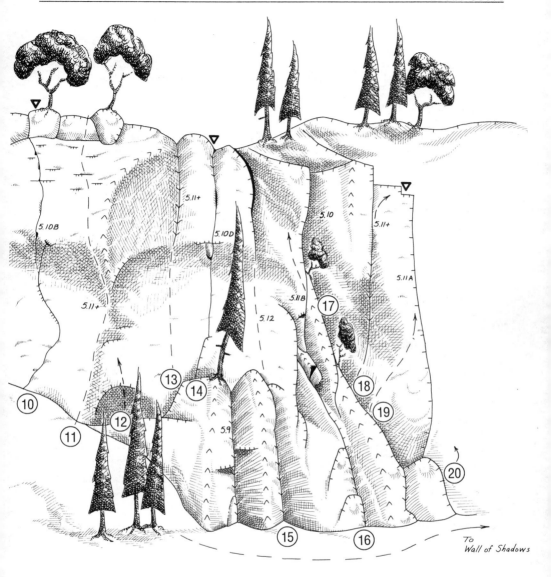

Breakfast Cracks

This small but historical amphitheatre offers several of the finest 5.10 cracks at the Butte.

1. **"D" and Rising** 5.10 B

2. **The Arete**
   3 QD's and #2 Friend
   A bolted arete at the left corner of this little amphitheatre. Looks climbable but not easily clippable.

3. **Blackberry Jam** 5.10 B ★★★
   Pro to 2"
   Very popular local favorite at the Butte. A steep crack system ending with a stiff crux exit move.

4. **Hot Tang** 5.10 C (variation)
A quick fingertips start to Blackberry Jam. Interesting.

5. **Expresso** 5.9 ★★
Pro to 2"
An obvious dihedral corner with a dirty exit move. Fun and quite popular. Climb the right facing corner.

6. **Red Zinger** 5.11 C ★★
Pro to 1"
An excellent and difficult undercling smear problem. Frequently top-roped and good for a quick pump. Start as per Expresso, but attack the seam that diagonals up right to a brushy slope.

7. **Orange Spice** 5.11 B ★
A top-rope face problem that ascends vertical rock diagonally to join with Lemon Twist. A good but short climb.

8. **Lemon Twist** (Direct Start) 5.10 B

9. **Lunge and Plunge** 5.11 (TR)

10. **White Rabbit** 5.10 B ★★★
Pro to 1"
One of the original all time favorites at Rocky Butte. Commence up right to a crack, then follow this up leftward then directly to the top of the cliff. Eases at about two-thirds height to sloping steps then a final vertical move.

11. **White Rabbit Buttress** 5.11+ ★★
An exciting climb ascending the outside face just to the right of White Rabbit. Start up thin holds just to the right of White Rabbit to several good large holds, then move up on sidepulls and clings until possible to move up left onto the slabs above. Continue to top.

12. **Unknown** 5.12 C (TR)

13. **Harder Than Life** 5.11 D (TR)

14. **Birds of Paradise** 5.10 D ★★★
Pro to 2"
A very popular, well deserving classic at Rocky Butte. One of the best. Start by angling up easy steps to a stance next to a fir tree (or by starting directly up a dihedral 20 ft. below the tree and hidden from view), then climb the crack on the left of the tree. Undercling through the crux and jam upward to the top of the crag.

15. _____ 5.12 (TR)

16. **Wisdom Tooth** 5.11 B

17. _____ 5.10
Prominent dihedral that diagonals up leftward to the summit. 100 ft. long.

18. **Trix are for Kids** 5.11+ (TR)
A beautiful, difficult overhang seam face climb partway up the same prominent dihedral. Step onto the right face at 1/2 height to ascend.

19. **Time of Your Life** 5.11 A (TR)
An excellent arete problem that starts up the aforementioned dihedral. Traverse to the arete near a patch of bright yellow lichen. Ascend via the left then right side of the arete.

20. **Swiss Miss** 5.10 B
Pro to 2 1/2" TCU's recommended
A crack that leads to the right side of the same arete. Makes use of natural pockets for protection. TCUs a must. Crux is a minor bulge 25 ft. up and may need pins.

Wall of Shadows

As the cliff curves west from Breakfast Cracks you will find the secluded Wall of Shadows. Several short and longer climbs exist, including some future potential for new routes. Though new housing development prohibits topping out on a few of the routes.

1. **Shadows in Space** 5.10 B
2. **Face Disgrace** 5.11+ variation
3. **Skywalker** 5.10 D
4. **Mystic Traveler** 5.11 (R)
5. **Spider Line** 5.11+
6. **Foot Loose** 5.9
7. **Joe's Garden** 5.6
8. **Hang Loose** 5.11+ (TR)
9. **Seventh Wave** 5.12 A

There are a minor selection of routes, some of good quality, that lay to the west near an area called The Grotto. Housing development has virtually curtailed any future ascents or activity in the area due to debris and water seepage and rough terrain. If you are interested in exploring this corner of the world see the **"Guide to Rocky Butte Quarry"** for information concerning those climbs.

Madrone Wall

This beautiful and highly accessible crag in the country, 15 minutes from I-205, is located in southeast suburban Portland, and has become a favorite winter stomping ground for the locals. Seasonally, the Madrone Wall (a.k.a. Red Bluff) is very much a quality winter destination. Comfortable winter temperatures on this southwest facing basalt crag are enticing, with a list of over 100 climbs to tantalize the year-round sports enthusiast.

The crag received sparse attention by early era climbers as long ago as the mid 1970's. Yet the difficulty and steepness of the routes precluded nearly all development of the crag.

In the continual quest for the perfect climb, route exploration took hold of the Madrone Wall late in 1986. Through the special efforts of Chuck Buzzard, John Jackson, Scott Smith, and friends they pioneered numerous excellent super classics such as **Beam Me Up, Mr. Scott** (5.11 C), **Mr. Noodle Arms** (5.11 B), **Ant Abuse** (5.10 A), **Catharsis** (5.11 C) and **Sheesh** (5.10 C).

The area remained a well kept secret until October of 1988. What followed may seem difficult to comprehend, but in just two years nearly 100 routes became established amidst the profusion of dirt, moss, rock and other flying objects. Chuck Buzzard, Wayne Wallace, Tim Olson, Robert McGown, Greg Lyon, Dave Sowerby, and many others were instrumental in creating great classics like **Where the Wild Things Roam** (5.11 D), **Scott Free** (5.12 B), **Full Spank Mode** (5.12 A), **Shining Wall** (5.12 A), **Nouveau Riche** (5.10 C) and **Divine Wind** (5.11 C).

Geographically, the Madrone Wall complex is just one long crag, but out of necessity, the cliff has been subdivided into six sections. They are as follows, from left to right: The Left Corner Wall, The Orange Wall, Fourth Class Wall, Madrone Wall (proper), Shining Wall and the Hardscrabble Wall.

Please do remember that the property is administered by Clackamas County, and it should be considered a privilege to have access available. We continue to hope for a peaceful resolution and co-existence on this land, so common courtesy, climber sense and safety are important factors to be stressed and maintained. In the best interest of all, respect the property and the laws, and maintain a clean environment when visiting here. You are responsible for your actions, and if placed out of control this could jeopardize the situation.

To reach this wonderland of rock, take Hwy. 212, the Clackamas exit from I-205, and drive east 3 miles to the Rock Creek Corner intersection. Turn south at the signal light onto Hwy. 224, toward Estacada, and drive to the small community of Carver. Approximately 2.2 miles further east of Carver on the main road and on the left side of the highway, you will find a large white metal gate with "No Shooting" signs on each side. Park along the highway shoulder only! Walk to the clearing below the Shining Wall. The left branch in the trail leads to the Madrone Wall proper, while the right fork leads directly to the Hardscrabble Wall.

Left Corner Wall

1. **Jackson's Daring Deeds** 5.10 A
   45' Pro to 2"
   This dihedral is located at the far left recesses of the wall.
2. **Patrick's Dihedral** 5.9 ★
   35' Pro to 1 1/2"
   A large dihedral that begins as an offwidth and climbs up past a narrow crux section to a madrone tree belay. Located to the right of a small rounded buttress.
3. **Sheesh** 5.10 C (PG-13) ★★★
   35' Pro to 1" including RP's
   Excellent climb. Definitely recommended. Sheesh is the clean, smooth dihedral with a small half-moon imprint on the left face. Thin crux.

4. **Identity Crisis** 5.10 B (R) ★★
   35' Pro to 1" including #4 Rock
   A fun climb. Recommended for all. Commence up the outside face to the right of Sheesh passing 2 bolts to an easy slab. Surmount a final bulge and move up left to a bolt belay.

5. **Mental Crisis** 5.11 D ★
   35' QD's and minor pro to 1"
   A good, short, difficult problem. Face climb over a substantial bulge past 2 bolts to join with Identity Crisis.

6. **Into The Black** 5.9 ★
   35' Pro to 2"
   A dark, contorted left-leaning crack system that joins with Identity Crisis.

7. **Talk, Talk, Talk** 5.12 A ★★
   30' 3 QD's
   A definite must on your list of climbs. This short, power packed line ascends up a rounded outside corner to a bolt belay. A harsh fingery crux.

Greg Lyon cruising Angular Motion (5.12 A)

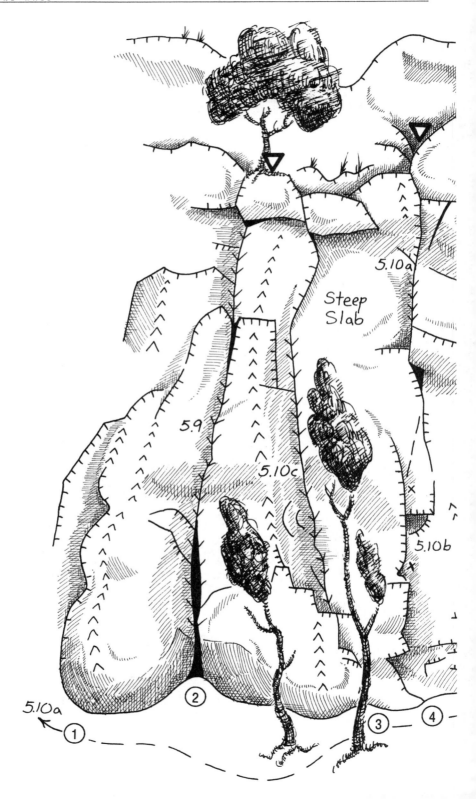

Brushy

Left Corner Wall

Poison
Oak

5.11d

5.9

5.12a

⑤

⑥

⑦

To
Orange
Wall

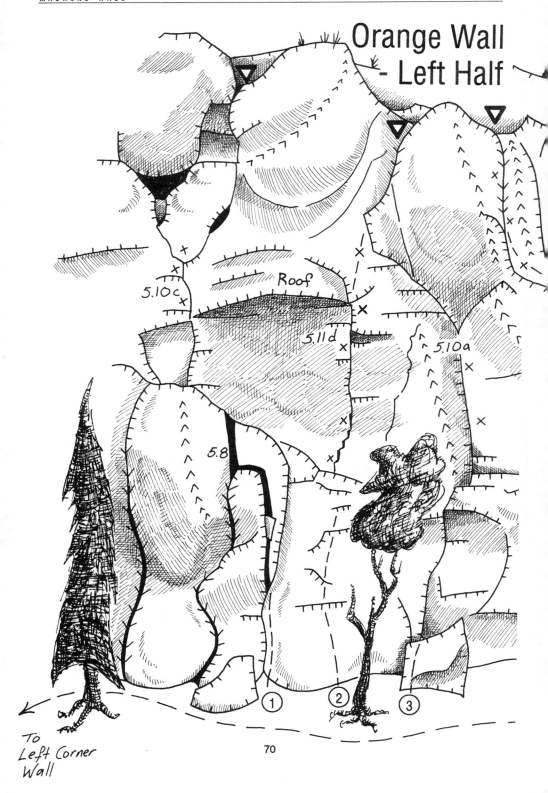

Orange Wall
- Left Half

Roof

5.10c

5.11d

5.10a

5.8

① ② ③

To
Left Corner
Wall

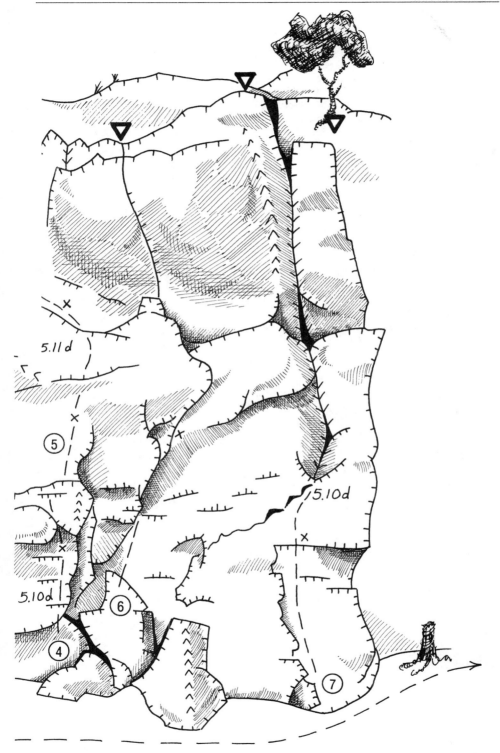

5.11d

5.10d

5.10d

5.10d

④ ⑤ ⑥ ⑦

Orange Wall - Right Half

Orange Wall

1. **Wild Blue Yonder** 5.10 C ★★
   45' Pro to 2"
   An interesting route with plenty of variety. Start next to a large boulder. Begin up a sickle shaped offwidth crack to a small ramp. Step left, then proceed directly up the broken face (3 pitons) just left of the large roof. From an alcove pull over an awkward bulge to a bolt belay.

Fourth Class Wall

5.10c

5.12b

5.10d

5.10d

5.9

Dirty

4th Class
To Summit

To
Madrone Wall

2. **Where the Wild Things Roam** (a.k.a. Wild Things) 5.11 D ★★★
45'   5 QD's and minor pro to 3/4"
One of the ten great classics at the Madrone Wall. Exhilarating problem ascending up a
brilliant orange face. Begin up an easy slab to the first bolt, then up a continuously overhanging face using numerous incut edges. Turn to the right side of the large roof and move
up a reasonable dihedral to a bolt belay. This is an excellent rainy day climb.

3. **Tangerine Dream** 5.10 A (PG-13) ★
   45' Pro to 1"
   A popular route. Start off a boulder and mantle over a crux bulge move, then continue up a dihedral (bolts) until able to angle up left to a bolt anchor.

4. **Direct Start** (to Tangerine Dream) 5.10 D ★
   15' QD's and pro to 1"

5. **Agent Orange** 5.11 D ★★
   45' Pro to 3/4" including TCU's
   A superb, demanding climb! Ascend Direct Start to a ledge then face climb up (1 bolt) past a horizontal crack, then up left to an overhung shallow double cornered dihedral (3 bolts) to a bolt anchor.

6. **Sub-Arachnoid Space** 5.12 B
   45' (TR)

7. **Midget Madness** 5.10 D (R)
   45' Pro to 2" including TCU's
   A tantalizing problem, yet does not see much climber traffic. Move up easy ground just left of an outside corner. Follow a right-leaning seam and pull an awkward mantle (questionable pro!) into a dihedral. Climb straight up to the top of the pillar to a small tree belay.

8. **Graduation** 5.9
   40' Pro to 1 1/2"
   A left-leaning dihedral with one fixed pin. Step up on large holds then make a quick crux move to easier ground up left. A little dirty near the tree belay, but still a fun climb.

9. **Chop the Monkey** 5.8+
   20' 5 QD's
   A pin protected corner up left from the 3rd bolt on Route Crafters.

10. **Route Crafters** 5.8 ★★
    40' 5 QD's
    A very popular and well-bolted route that wanders up steep ground via many ledges, then up a short dihedral to a bolt anchor.

11. **Cornick's Dihedral** 5.9 ★★
    40' Pro to 1 1/2"
    An interesting route that ascends the obvious deep dihedral just to the right of a large roof. Bolt anchor.

12. **Surfing with the Alien** 5.10 D (R) ★
    40' Pro to 1" RP's, TCU's recommended
    This technically demanding route is well worth the blast. Begin up the seam (immediately right of the large dihedral) that angles right to a vertical crack. Continue up a steep face and crack, then bail out left to the dihedral or proceed up through another crux via a thin seam to a bolt anchor.

13. **Wicked Little Nasty** 5.10 B (R) (variation)
    15' Pro to 3/4" TCU's recommended
    Located high and right around the corner from Surfing with the Alien. Rather short!

14. **Variations** 5.7 to 5.10 C

Fourth Class Wall

1. **Cut and Dried** 5.10 C
   40' Pro to 2"
   On the left side of this tiny section of cliff is a large dihedral. Climb up past a hard move until it eases. The quality deteriorates as the vegetation increases near the top.

2. **Severed Heads** 5.12 B ★
   30' 3 QD's
   Difficult arete climb.

3. **Short But Sweet** 5.10 D ★
   40' Pro to 1 1/2"
   An excellent climb. Proceed up the dihedral corner, moving past several small lips, step up left (1 bolt) and continue up easier vertical ground to a unique belay.

4. **Cult of Personality** 5.10 D ★
   40' Pro to 1"
   Ascend past a small bulge (1 piton), then exit up right along a right-facing dirty corner leading to a tree belay.

5. **Wolf of the Steps** 5.9
   35' Pro unknown

6. **Slippery Sage** 5.8
   30' Pro unknown

Madrone Wall

1. **Save the Whales** 5.10 A
   30' Pro to 3"

2. **Hungry for Duress** 5.10 A
   30' Pro to 3"
   Located 5 ft. left of Beam Me Up, Mr. Scott. A quick pump.

3. **Beam Me Up, Mr. Scott** 5.11 C (PG-13) ★★★
   65' Pro to 1 1/2" including TCU's
   One of the 10 super classics at the Madrone Wall. A fantastic, bold route of superior quality. Proceed up an overhanging face via incut edges (2 bolts) to a small stance. Desperately continue straight up the crack above (bolt) to a small ledge, then exit right to a tree belay above Rising Desperation.

4. **Scott Free** 5.12 B ★★★
   60' 5 QD's and minor pro to 3"
   Another excellent super classic. This one involves a fierce lunge! Start at the inside corner and move up right to a stance. Step up and left onto the central face and climb straight up. Lunge to a jug, then finish up an easy right facing corner to a tree belay.

5. **Rising Desperation** 5.10 A ★★
   60' Pro to 2"
   Interesting, fun, jagged crack system that ascends the vertical blocky section immediately right of Scott Free.

6. **Direct Finish** 5.10 A (variation)
   15' Pro to 2 1/2"

7. **Dr. Opus Goes Power Lunging** 5.11 C ★
   60' Pro to 1 1/2"
   An impressive climb with much variety. Begin up a smooth, clean 3 bolt face until possible to step out left onto a short (5.9) arete mantle move. From the upper ledge, power lunge your way up a very thin seam to the summit.

8. **Spectrum** 5.10 B ★★
   20' Pro to 3/4" including TCU's
   Excellent short problem. Start in a roof capped dihedral, then undercling out left and up the face (1 piton) to a fixed anchor on a ledge.

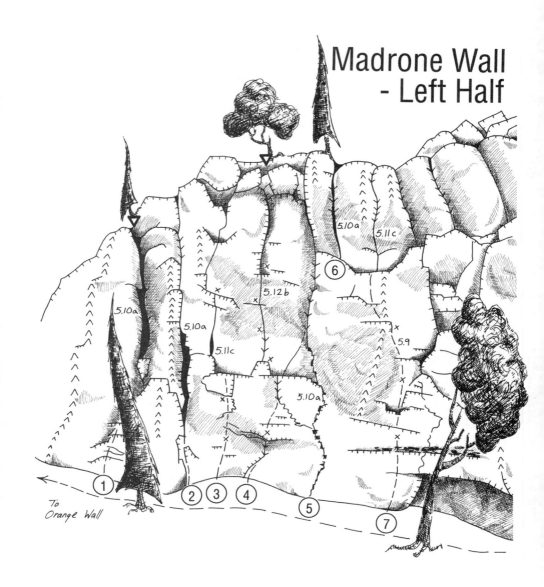

Madrone Wall
- Left Half

5.10a

5.11c

5.10a

5.12b

6

5.10a

5.11c

5.9

5.10a

1

To
Orange Wall

2 3 4

5

7

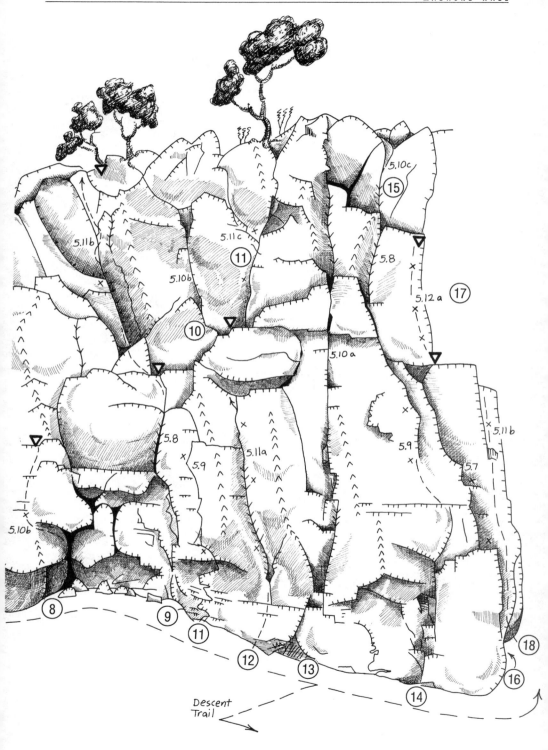

5.10c
15
5.11b
5.11c
5.8
11
5.10b
5.12a
17
10
5.10a
5.11b
5.8
5.9
5.11a
5.9
5.7
5.10b
8
9
11
18
12
16
13
14

Descent
Trail

77

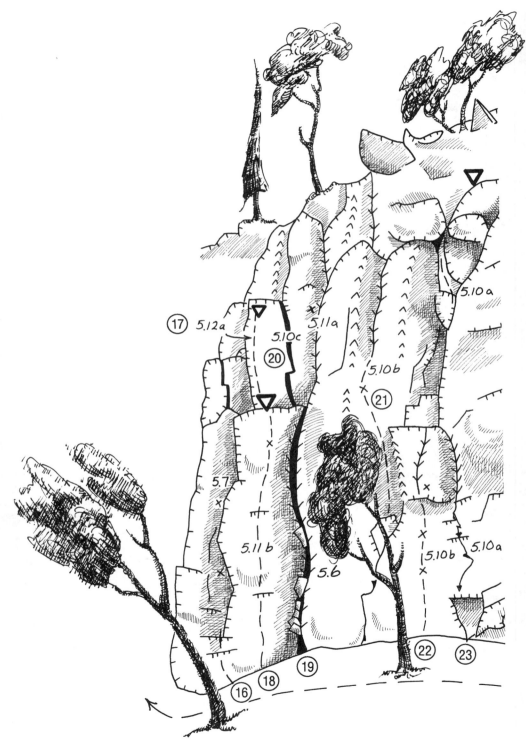

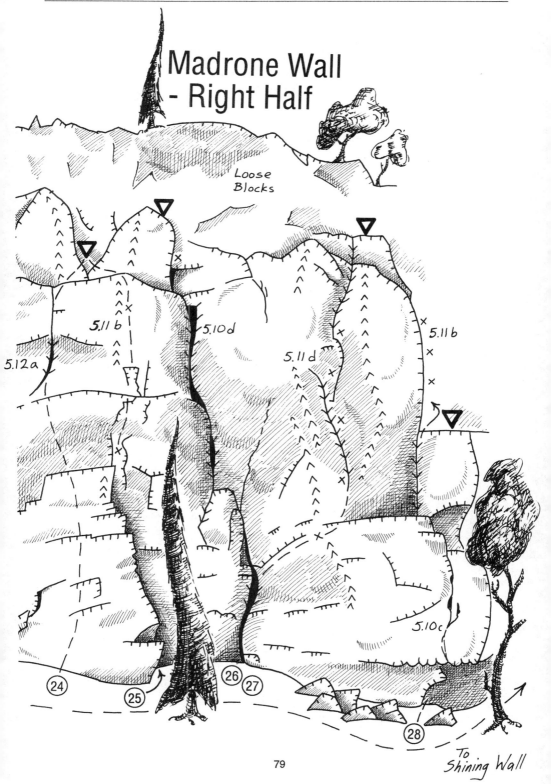

Madrone Wall
- Right Half

Loose Blocks

5.11 b

5.10 d

5.12 a

5.11 d

5.11 b

5.10 c

24

25

26 27

28

To Shining Wall

9. **Aerial Display** 5.11 B ★★
100' Pro to 1 1/2"
One of the few exciting roof climbs at the Madrone Wall. Start to the right of the deep corner (Spectrum) and move up an odd but easy (5.8) groove to ledges. Step left and embark up easy ground to the huge slanting roof broken by an undercling crack. Cling desperately out (1 bolt) and up to the ramps above. Continue up left to a tree belay.

10. **Mixing It Up** 5.10 B
100' Pro to 2"

11. **Catharsis** 5.11 C (PG-13) ★★★
100' Pro to 1 1/2" TCU's, RP's required
Mentally challenging and a serious lead. Begin up a vertical outside corner (5.9) broken with numerous holds (2 bolts) until you reach a ledge and belay. Step right and proceed onto desperate ground above, then angle up a difficult left seam (bolt) exiting to the top.

12. **Superstrings** 5.11 A
30' 3 QD's and optional pro to 1"
A frequently climbed shallow dihedral that ends on good ledges.

13. **Lost in the Delta Neighborhood** 5.10 A
100' Pro to 2"
Ascend a vertical corner crack system until you must pull over a semi-detatched set of blocks split with a crack. Wander up another dihedral and vertical ground to the summit.

14. **Sultans of Swing** 5.9
30' 3 QD's and minor pro to 1 1/2"

15. **Scotty Hits the Warp Drive** 5.10 C
100' Pro to 1 1/2"
Start at the Double Dutch belay ledge, step left and ascend a short dihedral to another ledge, then up a slightly overhung crack to the top.

16. **Double Dutch Left** 5.7 ★★
25' QD's and pro to 1"
Popular, easy dihedral with numerous ledges.

17. **Subway to Venus** 5.12 A ★★
18' 3 QD's
Just above the Double Dutch belay ledge is a unique but short arete problem. Bolt anchor.

18. **Trauma Center** 5.11 B ★
100' Pro to 1 1/2"
An excellent second pitch. The first pitch (5.11 A) climbs up a face (2 bolts) between the two Double Dutch routes. From the belay ledge, step right and finish up an orange dihedral (1 bolt) leading to (5.11 B) the top.

19. **Double Dutch Right** 5.6 ★
20' Pro to 4"
The obvious large offwidth corner.

20. **Primary Gobbler** 5.10 C
20' Pro to 6"
The second half of this large offwidth.

21. **Whatever Blows Your Skirt Up** 5.10 B (PG-13) ★
65' Pro to 1 1/2"
Ascends up easy rock left of Pillowtalk to a smooth face (1 bolt), then up a shallow dihedral capped by a small bulge.

22. **Pillowtalk** 5.10 B (variation) ★★
20' 3 QD's and pro to 1 1/2"
A popular trade route, though it is much more interesting when combined with Ant Abuse.

23. **Ant Abuse** 5.10 A (PG-13) ★★
60' Pro to 1 1/2" Cams recommended
This fun, clean route begins up the thin cracks immediately right of Pillowtalk. Pull up to the ledge, then move up a large open dihedral and step left to crank over an overhang (crux). Bolt belay.

24. _____ 5.12
50' (TR)
An incredible quality face climb with a short but difficult crux at a minor overhang. Bolt belay.

25. **Mr. Noodle Arm (goes limp)** 5.11 B (R) ★★★
50' Pro to 1" TCU's, RP's recommended
A route of staggering proportions. A very quality route and a must for everyone. Begin near a tall, thin fir tree. Climb a vertical broken arete (crux) to a stance, then move up left to a bolt anchor.

26. **Sisters of the Road** 5.10 D ★★
60' Pro to 1 1/2"
Highly recommended. Move up easy ground in a dihedral. The climb increases in difficulty with height until you encounter a deceiving crux in a pea-pod flare. From a small stance, pull through a mantle (piton) and finish up easy ground to a bolt anchor.

27. **Full Spank Mode** 5.11 D ★★★
65' 5 QD's and minor pro to 1/2"
One of the ten super classics. Start as for Sisters of the Road, but step right, lean out around on jug holds to a stance. Then embark up the difficult and slightly overhung face above. Eases to several ledges and a bolt belay.

28. **Arm Forces** 5.11 B (R) ★★★
65' Pro to 1" including TCU's, RP's
A superior climb and one of the ten famous classics. This bold and demanding route begins up a thin (5.10 D) vertical seam to a large ledge. Boldly march onto the sustained, overhung, rounded dihedral (bolts) leading to several ledges and a bolt belay.

29. **Cold Hand of Technology** 5.10 C.
70' Pro to 1 1/2"
Unique. Start at the large halfway ledge on Arm Forces. Step up right and ascend a dihedral until you can launch into a left leaning crack that turns a corner. Transverse left to the Arm Forces belay.

Shining Wall

1. **Arm Forces** 5.11 B (R)

2. **Cold Hand of Technology** 5.10 C

3. **Red Scare** 5.10 C (R)
25' Pro to 3/4" RP's and thin wires
Step off a large boulder and ascend a thin seam (1 bolt) to the large ledge. Finish up one of several routes.

4. **Domino Effect** 5.9
25' Pro to 1"

5. **Dirty Dancing** 5.9
80' Pro to 2 1/2"
Start at an overhang. Climb a corner up to the halfway ledges and step right to ascend a dirty meandering (5.7) corner system up a near vertical cliff. Bolt anchor at top.

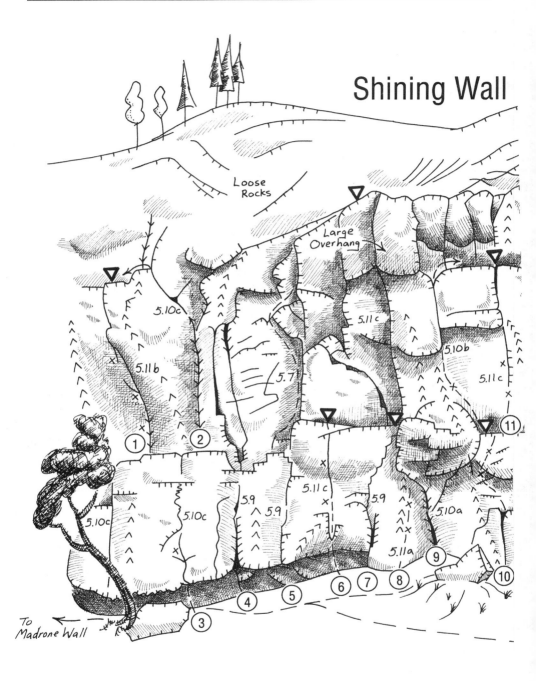

Shining Wall

Loose Rocks

Large Overhang

5.10c

5.11c

5.11b

5.7

5.10b

5.11c

① ②

5.10c

5.10c

5.9

5.9

5.11c

5.9

5.10a

5.11a

⑪

③ ④ ⑤ ⑥ ⑦ ⑧ ⑨ ⑩

To Madrone Wall

6. **Firing Line** 5.11 C (R)
   40' 2 QD's and minor pro to 3/4"
   An interesting bullet-scarred face. Runout and improper bolt locations. Pull through a flared overhung slot, move up a smooth face, then up a short, vertical crux until you can mantle up to a bolt belay.

7. **Lord of the Rings** 5.9
25' Pro to 3" Cams suggested
A short flare problem that angles up to join Dancing in the Lion's Jaw at the bolt anchor on a
ledge.

8. **The Gift of Time** 5.11 A (variation)
   15' 2 QD's and minor pro to 1"

9. **Dancing in the Lion's Jaw** 5.11 C ★★
   80' Pro to 1 1/2" including TCU's
   A bold lead for the serious climber. Start up a central dihedral on the Shining Wall (5.10 A) to a ledge and bolt belay. Commence up the prominent dihedral through two significant roofs. Pull wildly over the last bulge to a 'thank god' belay.

10. **Paleontologist** 5.10 B ★★
    60' Pro to 2"
    A popular climb, and rightly so. Start by stepping up onto a large rock platform. Move up left over a bulge (2 bolts) to a ledge and bolt anchor. Continue up left via a face then a crack to a large ledge with a bolt anchor on the right and above Rainman.

11. **Rainman** 5.11 B ★★
    25' Pro to 1"
    Outrageous, gripping climb. From the first belay on Paleontologist, step up right and climb a steep face to an easy vertical crack. Bolt anchor.

12. **Playing with Fire** 5.11 B
    60' Pro to 1"
    Good route. From the large platform, move up a deep dihedral (1 bolt) to a ledge. Continue up a fun curving finger crack system (1 piton) ending at an upper ledge. Step right and belay at anchor above the Shining Wall route. It is a 5.10 A if topping out above here.

13. **Shining Wall** 5.11 D ★★★
    60' 9 QD's
    A super classic. Climbs the obvious bolted orange face. A physically difficult route using many sloping edges only to end with a deceiving exit move.

14. **Cloudwalker** 5.11 C ★
    60' Pro to 1" TCU's recommended
    The first 15 ft. is the crux. Start near a group of madrone trees on the right side of the wall. Surmount a difficult start, step up left to a steep but reasonable crack with one hard move (5.10 B) at a bulge. Struggle over this to an easy dihedral and a bolt belay.

15. **Banana Belt** 5.10 C (R)
    60' Pro to 1 1/2" Needs bolts
    An inconspicuous prow that would make a fine climb were it bolted. Climb an easy offwidth to a ledge, then up a vertical prow broken with numerous edges. Belay at Cloudwalker anchor.

16. **Fits and Starts** 5.10 A
    30' Pro to 1 1/2"

17. **Beginner's Luck** 5.5
    60' Pro to 1 1/2"
    You can't miss it. Obvious wide chimney corner behind several madrone trees.

18. **Gym Rats From Hell** 5.10 C ★★
    40' Pro to 2"
    A unique climb. A great top-rope area because of its easy access from one anchor. This climb has two starts. The left is a steep crack, while the right is an easy approach via shattered flakes. From a halfway stance crank up a smooth face (bolts) and mantle using numerous sloping edges. Bolt belay.

19. **Plywood Jungle** 5.9 ★
    40' 3 QD's
    Fun lead.

Shining Wall
- Right Corner

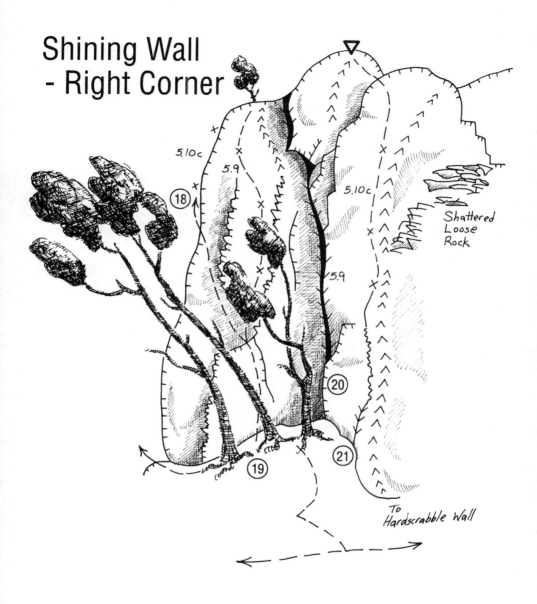

5.10c

5.9

18

5.10c

Shattered
Loose
Rock

5.9

20

21

19

To
Hardscrabble Wall

20. **Dihedral of Despair** 5.9
    40' (TR)
    The large yet somewhat loose dihedral. Top-rope only!

21. **Shattered Dreams** 5.10 C
    40' Pro to 1"
    A bit dusty, but otherwise a fun route. Start just to the right of Dihedral of Despair and
    ascend a short, jagged finger crack to a smooth face. A few tricky moves (bolts) and then
    traverse left to the bolt anchor.

Hardscrabble Wall

1. **Sacrifice** 5.10 A
   40' Pro to 1"

2. **Inner Vision** 5.11 A
   40' Pro to 1" including TCU's
   A bolted overhang left of Mind Games.

3. **Mind Games** 5.11 B ★★★
   40' Pro to 1" including TCU's
   One of the ten classics and a fun roof problem at that. Step up an easy slab, then ape your way out to the overhang (2 bolts) and straight up to easier ground. A final 5.8 move brings you to a bolt belay.

4. **Chicken** 5.7 (variation)
   25' Pro to 1" including TCU's
   The easy way around Mind Games

5. **Gym Droid** 5.9 (variation)
   25' Pro to 1"

6. **Life As We Know It** 5.8
   30' Pro to 1"
   Thirty feet to the right of Mind Games is a beautiful red-orange face broken by an overhang halfway up. The left variation is the easiest.

7. **Red Sun Rising** 5.10 B ★★
   30' Pro to 1 1/2"
   A great climb and very popular. Begin up an unprotected seam immediately right of the offwidth. At the roof, undercling out and surmount the overhang (1 bolt) via large jugs. Continue up and left to a bolt belay.

8. **It Takes a Thief** 5.10 D (PG-13) ★★
   30' QD's and pro to 1"
   A tantalizing route. Ascend the steep red face (bolts) past a hard move, then angle up and left to the anchor.

9. **American Girl** 5.9
   30' Pro to 1"

10. **Miss Adventure** 5.10 A
    35' Pro to 1 1/2"
    An interesting thin finger crack immediately right of the dihedral and behind several madrone trees.

11. **Primordial Soup** 5.9
    40' Pro to 1"

12. **Crystal Hunter** 5.10 B
    40' Pro to 1"

13. **Winds of War** 5.11 A ★★
    30' 4 QD's
    Quality face climb. Begin up just left of the Mountaineer's Route. Ascend a steep face and pull through a thin crux, then step right to a tree belay. The cracks on both sides detract slightly from the aesthetics of the route.

14. **Mountaineer's Route** 5.4
    30' Pro unknown

15. **Punters in Paradise** 5.9+
    50' Pro to 2"
    Proceed up the slightly overhung buttress via a crack just to the right of a poison oak bush. Angle up left and finish up an easy hand crack to a large fir tree near the summit.

16. **Red Fox** 5.11 A (PG-13)
    50' Pro to 1 1/2"
    An interesting climb with a nasty crux. Ascend a beautiful right-facing dihedral (has poison oak) and exit up left (crux) to easy slabs. Continue up a hand crack to the top.

17. **Windows of Your Mind** 5.10 A ★★
    40' Pro to 1 1/2" optional pro to 3"
    This great climb starts up a vertical crack broken with several large triangular "windows." Pull through a thin crux and finish up an easy offwidth. Bolt belay.

18. _____ 5.11 B
    40' (TR)

19. _____ 5.6
    40' Pro to 2 1/2"

20. **Electric Everything** 5.7 ★
    40' Pro to 2 1/2"
    Climbs up around the left side of the Guillotine Flakes topping out via an offwidth.

21. **Cast of Characters** 5.9
    20' Pro to 1"

22. **Nouveau Riche** (New Wealth) 5.10 C ★★★
    70' Pro to 1 1/2" TCU's suggested
    A super classic and well worth it. Superb, fun climbing. Begin at a large boulder near the head of the approach trail. Dance up a steep left-leaning crack to a stance, then up a crack splitting a smooth face. Step right, surmount an easy bulge. Wander up easy slabs just under a left-sloping roof, and move around a block then up to a tree belay.

23. **Stud** 5.7 (R) (variation)
    20' Pro to 3" Cams recommended

24. **Reinhold's Dihedral** 5.10 A
    30' Pro to 1 1/2"
    A short right leaning dihedral, followed by several ledges leading to a bolt belay.

25. **Eye of the Tiger** 5.10 C
    15' Pro to 3/4"
    The dull arete just to the right of 'Reinhold's.' A thin seam protects the moves. A little dirty.

26. **Fisticuffs** 5.11 C ★
    20' (TR)
    A short but physically demanding top-rope problem that ascends a smooth overhang split by a flared crux move.

27. **Goldfingers** 5.10 A ★★
    60' Pro to 1 1/2" TCU's recommended
    A fabulous and popular route. A must for all. Begin up an odd corner near four madrone trees. Move past a thinly protected seam (5.7) to a series of ledges. Proceed up a clean flared crack until able to step left to an offwidth. Pull up to a ledge and bolt belay.

28. **Girl Crazy** 5.10 A (variation)
    15' 2 QD's and minor pro to 1"
    An interesting variation that joins Reinhold's Dihedral with the Goldfingers offwidth section.

29. _____ 5.10
    20' Pro unknown

30. **Marginal Virgin** 5.10 C (R)
    15'
    Fascinating short solo problem that ascends a bulging clean arete near a large maple tree.

31. **The Arete** 5.9
    25' (TR)

Hardscrabble Wall
- Left Half

5.7

5.11a   x 5.11b

5.10A

5.9

5.9

Poison Oak

① ② ③ ④ ⑤

To Shining Wall

Dirty and Loose
No routes.

Dirty
Ledges

5.9

5.10a

5.9

5.11a

5.10b

5.10d

5.10b

5.4

Poison
Oak

Poison
Oak

6 7   8   9   10   11 12   13   14

Hardscrabble Wall
- Central

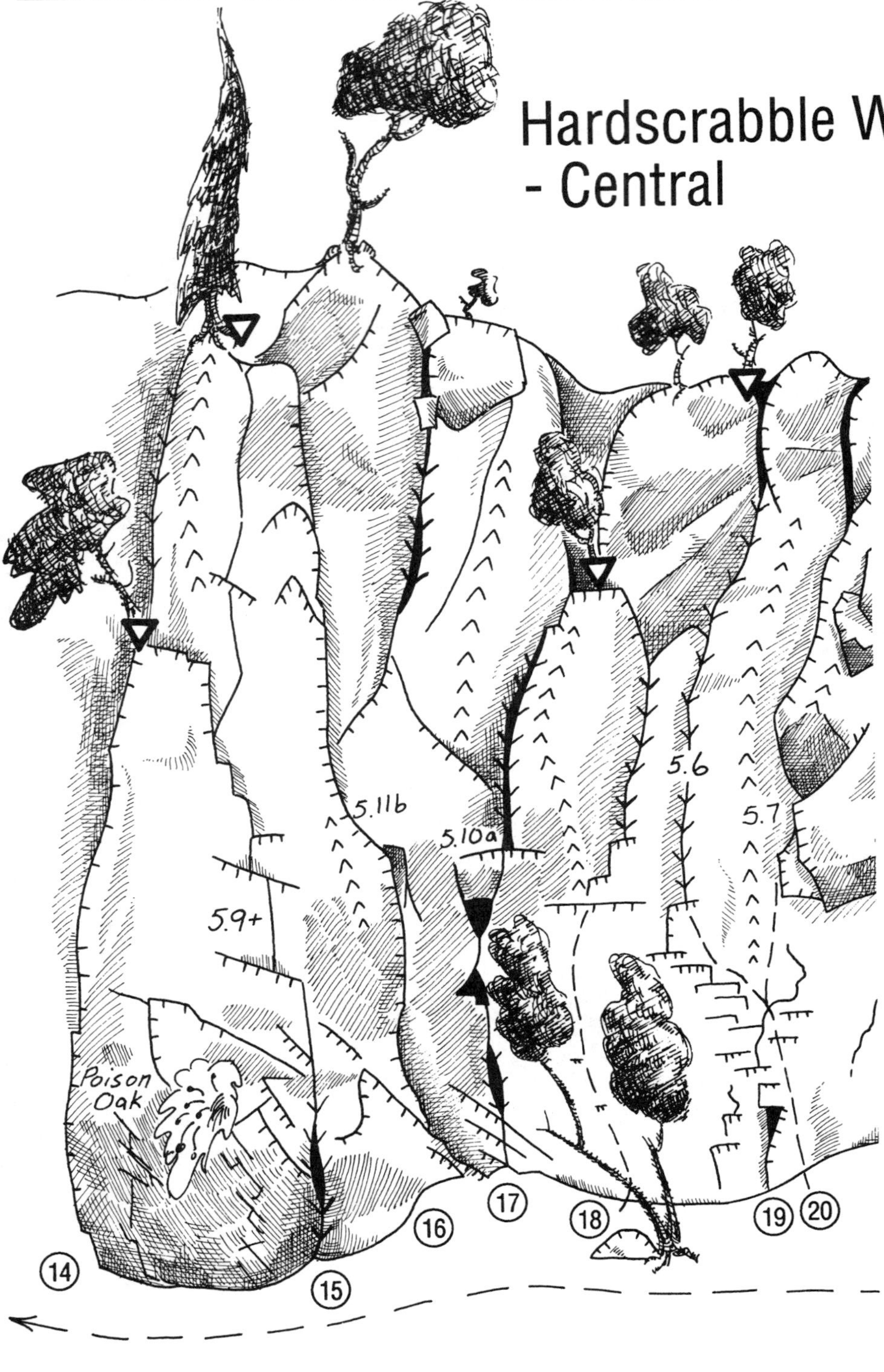

5.11b

5.10a

5.9+

5.6

5.7

Poison Oak

⑭

⑮

⑯

⑰

⑱

⑲ ⑳

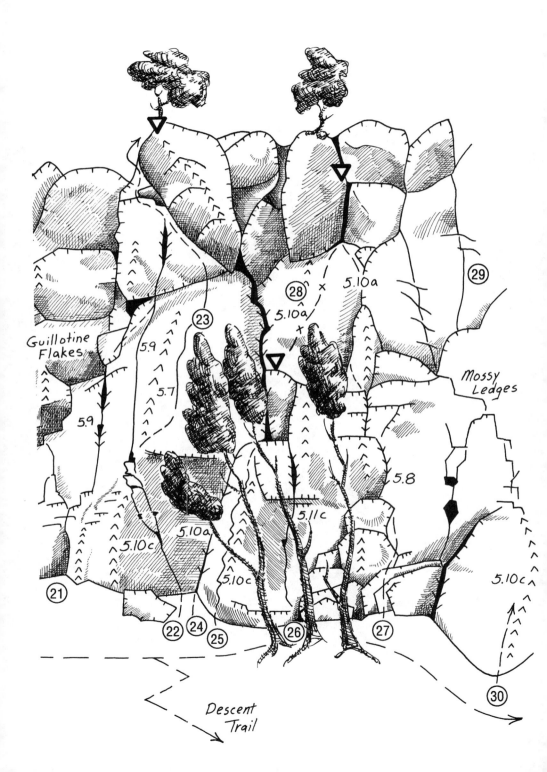

Guillotine
Flakes

5.9

5.7

5.9

23

28
5.10a
5.10a

5.10a

x
5.10a

x

Mossy
Ledges

5.8

5.11c

5.10c

5.10a

5.10c

5.10c

21

22   24

25

26

27

29

30

Descent
Trail

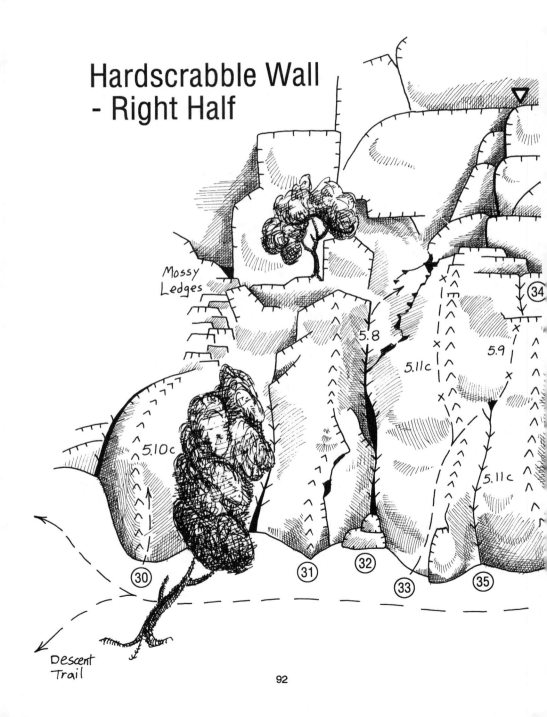

Hardscrabble Wall
- Right Half

Mossy
Ledges

5.8

34

5.9

5.11c

5.10c

5.11c

30

31

32

33

35

Descent
Trail

92

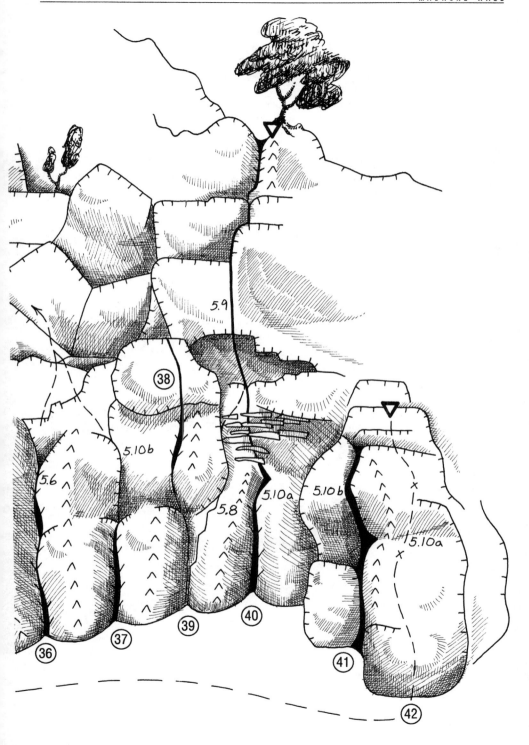

5.9

38

5.6

5.10b

5.8

5.10a

5.10b

5.10a

36

37

39

40

41

42

32. **Exodus** 5.8
    40' Pro to 1 1/2"
    A deep dihedral with a unique large jagged crack on the right face. Climb the dihedral until possible to exit up right to easy ledges. Step up to a bolt belay above Divine Wind.

33. **Divine Wind** 5.11 C ★★★
    40' QD's and minor pro to 3/4"
    One of the ten super classics. Begin on the left side of a minor outside corner. Move up to and ascend the bolted smooth arete, past a crux move to easier ledges. A very popular route. Bolt anchor.

34. **Tapestry** 5.9
    40' QD's and minor pro to 3/4"
    Start up Divine Wind but step right and venture up a separate line of bolts passing a bulge to easy ledges. Bolt belay.

35. **Direct Start** (to Divine Wind) 5.11 C (variation)
    15' Pro to 3/4" TCU's and RP's
    An odd but demanding problem. Originally led on-sight.

36. **Sisters of Mercury** 5.6 ★
    40' Pro to 1"
    A good quality climb for beginners. Ascend the obvious corner to the right of Tapestry.

37. **Chromesister** 5.10 B
    40' Pro to 1"
    Starts as an offwidth but involves a slightly overhung thin crack crux move.

38. _____

39. **Stampede** 5.9
    40' Pro to 1 1/2" Cams suggested

40. **Logjam** 5.10 A ★
    40' Pro to 3" Cams suggested
    This fun, wide crack is located immediately left of a dirty gully. Ascend this and angle up left to a stance below a steep upper section. Several quick jam moves lead to good ledges and a madrone tree belay.

41. **Dangerous Breed** 5.10 B ★
    30' Pro to 4"
    The next two climbs are located on the last climbable buttress at the southern end of the Hardscrabble Wall. Dangerous Breed is the "enjoyable" offwidth. Bolt belay.

42. **What's Your Motive?** 5.10 A ★★
    30' 2 QD's and optional pro to 1/2"
    The last climb, yet very satisfying and fun. Climb up the outside face of the buttress to a belay anchor.

Carver Bridge Cliff

The fabulous and elusive Carver Bridge Cliff. For generations this small crag remained well hidden under thick carpets of moss and vegetation. The base of the cliff was, in simple terms, a waist deep jungle of rotten logs, tall sword ferns, maple saplings and alder brush.

Though nearly impenetrable, early "pioneers" did venture to Carver and make forays onto this hidden crag. The occasional fixed piton attested to this fact. Even on the Yellow Wall (on Angular Motion) there was an old fixed 10 ft. rope hanging from a bashie, ascended in 1975 by Jeff Alzner and Terry Jenkins.

Late in the summer of 1987, I personally visited here and immediately realized its vast potential for free climbing routes. And in two seemingly short years, unbelievable amounts of vegetation were gardened away to produce a local climber's paradise. The superb classics are numerous and the climbing here is indeed excellent.

The Carver Bridge Cliff formation extends roughly along an east-west axis for several hundred yards in length. Minor outcrops do occur beyond the main sections described, but are not developed for climbing. The highest portion of the cliff (Rockgarden Wall) is approximately 130 feet. Carver has four sections of wall that have been named and developed for climbing purposes. They are as follows: the Rockgarden Wall, the Wall In-Between, Yellow Wall and Ivy League Buttress. The majority of the routes are rated from 5.9 to 5.12 and most are bolted or pinned. In other words, you may have to look hard to find an "R" rated climb at Carver.

The crag was predominantly developed by the author, hands down. Though, as for all climb areas, others such as Greg Lyon, Mike Pajunas, Robert McGown, Gary Rall and Wayne Wallace were instrumental throughout most of the 1987-90 seasons.

Here are several astounding classics to tease your fingertips: **Smerk** (5.11 A and one of the finest), **Angular Motion** (5.12 A), **Uncola** (5.11 C), **Notorious** (5.11 B), **Sea of Holes** (5.12 A) and **Rites of Passage** (5.10 B - First pitch). These and a host of other great climbs helped to set the area on edge and in motion!

Several important issues do need to be stressed. Carver is a very small, privately owned crag and future route development here is extremely limited. Needless cramming of more bolt routes is unnecessary, so please come to free climb only. Yes, the crag and the surrounding property are under private ownership. Continued freedom of access ultimately depends upon **your** willingness to obey the rules.

The situation could change, but as of this writing, climbing is open only to members of The Club. To join you must sign a liability release waiver available at the Portland Rock Gym or through the local climbers association.

When visiting, please do not litter (cigarettes included), despoil or vandalize anything. It is hopeful that all who visit will be courteous and respectful of the landowner's right to privacy. Use common sense and safety when climbing here. No excessive noise.

Be vigilant of unruly activities that may jeopardize access privileges. Only club members are allowed. Only responsible climbers who wish to maintain and preserve the area should plan to climb here. If you wish to climb dirty, go elsewhere!

Rockgarden Wall

1. **Crack in the Mirror** 5.9 ★★
   30' Pro to 1 1/2"
   At the far left side of the wall and just uphill is a unique looking "broken" flake start. Ascend this and exit right to an anchor at a ledge.

2. **Unknown** 5.10 A (variation)
   15' Pro unknown

Rockgarden Wall
- Left Half

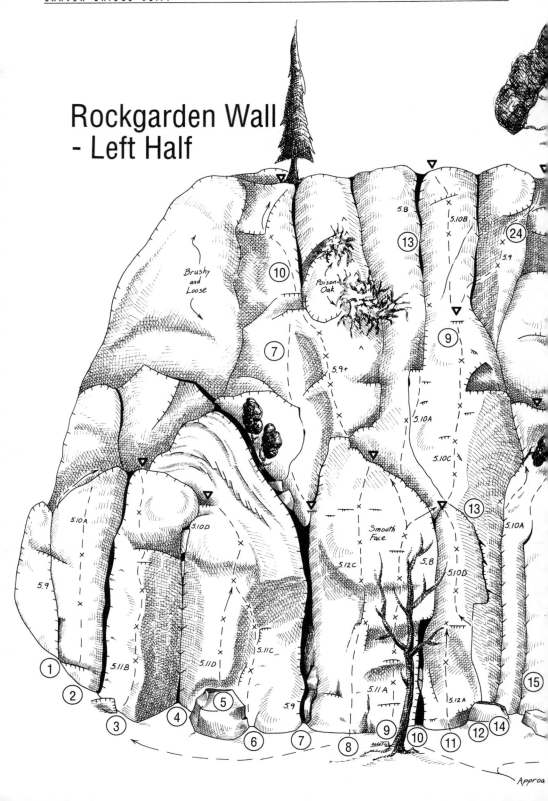

Brushy and Loose

Poison Oak

Smooth Face

5.8

5.10B

5.9

5.9+

5.10A

5.10C

5.10A

5.10D

5.8

5.12C

5.10A

5.9

5.10D

5.11B

5.11C

5.11D

5.9

5.11A

5.12A

Approa

(1) (2) (3) (4) (5) (6) (7) (8) (9) (10) (11) (12) (13) (14) (15) (24)

(10) (7) (13) (9) (9) (13)

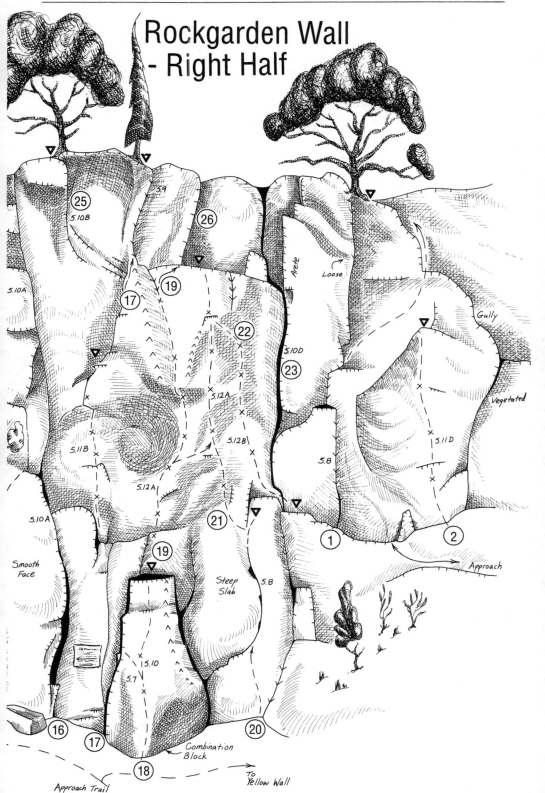

Rockgarden Wall - Right Half

25 5.10B

5.10A

26 5.9

19

17

22

5.10D

23

Arete

Loose

Gully

Vegetated

5.12A

5.11B

5.12B

5.12A

5.11D

5.8

5.10A

21

Smooth Face

19

1

2

Approach

Steep Slab

5.8

15.10

5.7

16

17

18

20

Combination Block

Approach Trail

To Yellow Wall

3. **Notorious** 5.11 B ★★★
35' 5 QD's
One of the great Carver classics. A very good climb! Climb the arete via large holds to a ledge and finish up left to an anchor.

4. **Margueritaville** 5.10 D
40' Pro to 2"
The deep overhung dihedral. A stiff crux. Join with Uncola.

5. **Cherry Cola** 5.11 D (variation) ★★
25' 4 QD's
This difficult problem begins off the top of a large boulder and joins with Uncola before ending at the bolt anchor.

6. **Uncola** 5.11 C ★★★
45' 5 QD's
One of the ten great Carver classics. Located just left of a large chimney. Move up to the top of the boulder, step right onto the face. Ascend the wild, slightly overhung, awkward face up left past a harsh crux. Bolt belay. An excellent route!

7. **Neptune** 5.9 ★★
40' Pro to 1 1/2"
The obvious wide offwidth. A fun climb. Stem, jam and body climb up to a bolt belay. A minor crack on the right face of the chimney offers good small pro.

8. **Smooth Torquer** 5.12 C ★★
45' 4 QD's
An excellent, desperate, physical "tips" climb just to the left of Smerk. Eases to a smooth slab after the crux. Bolt anchor.

9. **Smerk** 5.11 A ★★★
120' (40' 1st pitch) Pro = QD's
One of the finest classic routes at Carver Bridge Cliff. Very popular! Ascend a bolted face left of New Generation past a crux (5.11 A) exiting to the belay on the right. The second pitch (4 bolts) ascends directly up the headwall (5.10 C) to another bolt anchor. The third pitch (which requires a #3 TCU and #7 Rock) finishes straight up a smooth face (2 bolts) via a diagonal seam start. Bolt belay.

10. **New Generation** 5.9+ ★★★
120' (40' 1st pitch) Pro to 1 1/2"
A popular climb. Begin up an awkward start to a small corner and climb a sweet finger crack (5.8) to a bolt belay. Angle up left via a low angle ramp to another bolted face. Continue up this (5.9+) to a ledge, then finish up an arete (5.9) to a fir tree belay. Rappel or walk off.

11. **Free Ride** 5.12 A (variation)
15' 2 QD's
A bolted direct start to Scotch and Soda.

12. **Scotch and Soda** 5.10 D ★★★
40' QD's and pro to 1 1/2"
Fantastic crack and face climb. Start at a ledge beneath the Red Dihedral. Ascend a harsh finger crack until possible to maneuver left onto a small pedestal. Finish up a bolted face to an anchor.

13. **Tequila Sunrise** 5.10 C
120' Pro to 2"
Start as for Scotch and Soda, but traverse right to Red Dihedral, then up left around a minor corner to the New Generation anchor. Continue up easy ramps to the left then up and right (1 bolt) through a 5.10 A crux to a ledge. Move up a 5.8 crack and offwidth to the summit. Bolt belay.

14. **Red Dihedral** 5.10 A ★★
    60' Pro to 1 1/2" TCU's recommended
    Interesting dihedral. Originally named due to the red lichen on the rock. Pull up a crux start
    into the corner and ascend this up and then right to a stubby maple tree. Move past this and
    up a tight crux corner to a large ledge and bolt anchor on the right.

15. _____ 5.12 +
    60' (TR)

16. **Jungle Safari** 5.10 A ★★
    120' Pro to 3"
    An excellent LONG dihedral climb. Begin just left of the offwidth (Combination Block) and
    stem, jam your way up an awkward corner. The crux is a narrow section 80 ft. up. Finish up
    a steep but easy (5.8) fist crack to a tree belay.

17. **Night Vision** 5.11 B ★★
    120' (65' 1st pitch) Pro to 1 1/2"
    Not often climbed because it requires some pro, but is a superb route nonetheless. Com-
    mence up the offwidth crack on the left side of Combination Block. Follow a minor corner up
    and over a wild bulge then up a stiff face (crux) to a bolt anchor. The next pitch ascends a
    5.9 crack up right to the top of the cliff.

18. **Sanity Assassin** 5.7 to 5.10
    20' 2 QD's

19. **Sea of Holes** 5.12 A ★★★
    75' 7 QD's
    A beautiful classic and one of the finest at Carver. Begin from off the top of Combination
    Block and ascend the rounded buttress (crux) via unique pocketed face holds and edges.
    Enter a shallow dihedral where the route eases. Exit up right to a bolt belay. (Note: an
    exciting superior variation exists by connecting the lower half of Sea of Holes with the upper
    half of Wally Street. This demanding route is rated 5.12 C and is referred to as the "Sport
    Court" variation. 8 QD's.)

20. **Shadowfox** 5.8 ★
    25' Pro to 3/4"
    A short crack climb on a smooth slab. A good approach to the upper face climbs.

21. **Wally Street** 5.12 A ★★★
    70' 5 QD's and minor pro to 3/4"
    Start as for Shadowfox but enter up left onto a stiff, vertical face climb of quality proportion.

22. **Wally Wedding** 5.12 B
    20' 4 QD's

23. **Sweat and the Flies** 5.10 D (PG-13) ★
    20' Pro to 3"
    This bold flared offwidth is a surprising lead. Short and nasty, designed to dare anyone.

24. **Battleship Arete** 5.9 (variation)
    20' 2 QD's

25. **Night Life** 5.10 B
    35' Pro to 1 1/2"

26. **Holiday in Cambodia** 5.10 A
    20' (TR)

Wall In-Between

1. **Passport to Insanity** 5.8
   35' Pro to 2"

Ascend a perfect corner, mantle to a ledge, then mantle again, continuing up right, then left to an oak tree belay.

2. **Burning From the Inside** 5.11 D ★★
20' 3 QD's
This exhilarating problem dances up an overhung rounded face to a bolt belay. A great climb.

3. **Hinge of Fate.** 5.10 C ★★
25' 3 QD's and optional pro to 3/4"
At the top of a dirt gully you will find a dark, water streaked face. Ascend this past a crux, then lay back and smear your way up a flared seam (the hinge).

4. **Eyes of a Stranger** 5.10 A
40' Pro to 3/4"

5. **Shady Personality** 5.10 B
65' Pro to 1 1/2" Cams recommended
A unique climb that can be done in two short pitches. Move up a smooth slab (5.9) and up easy steps to a belay on a ledge. Continue up a slightly overhung crack that begins as a mantle into an offwidth pea-pod. Bolt belay.

6. **Rats in the Jungle** 5.10 A
20' Wide pro to 6"
The large chimney problem immediately right of Shady Personality.

Yellow Wall

1. **Call to Greatness** 5.10 C ★★
60' Pro to 2"
An impressive route. Classic thin hand jamming. Begin up a large brushing corner at the left edge of the Yellow Wall. Embark from a stance up the overhung crack system. Boldly climb around three small bulges, the hardest being the last. The main distraction is the Plastic Monkey anchor affixed to the wall at the crux exit move.

2. **Plastic Monkey** 5.13 A
60' 7 QD's
A very difficult problem and one of the hardest at Carver. Ascend the vertical bolted face on the left corner of the Yellow Wall.

3. **Rites of Passage** 5.11 C ★★★
80' 10 QD's
One of the finest, most popular routes at the crag. Commence up a face (1 bolt) and move right (or start up a jam crack to this point), then up a bolted face (5.10 B) until possible to move right to an anchor above Angular Motion. Step back left and continue up via a shallow corner (5.10 B) then up right to a flake to another bolt anchor just under an overhang. Rappel or charge up the thin crack above (1 bolt and pro to 1") leading to the summit.

4. **Digital** 5.12 D (variation) ★★
20' 4 QD's
A unique, yet difficult balance problem.

5. **Angular Motion** 5.12 A ★★★
40' 5 QD's
One of the most popular climbs here. Super classic! To the left of Chemistry Slab is an overhung face. Force your way up this until you must make a lunge to a jug then up right on tenuous holds to a ledge and a bolt belay. An exciting route with dynamic moves.

6. **Out on a Limb** 5.10 A ★
60' QD's and pro to 1 1/2"

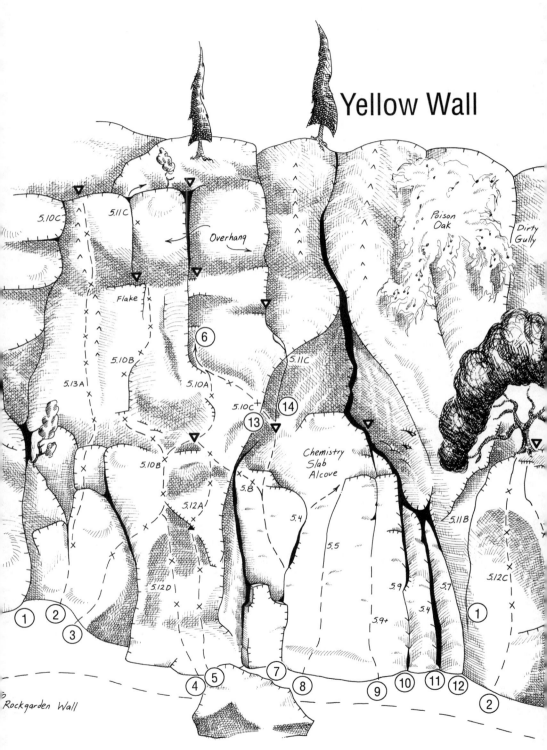

Yellow Wall

5.10C

5.11C

Overhang

Flake

5.10B

5.13A

5.10A

5.10C

5.10B

5.12A

5.12D

5.11C

Chemistry Slab Alcove

5.8

5.4

5.5

5.9

5.9+

5.7

5.4

Poison Oak

Dirty Gully

5.11B

5.12C

Rockgarden Wall

101

A good route. Start up the left side of Chemistry Slab alcove. Exit out left along a narrow ramp (crux) and up to a bolt anchor. Belay, then continue up a face (1 bolt) that leads to a dihedral above. Rappel from a bolt anchor under the final overhang.

The next six climbs are easy problems on the Chemistry Slab.

7. **Smooth Operator** 5.4 ★
   40' Pro to 1 1/2"
8. **Talent Show** 5.5 ★
   40' Pro to 3/4" TCU's and small wires
9. **Blue Monday** 5.9+ ★
   40' (TR)
10. **Crimson Tide** 5.9 ★
    40' Pro to 2"
11. **Spearfishing in Bermuda** 5.4
    40' Large pro
12. **Leaning Uncertainty** 5.7
    15' Pro to 2"
13. **King Rat** 5.10 C
    60' Pro to 1 1/2"
    An "out on a limb" route that exits the upper left side of Chemistry Slab alcove.
14. **Chariots of Fire** 5.11 C ★★★
    55' Pro to 2"
    An incredible and physical climb. A Carver classic for sure. Race up easy slabs passing a bolt anchor. Enter a hand jam crack leading directly up a desperately overhung wall. Exit past a block to a bolt anchor on a small ledge.

Ivy League Buttress

1. **Dreamscape** 5.11 B ★★
   30' Pro to 1 1/2"
   A beautiful tips crack that breaks the right outer face of Chemistry alcove. Ends at the maple tree belay.
2. **Rip Grip** 5.12 C ★
   30' 4 QD's
   A bolted face immediately right of Dreamscape. A desperate tips ripper.
3. **Rubicon** 5.9 ★★
   30' 3 QD's and minor pro to 3/4"
   A very popular easy climb for everyone. Ascend the outside corner (1 bolt) to easy edges, then up a steep face (crux) until you can grab the base edge of a thin crack. Tree belay.
4. **Edge of the Reef** 5.10 B ★★
   45' Pro to 1" TCU's recommended
   A really good climb. Challenging but not extreme. Move up the curved starting crack (numerous edges) then straight up a crack past a face crux with 1 bolt. Finish up a thin crack that rounds to a slab and bolt anchor.
5. **Great Barrier Reef** 5.7 (R)
   30' Pro unknown
6. **Penguins in Heat** 5.12 A
   30' 4 QD's
   A difficult problem located above the first pitch of Edge of the Reef.

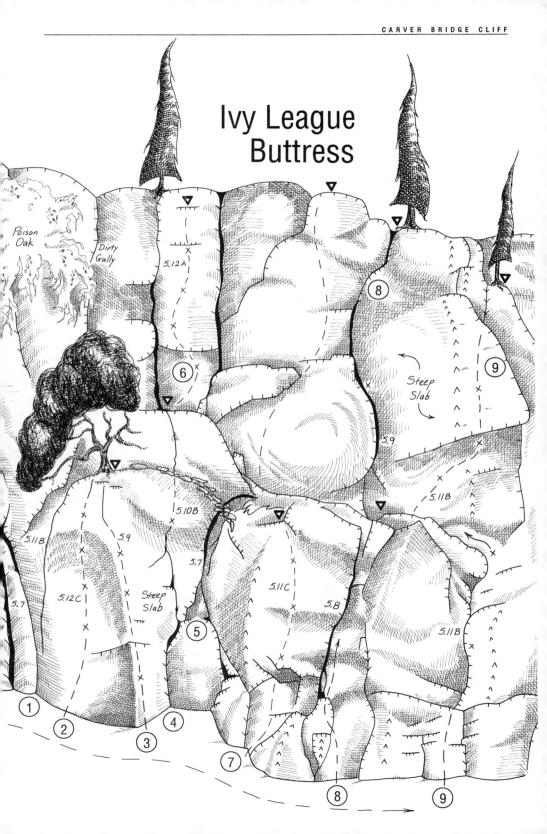

Ivy League Buttress

7. **Challenger** 5.11 C ★★
30' 3 QD's TCU's optional
The name describes the route very well. This quality climb begins up easy steps until you must enter a smooth face broken with unusual edges. Finish up and left to exit at a bolt anchor.

8. **Last of the Mohicans** 5.9 ★
100' (40' 1st pitch) Pro to 2 1/2"
A good, enjoyable climb to learn the basics. The first pitch (5.8) is the most popular. Ascend a broken crack system with a bulge on the right side. Move up and belay at bolts. The second pitch is more unusual, involving some poison oak and flared offwidths. Climb a crack system directly above the anchor until you can top out. Bolt anchor up left on a boulder. Overgrown at the top of the cliff.

9. **Riders of the Purple Sage** 5.11 B ★★
80' QD's and pro to 1" TCU's recommended
This is Carver's unknown and seldom climbed classic. Step up easy ground to a considerably overhung short corner (1 bolt). Stem and layback through and continue up right then left to the bolt anchor for Last of the Mohicans. Step right onto a smooth face (crux) and ascend over a bulge to a slab that leads to a thin fir tree. Rappel from here.

10. **Hexelerator** 5.11 C
110' (40' 1st pitch) QD's and pro to 1 1/2" Needs hangers
A bizarre climb with much variety. Ascends a steep face and along an arete to a bolt belay. Then continues up a sweet looking slab and vertical crack on a smooth face (5.10 D). Rappel from a fir tree. Overgrown with brush and poison oak.

12. **Aphid City-O**
5.10 B (R)
40' Pro to 1" Needs hangers

Gary Rall climbing Angular Motion (5.12 A)

Beacon Rock

The Portland climber could not have asked for a finer big wall crag than Beacon Rock. This is the place! The best technically demanding and sustained dihedral climbing can readily be found here on the huge 400' vertical south face.

Beacon has enchanted and hauntingly enticed generations of climbers ever since the first ascent of the **SE Face** in April of 1954 by John Ohrenschall and Gene Todd. This historical monument of rock was first sighted and named by the Lewis and Clark expedition of 1805-1806. It stood as a final "beacon" to early pioneers seeking the Oregon Country. In 1915 Henry J. Biddle initiated the building of the present day trail which leads to the summit of the rock. In 1935 the rock was established as part of the Washington State Park System, so that all could enjoy the beauty and wonder of this majestic monolith.

In 1961, J.F.K. was president of the U.S., the Beatles were nearing world fame, yet closer to home, the roots of rock climbing at Beacon had just begun. The spectacular efforts of Eugene Dod, Bob Martin, and Earl Levin came true when they succeeded in ascending a prominent dihedral crack and offwidth system near the Arena of Terror. To this date, **Dod's Jam** (5.10 C) stands as a remarkable and classic example of early route pioneering achievement.

Throughout the latter half of the 1960's an inner core of climbers continually broke major barriers via mixed free and aid climbing technique. They created instant attractions like **Flying Swallow** (5.10 D), **Right** and **Left Gull** (5.10 A), **Jensen's Ridge** (5.11 B), culminating with a remarkable winter first ascent of **Blownout** (5.10 A) in January 1969 by Steve Strauch and Danny Gates. Dean Caldwell, Dave Jensen, Steve Strauch, Kim Schmitz, Bob Martin and others involved in the scene shall forever live in the climbers' hall of honors.

The next decade (1970's) provided an even wider variety of mixed free and aid ascents. Two such notable feats certainly would have to be Les Nugent's ascent of **Steppenwolf** (5.10 D) and **Free For All** (5.8) in 1973 by Dean Fry and Steve Lyford. The mid 1970's brought a new group of climbers to the crag as they ascended superb routes like **Flighttime** (5.11 C), **Pipeline** (5.11 A), **Blood, Sweat and Smears** (5.10 C) and **Free For Some** (5.11 A). Jeff Thomas, Mark Cartier, Ted Johnson, Avery Tichner, Alan Kearney, Jim Olson, Mike Smelsar, Robert McGown and others frequently turned toward the countless old aid lines, discovering that these routes produced excellent free climbs. Free climbing was now the vogue.

The following decades have continued to bring an even wider spectrum of climbers to Beacon to join forces. From this new generation of climbers came quality routes like **Cruisin'** (5.7), **Fear of Flying** (5.10 B), **Bladerunner** (5.10 C), **Winter Delight** (5.10 B), **Borderline** (5.11 B), **Excalibur** (5.12 B), **Flying Dutchman** (5.10 B) and **Windsurfer** (5.10 B). Those who continued to astonish in the 1980's and 90's were mainly Ron Allen, Scott Tracy, M. Cartier, Darryl Nakahira, Jim Opdycke, R. McGown, Wayne Wallace, Nathan Charleton, Tim Olson and Jim Yoder. Uncountable tales have yet to be told in the years to come, as only time will tell. So stay tuned to Beacon Rock.

Beacon Rock is a part of the Washington State Park System. The following park rules are to be observed while climbing here.

1. State law requires climbers to sign in and out. A bulletin board and climbing register have been set up at the eastern end of the restroom parking lot to simplify procedures.

2. Climbing is presently limited to the river or south face because of state management policy. Climbing elsewhere would endanger hikers on the west side trail and motorists at the north side facilities.

3. The park discourages climbers from parking in the boat ramp and camping area west of Beacon Rock. The amount of space for automobiles is limited and the railroad company does not like climbers walking along its tracks.

Obey the rules. Any violation would seriously jeopardize the privilege of climbing on Beacon Rock. For those seeking resolutions to this policy contact:

Washington State Parks and Recreation Commission
7150 Clearwater Lane
KY-11
Olympia, Washington 98504-5711

There are two objective hazards to climbing on the south face of Beacon Rock: poison oak and rockfall. Take the necessary precautions and learn to avoid both. Hard hats are recommended for personal safety (see introduction). Do not be dissuaded from climbing at Beacon Rock, for these are minor drawbacks.

Beacon offers technically difficult climbing on extremely sound rock. Competency is a must! Climbing here is not for the faint of heart or for novices. The routes are often multi-pitch, demanding and sustained. Yet Beacon is quality time for the money and well worth the drive. The scenery of the Columbia Gorge is superb, while the literally hundreds of dihedral crack systems are sure to tantalize many climbers for generations to come.

The directions are as follows. Beacon Rock is 28.8 miles east of Portland from I-205 on the Washington side of the Columbia River. For those with a strong appetite to climb, drive east from Vancouver on State 14 (30 min.) or east on I-84 to Bridge of the Gods, then west on State 14 to this famous andesitic monolith of the Gorge.

Climb safely and enjoy your stay.

The following routes are described from right to left and begin near where the east side hikers' trail meets the base of the southeast buttress. The great forboding east face, with its spectrum of illegal routes, lies just to the right.

1. **Pacific Rim** II 5.10 C ★★
   Multi-pitch QD's and minor pro to 1"
   A fantastic route that will keep you on the edge all the way. Begin under the well protected overhangs (of the east face) twenty feet downhill and left of a large alcove. Commence up a shallow corner then face climb (bolts) up right along the virtual edge of the abyss directly below. Belay at a 2 bolt anchor. Rappel 60' or continue up right (bolts) until you can climb a vertical corner that eases to a dihedral. Bolt belay up right on a ledge. Rappel with two ropes 120'. The upper headwall has yet to be completed, yet holds excellent promise.

2. **Boardwalk** 5.6
   Pro to 2" Two rope rappel (120')
   A long, obvious right facing dihedral approx. 40' uphill from the trail. Climb the corner up to a roof, step right then up to a bolt anchor. Rappel.

3. **Southeast Buttress** Abandoned project

4. **Unknown**

5. **Obnoxious Cubbyhole** 5.7 A2
   Protection unknown
   Nail up to the right of Stone Rodeo until the two routes meet at the large roof. Not recommended.

6. **Stone Rodeo** 5.12 A ★★★
   65' QD's and minor pro to 3" Friends recommended
   A supreme example of physical endurance. As the hikers' trail meets the cliff beneath Cruisin', look to the right 25 ft. past an oak tree. Beyond is a bolted overhung face that leads up through a roof split with a crack. Climb this and enjoy. Excellent rock. Pro needed for roof.

7. **Rock Police** II 5.10 C ★
   QD's and pro to 1" TCU's required Poor hangers
   To the right of the same oak tree 15 ft. is a bolted face that follows a right leaning arete.

Unusual climb but still fun. Poor hangers. Climb up a face (to the left of Stone Rodeo) to a bulge crux move (bolt). Angle up right on a steep slab staying near the arete (crux), eventually easing to a ledge and bolt anchor. Rappel 65 ft. or angle up left to the second belay on the SE Face route. From there move up right (5.9) to a slabby right-facing arete. Rejoins with SE Face near the top of the slab.

8. **Return to the Sky** 5.10 A
   65' Pro to 1 1/2"
   A seldom climbed route that angles over several dihedrals then up a corner. Start behind the oak tree and climb up right past a bolt (crux) then upward to a bolt belay. Rappel.

9. **Sky Pilot** 5.11 A
   95' Pro to 2"
   Start as for Return To The Sky except storm through a weakness in the overhang above. Obscure.

10. **Couchmaster** 5.9
    100' Pro to 1 1/2"
    Start up slab behind oak tree, step left and turn corner stemming up (crux) to join with Cruisin'.

11. **Jingus Jam** 5.9 (variation)
    35' Pro to 2"

12. **Cruisin' Direct Finish** 5.11 C (variation)
    25' Pro to 3/4" Needs pitons

13. **Cosmic Dust** 5.10 B (variation)
    25' Pro to 1"

14. **Cruisin'** (a.k.a. Cruisemaster) 5.7 ★★★
    100' Pro to 2"
    An excellent local favorite. And rightly so. Start up a fun slab 15 ft. left of the large oak tree. Follow a thin crack (crux) to an overhang. Move left to sidestep the roof, then continue up a dihedral to easy ledges. Belay at the established anchors on the SE Face.

15. **Stardust** 5.8 ★
    100' Pro to 1 1/2"
    Start up a left facing corner to a small roof. Turn this by sidestepping around to the right and continue up until it joins Cruisin'.

16. **Rock Master** 5.11 C (PG-13) ★★
    100' Pro to 2" TCU's required
    Technically very bold. Stem up a left facing corner (crux) using very unorthodox maneuvers to succeed (#0 TCU). Pull through a difficult roof move and up a crack system that eases and joins with the SE Face route.

17. **Rookie Nookie** 5.10 C (PG-13) ★★
    100' Pro to 2"
    Slightly uphill and left of Rock Master is a prominent left-facing dihedral with one fixed piton. A great climb. Joins with the SE Face route.

18. **Icy Treats** (a.k.a. Frozen Treats) 5.10 D (R) ★
    100' Pro to 1 1/2" Needs more fixed gear.
    Look for a shallow corner with two bolts near the start. A difficult stem problem with hard to place pro and a little runout in places. Climb up past the bolts to a halfway stance. More awkward, desperate smears lead to the top where it joins the SE Face route.

19. **Switchblade** 5.11 A (PG-13)
    110' Pro unknown

20. **Bladerunner** 5.10 C ★★
    110' Pro to 2"

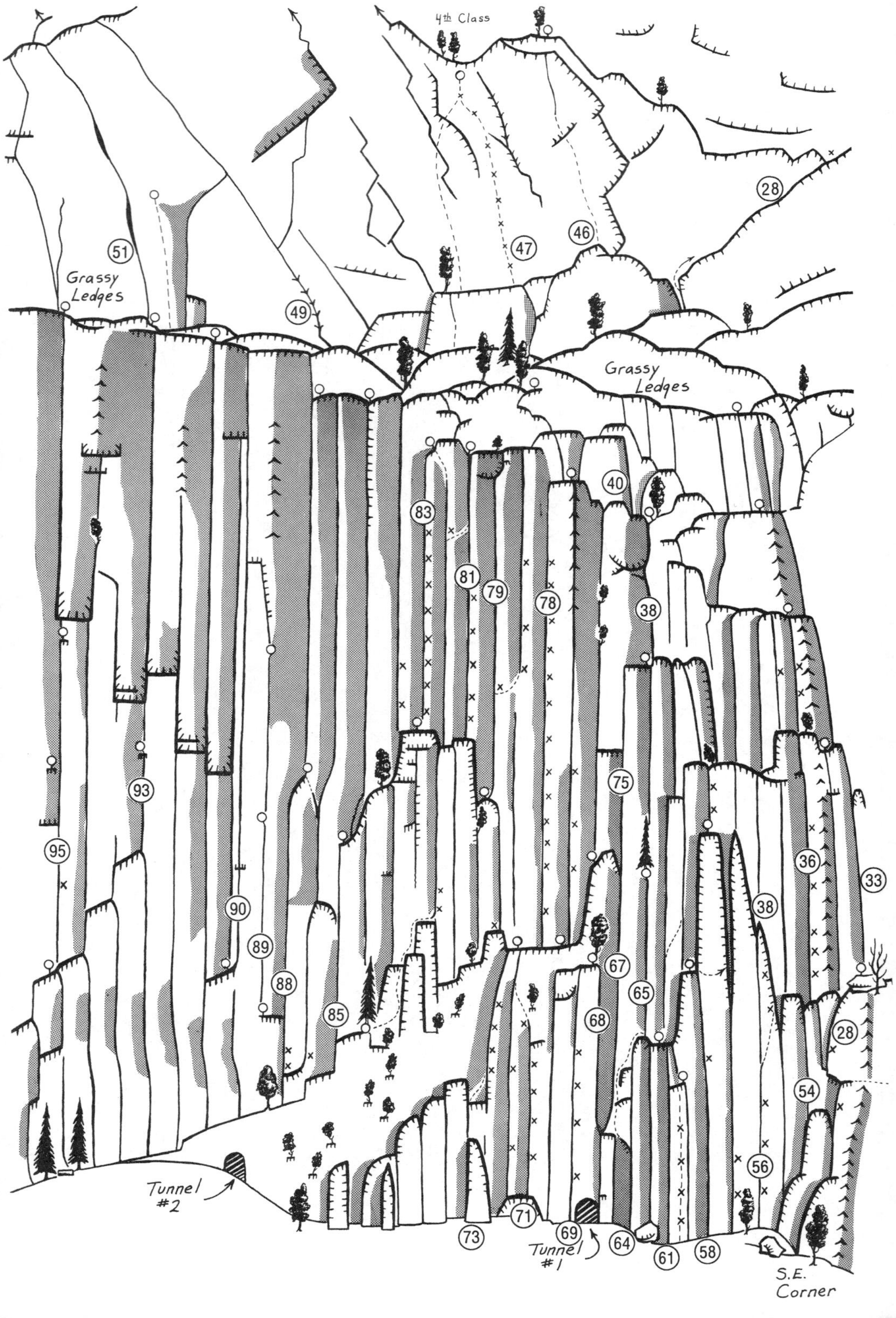

4th Class

Grassy Ledges

Grassy Ledges

51

49

47

46

28

83

81

79

78

40

38

38

75

93

95

90

89

88

85

36

33

38

67

65

68

28

54

56

73

71

69

64

61

58

Tunnel #2

Tunnel #1

S.E. Corner

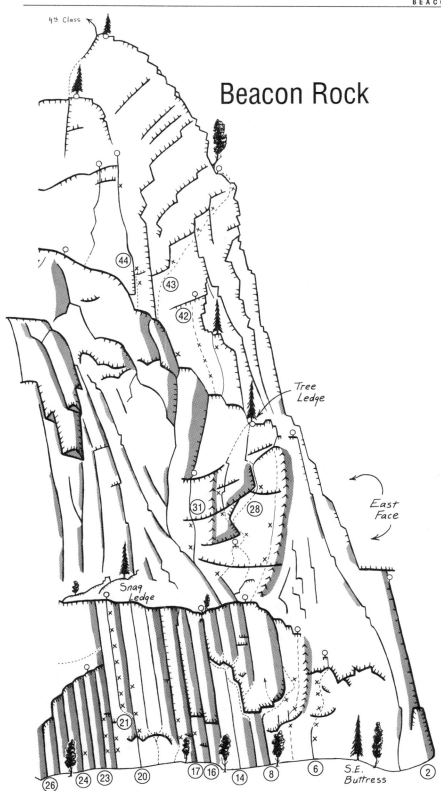

4th Class

Beacon Rock

44

43

42

Tree Ledge

31

28

East Face

Snag Ledge

21

26 24 23 20 17 16 14 8 6 S.E. Buttress 2

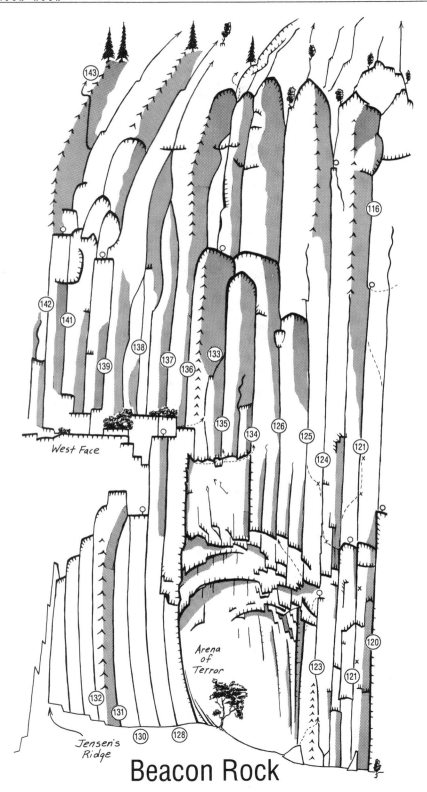

West Face

Arena
of
Terror

Jensen's
Ridge

Beacon Rock

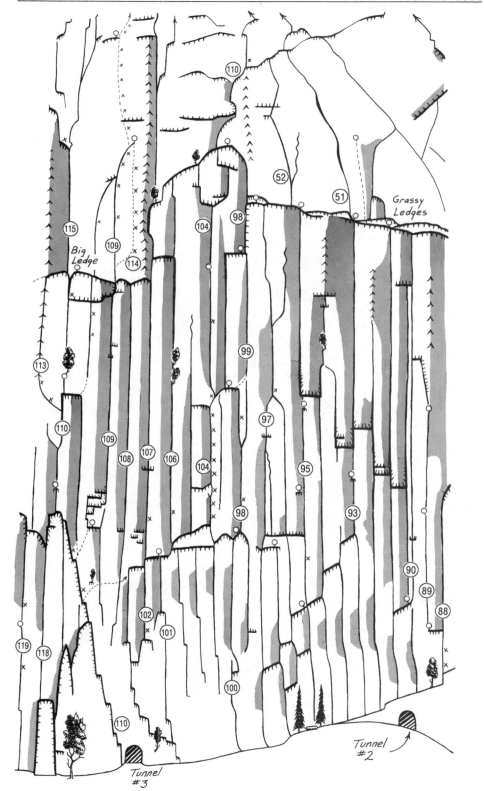

Tunnel #3

Tunnel #2

An incredible route and an excellent prize. Begin up and pull through (1 bolt) a loose section of rock to a stance. Angle up left then straight up a seam (2 bolts and crux) until the crack widens and eases in difficulty. Belay at bolts just below Snag Ledge tree.

21. **Fire and Ice** 5.11 B ★★★
110' QD's, small wires, and TCU's to 1"
A demanding, exciting and high quality classic. A staggering modern climb on the smooth, rounded arete slab left of Bladerunner. Climb up Bladerunner to the second bolt, traverse left onto the face and go straight up the bolt line. From a stance above the halfway crux, step left to finish up a thin seam (pitons) which ends at the hidden anchor near the Snag Ledge tree.

22. **More Balls Than Nuts** 5.11 B (R)
50' Thin pro to 1"

23. **No Balls, No Falls** 5.11 A
50' QD's and pro to 1"

24. **Levitation Blues** 5.10 D
50' QD's and pro to 1"

25. **Repo Man** 5.10 C
40' Pro to 1"

26. **Cigarette** 5.10 A
30' Pro to 1"

26. **Lethal Ejection** 5.9
60' Pro to 2"

28. **Southeast Face** III
5.7 ★★★
Multi-pitch Pro to 2"
The first established climb on Beacon Rock. Interesting route that meanders up 600' of rock to the west side hikers' trail. Begin west and uphill of a prominent corner near the railroad tracks. Climb easy steps (2 fixed pitons) on clean rock 80 ft. to a bolt belay at a ledge. Traverse rightward (NE) along gravel ledges 70 ft. to another bolt anchor. Belay. Move up a slab to the left (or surmount bulge directly above via bolt), step right (crux), then up around a roof and continue up a slab corner system. When possible work rightward to turn an exposed corner (SE

Cindy Olson climbing Winter Delight (5.10B)

Buttress directly below) then up to the Tree Ledge belay. Follow a left leaning dihedral ramp system to Grassy Ledges. Belay. Wander up and left through an OW chimney move. Continue up a right leaning low angle ramp (1/4" bolt near top). Exit left here along small grassy steps, bushes and 4th class ground until it eases. Or move right to a tree belay, then straight up to a notch and scramble into the woods beyond.

Note: please be aware that there is much loose rock on Grassy Ledges. It is easily disturbed by foot or with ropes and will continue to be a serious danger to climbers below. In the interests of all, please rappel from Grassy Ledges.

29. **Variation** 5.9
25' Pro to 2"

30. **Desdichado** 5.10 C
40' QD's and pro to 1 1/2"
A unique short climb with poor hangers. Located about 1/3 of the way up the crux pitch of the Southeast Face on a slightly overhung corner.

31. **Dynaflux** 5.11 B
50' QD's and pro to 1 1/2"
Up left from the second belay on the Southeast Face is a bulging face with a vertical crack in it. Two bolts protect the hardest moves. Rappel from bolt anchor.

32.

33. **Jill's Thrill** 5.9
160' (2 80' leads) Pro to 2"
A fun route, especially the second half. Start at Snag Ledge belay. Move up to and climb a minor corner with 2 fixed pitons. Belay at anchor on a ledge to the left at 70 ft. Step back right and continue up a flared slabby crack system 70 ft. to a large gravelly ledge and bolt anchor. Rappel.
Note: This is one of the finer established 80 ft. rappels on Beacon Rock from Grassy Ledges. There are many rappels, but this one is far more safe, less exposed and conveniently oriented near the SE Face.

34. **Tooth Faerie** 5.10 A
70' Pro to 2" #0 TCU recommended
Ascend a clean crack directly above belay anchor. At the flakey overhang face climb up the left side of crack to join with Jill's Thrill.

35. **To the Edge and Beyond** 5.11 B
70' Pro to 2" including TCU's
Somewhat contrived, but challenging.

36. **Fear of Flying** 5.10 B ★★★
160' Pro to 1 1/2"
A superb Beacon Rock climb involving exciting stemming and fixed pitons to ease your fears. Step left from the Snag Ledge belay and commence up a dihedral protected with 4 fixed pins. From a belay ledge at 65 ft. continue up a thin, desperate crack (2 pitons) until possible to step right and join with Jill's Thrill.

37. **Desperado** 5.10 D (R)
160' Thin pro to 1 1/2" Needs pitons

38. **Right Gull** III 5.10 A (or 5.7 A0) ★★★
Multi-pitch Pro to 3"
A very popular route with plenty of variety. From the Snag Ledge belay step left around a corner and enter a large right-facing corner. Climb this until it tops out on a pedestal, then gingerly move left to a bolt anchor. Either A0 or free climb (5.10 A crux) past 2 fixed pitons to a ledge. Above are several options. On the right is an offwidth (4"); in the center, a slightly dirty left leaning crack; or on your left is a fist crack (3"). All of these are approx. 5.8. At the top of these options, step left to a bolt anchor on a comfortable ledge. Bluebird and

several other routes end here as well. Continue up a wide crack pulling through an awkward bulge to a rocky ledge with a small oak tree. Wander up behind the tree and leftward via a series of steps to another bolt anchor and Grassy Ledges.

39. Vulcan's Variation 5.8
12' Pro to 3/4"
A rather convenient way to bypass the crux on Right Gull. Climb a thin crack to the right of the second belay and above a sharp ear of rock.

40. Muriel's Memoir 5.9
25' Pro to 1 1/2"
When Right Gull eases to the rocky ledge near a small oak tree, look to your left. This is the good looking clean corner crack. Rejoins with regular route.

The following 13 routes are located above Grassy Ledges beginning near Tree Ledge and ending at Flying Swallow.

41. Synapse 5.10 C 35' Pro to 1"

42. Death and Taxes 5.12 C ★★
45' QD's and minor pro to 1"
This short, premium quality face climb utilizes a series of incipient seams and edges. A very unusual climb to be found here at Beacon. It is located approximately 40 ft. up and left of Tree Ledge (SE Face route).

43. Lost Variation II 5.8
Pro unknown
An indisputable route so named because numerous parties were unable to find it.

44. Elusive Element 5.10 D (R) ★
80' Pro to 1 1/2" including TCU's
A fabulous yet easily missed route roughly 100 ft. up left from Tree Ledge. Lead up a right facing corner (crux) past 2 bolts to an easy slab. Continue up the crack to a short steep section (crux) and reach a bolt anchor just beyond. A really good climb except for the weird hangers and runout sections.

45. Cloud Nine 5.9
80' Pro to 2" Pitons needed for belay anchor
A bit mossy, but still a neat crack climb on a long slab. Located immediately uphill and left of Elusive Element. No fixed belay at present.

46. High and Mighty 5.11 B ★★
80' TCU's and wires to 1 1/2" Bolts or fixed pins needed
An excellent route high above Grassy Ledges. Located up left from the easy 5th class offwidth move on Grassy Ledges (SE Face route). Climb a wandering set of seams on a steep smooth face until possible to turn a corner leftward then up a crack on a slab. No fixed belay anchor at present.

47. Sacrilege 5.10 D ★★★
80' 8 QD's
A fantastic face climb on very steep terrain. Incredible lead and one of the few totally bolted Beacon classics. To the right of Diagonal Desperation is a large hidden terrace with an oak tree on it (little peoples ledge). This is the bolted route on the right side of the ledge.

48. _____ 5.12+
80 (TR)

49. Diagonal Desperation 5.10 D A0
Pro to 2" including pitons
Located just to the right of the upper pitches of Smooth Dancer. Climbs a left-leaning crack, then zig-zags before topping out. Yet to be freed.

50. _____

51. **Riverside** 5.10 B
    Multipitch (80' 1st pitch) Pro to 2 1/2"
    Probably one of the most unusual Beacon climbs available. Climbs a continuous and
    awkward flared left-leaning crack system near the left end of Grassy Ledges. Rappel after 80
    ft. or continue to the west side trail.

52. _____ 5.11+
    80' (TR)

53. _____ 5.12+
    80' (TR)

The following routes are described right to left beginning immediately left of the SE Face route.

54. **Little Wing** 5.8 ★★
    80' Pro to 2"
    Immediately left of the SE Face route is a fun little classic climb that begins up easy slabby
    steps. Follow this and finish up a shallow well-protected corner until possible to step right at
    the Snag Ledge belay. The next pitch (needs pins) ascends a thin seam (5.10 B) above a
    small ledge directly above the first pitch. Joins with Fear of Flying.

55. **Broken Arrow** 5.10 A
    60' Pro to 1"

56. **Idiot** (a.k.a. Magester Ludi) 5.12 A
    120' QD's and pro to 1"
    Uphill and left of the SE Face is a smooth face with several thin climbs. The right is the Idiot
    and the left is Magic Fingers. Ascend the difficult face (bolts and pitons) 40 ft. until you can
    reach over and use the outside corner of Right Gull. Layback up this (2 bolts) until necessary
    to join the Gull route.

57. **Magic Fingers** 5.12 C
    110' Pro to 2 1/2"
    This is the serious and demanding 2 bolt seam just left of the Idiot. Opens up to a large
    chimney on the last 25 ft. of Left Gull.

58. **Wrong Gull** II 5.10 C ★★
    110' Pro to 2 1/2"
    No two ways about it, a terrific climb with excellent pro. Start in the minor corner near an old
    tree stump. Stem up 80 ft. to a bolt anchor on a ledge. Then, if you're very bold, jam up the
    left side of a detached free standing pillar. Joins Right Gull.

59. **Sorcerer's Apprentice** 5.10 C
    40' Pro to 1"
    A thin seam crack immediately left of Wrong Gull.

60. **Old Warriors Never Die** 5.12 B ★
    80' QD's and minor pro to 1"
    A great bolted climb located on the outside of a minor rounded corner. Climb 45 ft. up the
    steep face and short dirty corner to a ledge. Belay at anchor. Rappel or continue up right
    (bolts) via dubious cracks to join with Wrong Gull at the bolt belay. Rappel.

61. **Seagull** II 5.10 C ★★★
    45' 1st pitch Pro to 1 1/2" Cams suggested
    This and the following climb are superb classics. They accurately portray Beacon stem
    climbing at its finest. The route ascends a double cornered crack system (5.10 C) just to the
    right of a large boulder. Bolt belay on ledge (45'). Rappel or climb a thin crack above (5.10
    D) to join with Right Gull.

62. **Tennessee Walker** 5.10 D (PG-13) ★★
    45' Thin wires and pro to 1 1/2"
    A fabulous route. Pure stemming on thin but good protection. Ascend the corner just left of

the large boulder. Several fixed pitons after the crux. Beware of minor poison oak near the top of the climb.

63. **Too Close for Comfort** 5.12 A
(TR) No hangers
This is the outside corner left of Tennessee Walker.

64. **Left Gull** III 5.10 A or 5.8 AO
Multi-pitch Pro to 3"
An unusual but fun climb. Some poison oak and chimney climbing to contend with. Starts up broken corners and ledges immediately right of the first tunnel and joins with Right Gull at its second belay on the pedestal.

65. **Summer Daze** (a.k.a. Christmas Tree Crack) 5.11 C or C3 ★★
95' Thin wires and TCU's to 2 1/2"
Great climb with a desperate thin start. From the belay ledge at the top of Tennessee Walker / Seagull step left then proceed up the seam (piton). The crack widens and passes a fir tree halfway up before it joins with Right Gull at a ledge belay.

66. _____ 5.12
130' (TR)
An outside arete and face between Summer Daze and Bluebird.

67. **Bluebird Direct** 5.10 D (R) ★
160' Pro to 2 1/2"
Directly above the first tunnel is a long dihedral. Commence up a thin seam on the tunnel's right side to a ledge 20 ft. up. Stem up a poorly protected dihedral to where it joins with the standard Bluebird route. A good climb but a little runout.

The following five routes, known as the Five and Dime Wall, offer high quality and only moderately difficult climbing. All are unique, several are serious but most are quite fun to lead.

68. **Spring Fever** 5.10 A ★★
55' Pro to 1 1/2"
Ascend the thin seam just to the right of the first tunnel. At the small ledge 20 ft. up step left and continue up a weird crack to a maple tree belay. Rappel.

69. **Winter Delight** 5.10 B (PG-13) ★★★
55' Pro to 1 1/2" (#2 TCU required)
A prize worth attaining and a delight to climb. Climbs a partly bolted seam immediately left of the first tunnel. Rappel from the small maple tree.

70. **Sufficiently Breathless** 5.10 A ★★
55' Pro to 1 1/2" Doubles at 3/4"
Superb route with excellent protection. Ascend via a minor crack and corner system just left of Winter Delight. Several fixed pitons. Exit right to the maple tree belay.

71. **Fall Guy** 5.10 D ★★
65' 5 QD's and optional pro to 3/4"
An exciting definitive face climb. Climb a shallow vertical corner to a sloping stance (loose rock just above) stepping up left and around corner to join with Aging Fags. Rappel from bolt belay.

72. **Aging Fags** 5.10 D (PG-13) ★
65' Pro = RP's, small wires and TCU's to 1"
A wide dihedral that is quite bold to lead. Starts off from a ledge 15 ft. left of the tunnel.

73. **Blownout Direct** 5.9
65' Pro to 1 1/2"
Climbs a free-standing thin flake, then pulls into a corner stance before ascending a piton protected seam. Rappel from bolts.

74. **Tombstone Territory** 5.7
25' Pro to 2 1/2"

75. **Bluebird** II 5.10 A ★
Multi-pitch Pro to 4"
One of the original Beacon favorites. An excellent 35 ft. crux pitch. The old starting point was located at a fir tree next to the base of Wild Turkeys. From there it traversed rightward via brushy, sloping ledges and minor downsteps. Otherwise climb one of a number of routes near the first tunnel to approach.

76. **Variation** 5.9
40' Pro to 3"
Halfway up the crux pitch of Bluebird, step left onto a good ledge and finish up a deep dihedral choked with bushes.

77. **Bridge of the Gods** 5.12 B or 5.11 A2
110' Pro to 4" Needs more bolts
High above the first tunnel is an impressive shallow corner system that eventually widens to an offwidth crack splitting an arete. Two rope rappel. Approach via one of the lower variations.

78. **Pirates** (a.k.a. Rock Pirates) 5.12 A (R)
110' Pro to 2" Runout and poor pins
Probably one of the three most serious, awkward climbs at Beacon Rock. A very long lead with many fixed pitons. Still worthy of top-roping. Approach via one of the lower variations. Two rope rappel.

79. **Blownout** II 5.10 A ★★★
Multi-pitch Pro to 2 1/2" Doubles recommended
One of the ten supreme classics. Commence up Blownout Direct (or another nearby option) to a bolt belay. Move up left, then straight up a jagged hand crack to a belay in a protected corner beneath the great upper dihedral. Step forth and climb the obvious corner 120 ft. (crux) until possible to exit right onto a gravelly ledge. Bolt belay to the left. Rappel.

80. **Second Wind** 5.11 D ★
100' Pro to 2"
Twenty feet up the last pitch of Blownout (1/4 bolt), traverse right around the arete and finish up a strenuous thin finger crack. Extreme.

81. **Borderline** II 5.11 B ★★★
80' 5 QD's and pro to 1 1/2"
A staggering and most excellent climb. Begin at the lone fir tree immediately right of the Wild Turkeys start. Climb up right onto a detached flake and climb (pitons) 40 ft. up (5.10+) to a belay on the "Beacon Towers" ledge. Step right and embark up the beautiful second pitch (bolts) via face climbing and laybacks to the top. Rappel.
Note: this rappel from Grassy Ledges is convenient, hassle free and can be done with one rope. 80 ft. exactly!

Nathan Charleton on Excalibur (5.12B)

82. **Grunge Book** III 5.10 A A3
Virtually all of this route (except 40 ft.) has now been free climbed and should be done so using natural protection only.

83. **Excalibur** 5.12 B ★★★
80' QD's, small wires, TCU's (and Friends to 2 1/2")
Incredible! An extreme line and one of the most difficult at Beacon. Start on the "Beacon Towers" immediately right of Wild Turkeys. Face climb straight up until it eases and widens gradually near the top. Rappel from bolt belay.

84. **Crankenstein** 5.11 A (TR)
35'
Immediately behind the lone fir tree at the start for Borderline is a minor dihedral corner.

85. **Wild Turkeys** III 5.10 C A2
Multipitch Pitons and pro to 1 1/2"
One of the original Beacon aid routes. The popular first pitch goes free at 5.10 C, but the second has still yet to be freed. Probable 5.12+. Ascend an interesting corner left of a fir tree. Climb 25 ft. to a belay on a sloping ledge. Continue up right via easy steps to the "Beacon Towers." Belay then nail the seam left of Excalibur.

86. _____ 5.12 A
120' (TR) Needs bolts
A terrific, extreme climb requiring superb technique. From the first belay on Wild Turkeys commence directly up a shallow dihedral. It soon straightens to a vertical seam on a perfect smooth face.

87. **Psychic Wound** 5.10 B
80' Pro to 1 1/2"
This climb and the following several routes are located above the second tunnel. From a stance at a thin oak tree step up right and climb a left facing corner (piton) to a stance. Finish up a weaving corner system until possible to exit left to the Flying Dutchman bolt belay.

88. **Flying Dutchman** 5.10 B ★★
80' Pro to 1 1/2" Small wires and TCU's suggested
An enjoyable route. Excellent rock. Begin at the thin oak tree and climb up past two pitons to a stance. Continue straight up a left facing dihedral to the bolt anchor. The upper pitches of the previous two climbs have yet to be freed.

89. **Bears in Heat** II 5.11 B ★★
80' first pitch Pro to 2 1/2" Cams suggested
A great climb. The name describes accurately the second pitch bear hug. Start as for Flying Dutchman past the pitons to a stance. Step left, then ascend an unusual crack system to a crux move just shy of the anchor. Rappel or continue up (35 ft.) the second pitch bear hugging and jamming to reach a final belay. Rappel.

90. **Smooth Dancer** III 5.9 A2
Multipitch Pitons and pro to 1 1/2"
A long, multi-pitch aid route immediately right of the great roofs in the center of the wall. The two pitches above Grassy Ledges offer good free climbing.

91. **Dirty Double Overhang** III 5.7 A3
Multipitch Pitons and pro to 2"
This is the other sustained two-pitch aid route on the central face.

92. _____

93. **Takes Fist** III 5.10 D ★
Multi-pitch Pro to 3"
This wild climb leads through a fist crack in the 'great roof' area. A little brushy on the first pitch. Start near the twin oak trees angling up right to a vegetated dihedral. Commence

upward and through the overhang to the top. Rappel via another established safer rappel on Grassy Ledges.

94. _____

95. **Ground Zero** III 5.11D ★★★
Multi-pitch   Small wires, TCU's and double sizes recommended to 2 1/2"
One of the super classics at Beacon. A very physical lead. Each pitch is more extreme than the previous culminating with a crux at the roof. Start near the twin oak trees up easy 5.9 slabs to a piton belay 80 ft. Continue up to a small lip (5.10 C) and some difficult climbing to a bolt anchor on the left 80 ft. Another 25 ft. lead to an anchor underneath the roof. Smear left (crux) around the corner, then finish up a very steep crack to the top 50 ft. Rappel with two ropes. Note: do not allow your ropes to overlap and be sure to set the knot over the edge.

96. **Nuke-U-Later** 5.10 C (R)
120'   Pro to 1 1/2"
Start as for Ground Zero but a thin crack that leads up through flaky, hollow rock. Anchor just below a small overhang. Rappel.

97. **Iron Maiden** III 5.11 A4
KB, LA, Baby Angles and Pro to 3/4"
Step left from the Nuke-U-Later belay and nail up a seam on a blank face.

98. **Flying Swallow** III 5.10 D (PG-13) ★★★
Multipitch Pro to 3" Extra set of thin to medium wires
One of the finest Beacon Rock classics. The original route started up the 5.6 section of Dod's Jam then traversed rightward across to the top of Black Maria, Reasonable Richard and Local Access. But it is now much more direct and fun to climb one of these three options mentioned above. From that bolt anchor traverse up right to the base of a 60 ft. dihedral. Belay, then have at it. Stem upward (crux) to a sloping ledge and bolt anchor. Above is a slightly overhung finger crack that opens to an offwidth. Climb this to another ledge and belay. Then continue up a nice left-facing corner 20 ft. to Grassy Ledges. Belay. Rappel via an established descent route or finish up a flared chimney system to join with Dod's Jam.

99. **Variation** 5.10 B ★
60'   Pro to 2 1/2" Extra wires

100. **Direct Start** (to Flying Swallow) 5.11 A
100' (TR) Needs bolts

The following three climbs are good direct start options to Flying Swallow, Flighttime and Blood, Sweat and Smears.

101. **Local Access Only** 5.10 A
110'   Pro to 1"
Wanders up easy but unprotected slabs to a small corner dihedral.

102. **Reasonable Richard** 5.9 (PG-13) ★★
110'   Pro to 1 1/2" TCU's recommended
Commence up easy slabs to a stance, then embark up a minor crack (1 bolt) on a rounded face leading to a bolt anchor. An excellent climb.

103. **Black Maria** 5.9+ (PG-13)
110'   Small wires, TCU's and Friends to 3"
A minor corner directly below True Grunt and just left of Reasonable Richard. Start up easy slabs but work left from a stance into a dihedral. Continue up this until you can exit right to the anchor.

104. **Flight Time** II 5.11 C ★★
Multi-pitch Pro to 1 1/2"
For the climber with strong wings here is a terrific and well-protected route. Move up right

(from the belay at Reasonable Richard) along dirty ledges to a mostly fixed crack. This is the wild one. Desperately climb up using the right crack when necessary to a sloping ledge and belay. Step back left and continue up a stiff dihedral to a hanging belay. Rappel or continue up and exit out right under a roof to join with Flying Swallow.

105. _____

106. **Flying Circus** III 5.10 C (R)
Multi-pitch Pro to 4" Extra set of wires
Above Reasonable Richard is a crack (with a small bush growing from it) that opens up to an offwidth. A long lead. 165 ft. rope required. Joins Dod's Jam route in the great amphitheatre.

107. **Blood, Sweat, and Smears** II 5.10 C ★★★
165' Pro to 3" Double set of wires
A most excellent route and one of Beacon Rock's finest. Traverse up left from Reasonable Richard belay. Enter and climb the dihedral passing through several small overhangs and thin sections. Belay on Big Ledge.

108. **True Grunt** II 5.11 A (PG-13)
165' Pro to 2" Extra wires
A difficult and technical crux. Unique but seldom ascended. A very long lead.

109. **Steppenwolf** IV 5.11+ A0 (5.10 C to Big Ledge) ★★★
165' first pitch Pro to 2" Extra wires
This superb route is one of the best prizes at Beacon Rock. Start up the 5.6 section to Dod's Jam until possible to angle right to a bolt belay under a roof. Step up right around the roof and climb a long exhilarating dihedral. Pull through a final overhung jam crack to Big Ledge. Belay. Above are two beautiful cracks than join halfway up and then angle to the right. The right crack is Steppenwolf, while the left is a continuation of Journey to the East. Free climb up the right crack (5.11+) 60 ft. to a bolt anchor. Above are several more pitches of mixed free and aid climbing up the "Norseman's Head" to the west side hikers' trail.

110. **Dod's Jam** III 5.10 C ★★★
Multi-pitch Pro to 3"
One of the all time Beacon classics. Very popular. Start up easy slabs (from the 3rd tunnel) leftward along a series of corners and small ledges. When you reach the base of the main dihedral (Free For All joins here) step up to a bolt belay. Climb a crack that quickly becomes an offwidth (5.9) to a ledge aptly called "The Perch." Climb up past a tree via a crux (5.10 C) jam crack. Belay at Big Ledge. Rappel or climb the next pitches. Step right around corner and move up a series of wide cracks and offwidth chimneys (5.7 - 5.9) then angle up right along slabs to a sling belay. The far left side of the amphitheatre offers an offwidth-crack with numerous holds (5.9) while the right side has a short curving crack in a bulge. Above are numerous ledges and short hard sections (5.8) that eventually lead to the West Side Trail. Note: use caution on the last section because of loose rock.

111. **Dod's Deviation** 5.9 (variation) ★
45' Pro to 3"

112. **Journey to the East** IV 5.11 A4 Pins, Rurps and Hooks to 3 1/2"

113. **Devil's Backbone** 5.12 A ★★
80' Pro to 1 1/2" Needs bolts
Probably the finest example at Beacon of a crack that splits an arete. Approximately 20 ft. above the first belay on Dod's Jam move left via underclings to an arete. Climb straight up to Big Ledge. An incredible climb!

114. **The Norseman** 5.12 B ★★
60' 5 QD's and minor pro to 1 1/2"
This is the bolted route on the buttress of the "Norseman's Head." From Big Ledge climb up Steppenwolf until possible to move right to a rounded buttress. Ascend this to a bolt anchor. Excellent climb.

115. **Dastardly Crack** 5.9 ★★
165' Pro to 2"
Directly above Dod's Jam
from Big Ledge is a large
dihedral. Climb the corner,
angle left and up easy steps
to a bushy corner that leads
to the west side hikers' trail.

116. **Squeeze Box** 5.10 B
(PG-13) ★
165' Pro to 2"
An interesting fist crack
through a roof. From Big
Ledge angle down left until
possible to turn a corner.
Climb a dihedral and
overhangs to rejoin with
Dastardly Crack.

117. **Edge of Fear** IV 5.11 A4
100' Pro to 1 1/2"

118. **Free For All** 5.8 ★★★
150' Pro to 2"
Excellent route. A must for
everyone! Just left of a large
oak tree (left of the 3rd
tunnel) is a detached free
standing 25 ft. pillar. The left
side is the Direct Start (5.10
A), while the right side is 5.8.
Climb either and from the top
of the pillar continue up the
obvious crooked hand crack until it joins with Dod's Jam at the first belay.

Robert McGown on 2nd pitch Free For Some (5.10C)

119. **Free For Some** 5.11 A (PG-13) ★★★
140' Pro to 2" TCU's recommended
A remarkable and demanding lead with excellent protection. Immediately left of Free For All
is a thin seam. Climb this to a bolt anchor at 65 ft. then ascend the second half (5.10 C) or
rappel.

120. **Windsurfer** 5.10 B ★★★
120' Pro to 3" Double set of wires
A popular and exciting climb. To find this good route look for a left-facing dihedral with three
small roofs. Begin up a wide crack that ends at a ledge and bolt belay.

121. **Fresh Squeeze** (a.k.a. Squeeze Box Direct) II 5.11 D ★
120' first pitch Pro to 2" Needs bolts
On a face between Pipeline and Windsurfer are two crack systems. The right is Fresh
Squeeze. Ascend the first pitch (5.11 C) to a ledge and belay. The second pitch steps up
above the anchor, moves right and climbs a vertical face broken by a seam. Eventually
enters a dihedral and eases (5.10) until it joins with Squeeze Box. Second pitch is 140 ft.

122. _____

123. **Pipeline** 5.11 B ★★★
60' Pro to 1 1/2"
Superb classic. A must for everyone. On the right side of the Arena of Terror is a thin,

difficult finger crack that ends at a bolt anchor next to several overhangs. Ascend this and enjoy!

124. **Pipe Dream** 5.12 A ★
160' 1st pitch Pro to 1 1/2"
Little is known about the quality of this route, but it looks just incredible! The route has been free climbed in very bold style (ground-up and red-point). From the belay ledge for Fresh Squeeze (1st pitch) step left and ascend a remarkable crack on a smooth face to an anchor at the base of an easy dihedral. Rappel with 2 ropes or continue up and join with Dastardly Crack.

125. **Pipeline Headwall** III 5.11 B
Multi-pitch Pro to 2"

126. **Silver Crow** IV 5.10 D A3
KB, LA, Rurps and pro to 4"

127. **Axe of Karma** IV 5.10 C A3 ★
Multi-pitch KB, LA and pro to 4"

The following six climbs are located left of the Arena of Terror. The leftmost is the easy (5.7) approach arete to Jensen's Ridge and the other west side routes.

128. **Red Ice** 5.10 D ★
145' Pro to 2 1/2"
Just left of the Arena of Terror. Ascend easy ground to a loose, hollow section. Move up left and finish up a beautiful finger to hand crack in a dihedral. Bolt Anchor. Rappel with 2 ropes or ascend one of the upper climbs on the west face.

129. **Doubting Thomas** 5.10 C
145' Pro to 1 1/2"

130. **Boys of Summer** 5.10 B
145' Pro to 2"

131. **Fingers of a Fisherman** 5.10 B
145' Pitons and pro to 2"

132. **Crack of Dawn** 5.9
145' Pro to 2"

133. **Jensen's Ridge** III 5.11 A ★
Multi-pitch Pro to 4" including TCU's and big pro for OW
The physical crux is a thin tips crack on the second pitch, while the offwidth just beyond is certainly the psychological mindbender. Commence up an easy ridge (loose) to a bolt belay. Step right (nearly off the platform) and ascend the desperate thin crack 20 ft. to a ledge. Enter into a deep dihedral that opens to a wide offwidth. Belay at bolts just where Lay Lady Lay joins. Continue to the hikers' trail via two options. Both are 5.9+.

134. **Updraft to Heaven** III 5.10 D A1 (R)
160' KB and pro to 6"

135. **Mostly Air** 5.10 B (PG-13)
160' Pro to 2 1/2" (poorly protected)

136. **Lay Lady Lay** II 5.10B ★★★
100' Pro to 2 1/2"
A quality route except for the poison oak that plagues the start of this and the following three routes.

137. **Synchronicity** II 5.8 A2
Multi-pitch KB, LA and pro to 4"

138. **Rip City** II 5.10 A ★★
80' Pro to 1 3/4"

139. **Hard Times** II 5.10 C
80' Pro to 2 1/2"

140. **Rag Time** II 5.10 C
80' Pro to 2 1/2"

141. **Boulder Problem in the Sky** II 5.10 D ★★
Multi-pitch Pro to 2 1/2"
An excellent stem problem with a captivating roof crack exit move.

142. **Iron Cross** (a.k.a. On the Move) II 5.11 B (PG-13) ★★
Multi-pitch Pro to 4"

143. **Variation** 5.9
80' Pro to 2 1/2"

Climbers on Horsetail Falls, Columbia Gorge Ice.

Columbia Gorge Ice

Winter ice climbing in the Columbia River Gorge. It brings to mind subzero temperatures and bitter cold winds that easily send chills down the spine. Yet the Gorge is a remarkable, photogenic wonderland of the Pacific Northwest, that continues to attract an ever growing number of ice climbers with each freeze.

There were occasional historical ventures into this vast arena of ice during the 1970's. Yet through the recent high-tech breakthroughs in ice-climbing hardware, climbers took to the ice seriously during the mega-freeze of January 1979.

The Columbia Gorge offers a wide spectrum of possibilities from enjoyable wet plastic ice to vertical ice pillars or thin smears to multi-pitch desperate grade IV and V climbs still seeking a first ascent.

Many locals gained their skills and proficiency at distant places such as Lee Vining, Ca., Telluride, Co., the Tetons of Idaho or even Banff in Canada. But during the summers, locals-in-residence usually suffice by visiting Eliot Glacier (on the north side of Mt. Hood) to test their skills. The glacier offers easily accessible crevasse or serac climbing with generally mild summer temperatures. And for the hard core enthusiast seeking the edge of adventure, visit the glacier from mid-September thru October. Superb ice conditions can be found upon the Coe Glacier, while extreme mixed rock and (black) ice conditions are available on the upper reaches of the Eliot Glacier.

For 15 years many have ventured here to climb on this realm of ice. Often only the names ring in our ears, like the whispering winter wind. Jay Carroll, Mark Cartier, Ken Currens, Alan Kearney, Monty Mayko, Jim Mayers, Robert McGown, Mike O'Brien, Jim Olson, Ed Newville, Jeff Thomas, Scott Woolums, Ian Wade and the many others who made frequent forays.

Whenever possible this chapter will record known first ascent information after each route. Most first ascents and titles of climbs are seldom available though, even on the popular ice routes. Therefore, for the sake of locating and identifying climbs for the reader, the author will try to use nearby places or subject matter for a given route such as **Benson Lake Icefall**. (Located 1/2 mile west of Multnomah Falls and adjacent to Benson Lake on the scenic highway.) This should help to alleviate the potential problems of using "unnamed" too often, creating monotony and confusion.

Logistics

The region of the greatest interest to ice climbers in the Columbia Gorge starts near Crown Point, ends near Bonneville Dam and includes both sides of the river. The author has chosen to describe this area in detail because of the concentration of ice routes as well as easy access due to the scenic highway which runs parallel with I-84 through this portion of the Gorge. To the Portlander, convenience usually dictates the choice.

A fair number of excellent options do exist further afield and are highly recommended. These are as follows: Both east and west of the I-84 Corbett exit for roughly 2 miles, there are numerous low angle ice seeps and/or creek drainages. They freeze quite solidly and offer good practice or solo problems. Along the Mt. Hood scenic Highway 35 is the summertime crag called **Pete's Pile.** But during the hard winters ice does consolidate here in several places yielding excellent TR problems as well as several long, steep desperates. Pete's Pile is located uphill on the east side of the highway approximately 3/4 mile south of the Cooper Spur intersection. This is the one place where you can usually find ice consistently each year in some form (thick or thin). Look up near the far right side of the crag for starts. A summertime trail has been established and is generally still usable even in winter, if the snow is not too deep.

At **Mirror Mountain** (a.k.a. Ski Bowl) near Government Camp, there is a small prominent basalt crag just to the west of the main ski course. When the conditions are cold, you will find ice here. This is a north facing crag with short but often thin and extreme leads as well as deep snowy corners.

There are several roadcuts along the Mt. Hood highway that do offer some ice bouldering problems. Search and you shall find.

Season

Ice climbing in the Columbia Gorge is without a doubt quite fickle. And when compared (should it not be?) with rock climbing it might even seem a bit trivial. But alas, when the great northern continental air mass descends upon the Pacific Northwest, ice climbers will madly scramble to sharpen their tools and race to the Gorge.

The northern arctic winds tend to come between December and February. In roughly 2-3 days, with a steady surge of cold wind, the ice routes are ready to be approached and tested. It will normally last one to two weeks with temperatures hovering from 20° to 30° F. Every year some ice does consolidate, but the severe cold spells which climbers depend upon generally arrive in four year intervals. During 1978, 1979 and recently in 1988 and 1990 this trend proved otherwise to the benefit of the ice climber.

When the snap first arrives, the temperature lingers in the lower teens several days, then gradually rises up into the mid 20s. A rather stiff, penetrating 15-40 mph east wind will blow much of the time, making it uncomfortable to stand about. Luckily, many routes are somewhat hidden in corners or enveloped in a forest of trees, just enough to break the main force of the growling wind.

Water ice varies considerably from day to day in the Gorge, as well as from one climb to the next. On one route you may experience brittle "dinnerplate" ice or even see 5' fracture marks race across the ice as your tool strikes into the surface. A day later, you could find wet plastic ice which sucks up any tool thrown at it. Generally, the greater the amount of water in the falls, the less likely it will be ascended. A small seepage on a wall creates a beautiful thin

Wayne Wallace leading Life Shavings, Columbia Gorge Ice

delicate smear, whereas Multnomah or Latourrell Falls are simply unclimbable in their entirety, but may offer leads to the right or the left of the main watercourse. Expect to have a crackly suit of ice armor after such a climb! Most of the easy to moderate ice routes have water dripping down the face or have small streams flowing near the top such as Benson Icefall or Crown Point. If the climber will look beyond the obvious routes, he or she will then see the many smaller seeps that often are quite solid and drip much less than usual. Once the climbing ropes get soaked they quickly become stiff "steel cables," refusing to feed through even the largest belay device.

On several of the grade IV and V routes, an extended cold spell and/or water conditions may be needed to slow the running water.

Get a jump on the most popular routes, for they could see 15-20 or more ascents in just a few days. And since the sport is so short lived, do bring your cameras and take many photos to show your friends and for future memories.

Ice Ratings

In **The Ice Experience** (1979) by Jeff Lowe, two systems are incorporated to achieve a rather comprehensive and useful Americanized grading standard. They are the Yosemite Decimal System (mentioned in the Introduction) and the Scottish grading for ice. Let's take a quick look at the grading in detail.

The **length or vertical relief** (whether 60' or 600') conveys to the climber a picture of general route difficulties. Each person then must evaluate their commitment level towards the completion of the concentrated difficulties involved.

The **overall difficulty** grading (I to VI) should indicate to the climber the approximate time necessary for such an ascent.

The **hardest rock or ice** move (or both) will prepare you for the technical problems encountered on the climb and will be shown as WI (water ice) 1 to 7.

If aid climbing is part of the route, a rating of such will be added as well.

For example, the final name and rating could look as such:

Ice Man   600'   IV+   WI 5   5.10 B   A2

As a reminder, since ice is a constantly changing medium, no rating should ever be considered absolute, but used constructively as a reference tool for your own tastes and ability.

Equipment

Basically, any ice climbing gear will do the job. Optimally speaking, improved modern equipment (as well as good technique!) improves efficiency.

Bring at least two ropes (everdry ropes are the best), storing a third one in your car, especially if you are considering several wet routes in one day. While climbing, properly manage your rope by keeping it from direct contact with water as long as possible. One frozen rope is better than two. Carry the second rope in your pack until you need to use it. When the day is over toss the stiff ropes in a clothes dryer for an hour or so to dry them out again. It works!

Eight ice screws are usually sufficient for most leads, yet extras are always nice to have. Titanium screws are supreme. Snargs work great in a tight situation unless you hammer into an air pocket. A small selection of QD's, several loose carabiners and you're set. The slings are handy since most ice climbs are liberally blessed with thick bushes or trees to clip into for safety. Bring along several yards of old 11mm rope to leave as rappel anchors. Rappel rings are non-existent at the tree anchors and old climbing rope withstands repeated descents and other punishment better than slings. Old rope works well in ice bollards, too. Often the dripping water quickly settles around the rope and refreezes. Do not rappel directly from the bollard; leave a sling or piece of rope behind.

Pitons are helpful, especially on extreme routes or when you need a fixed belay at a rock wall. A bolt kit, though seldom used, could be handy if you desire a more permanent anchor.

Another unique (and unsightly) option for rappel anchors is 3/4" metal conduit tubing. Cut it into 2' lengths. Hammer two of these in perpendicular to the ice and let the ice refreeze to the tubing. Clove hitch a sling to this and rappel. The cost is many times less than leaving an ice screw, especially if there are no trees nearby.

Reverse curved ice tools are the best choice for climbing, while plastic boots (or full shank leather boots with footfangs (or other crampons) are pretty much standard fare.

Remember, experience is gained by climbing, while efficiency depends on the climber's experience and reliable equipment.

Clothing

When you visit the Gorge for the first time, the bitter cold east winds will feel bone chilling and brutal. Therefore, you need to be properly equipped with the necessary amount of clothing to be comfortable and functional. Each person has a different comfort range. For your survival you should have all or most of the following: Gloves, overmitts, balaclava, windbreaker, windpants, wool hat (hard hat as well), pile jacket, polypropylene, wool garments or other clothing and sturdy **warm** boots. There is a fine balance between feeling the cold temperature and being seriously chilled. Finally, before embarking immediately up an ice climb, warm up a bit by bouldering on the ice first; otherwise, your hands in particular may not adjust to the cold easily.

Let's face it: most ice climbers who visit this ice arena in the Gorge want to climb only one route, maybe two in a day. But for those hardmen who like to grit their teeth at extreme climbs, an early morning start (7 AM) allows you to do 3-4 or even 5 different 1-2 pitch ice routes in a day. If you begin more casually (9-10 AM), after breakfast stops and other look-see stops, as well as last minute clothing adjustments, the time will be shortened for climbing.

Of course, what you intend to accomplish dictates your time goals for the day. Is it a day for learning the sport, advancing some skills, to climb a few routes, or to knock off as many ice classics as possible before it all falls down? Time, then, begins to make a considerable difference.

On many of the grade IV and V ice routes you will generally need a full day for success. You may need to start before sunrise and finish after dark on a few.

Be prepared by studying the specifics of a climb. Is the ice solid? Are there any ice pillars, or huge umbrellas of ice to surmount? Is the route all there? Is it too difficult for you to ascend? Guarantee your retreat options. This applies to shorter routes as well as the huge logistical monsters.

Let your friends know what you're up to. If the climb is exposed, with serious objective hazards involved, you may breathe easier if someone back home is awaiting your safe return.

Remember you can go out and spend a lot of time climbing, or you can just plain spend a lot of time. Either way, the majestic ice arena in the Columbia Gorge won't remain long!

Vandalism

Beware of the thief in the night. Or in our case, during the day. Climbers, leave **nothing** of value in your car to be seen by stealing eyes. Break-ins are a common occurrence here, during the summer as well as during the winter. Sometimes cassettes are taken, or radios, or even items beyond logic (car registration!)

Here are several ways to counter a possible break-in. Park where you can keep an eye on your vehicle. Park near tourists or busy intersections. Lock your car! Stow your valuables in the trunk out of sight. Out of sight, out of mind. In the case of most thieves, they do lack brains any way. The thief tends to notice the expensive, newer make vehicles, so drive a junk car.

All said and done. Let's go ice climbing!

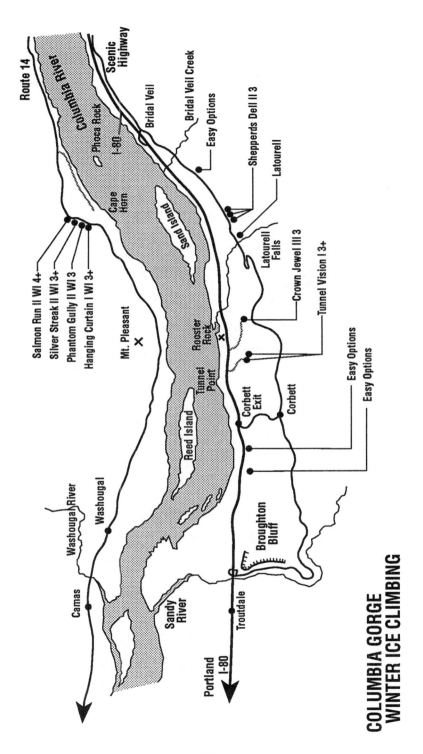

Route 14

Columbia River

Scenic Highway

Phoca Rock

I-80

Bridal Veil

Bridal Veil Creek

Easy Options

Shepperds Dell II 3

Latourell

Cape Horn

Sand Island

Latourell Falls

Crown Jewel III 3

Tunnel Vision I 3+

Salmon Run II WI 4+
Silver Streak II WI 3+
Phantom Gully II WI 3
Hanging Curtain I WI 3+

Mt. Pleasant

Rooster Rock

Tunnel Point

Corbett Exit

Corbett

Easy Options

Easy Options

Reed Island

Washougal River

Washougal

Camas

Sandy River

Broughton Bluff

Troutdale

Portland
I-80

**COLUMBIA GORGE
WINTER ICE CLIMBING**

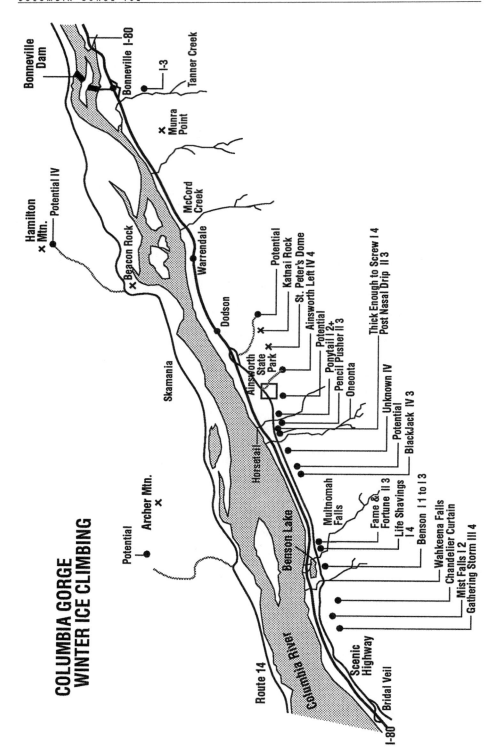

COLUMBIA GORGE
WINTER ICE CLIMBING

1. **Tunnel Vision**
   120' I WI 3 FA Jan. 1993 Wayne Wallace, Tim Olson
   Park on the south side of 1-84 approximately 1/4 mile east of Tunnel Point. This is where the railroad tracks cut through an outcrop of rock along the freeway. Cross the railroad tracks and walk east until you see the icefall on your right. Two gullies on the far left amongst the trees are low angle smears, yet do lead nearly to the top of the mountain (500' in length).

2. **Crown Jewel** (a.k.a. Crown Point)
   300' III WI 3 FA Jan. 1979 Alan Kearney, Chuck Sink
   A super classic and very popular ice climb in the Columbia Gorge. This moderately difficult icefall is quite obvious from the highway and holds a spectacular position for all to see. Because of the numerous parties ascending the route, it is wise to make an early start. Park immediately across from the Rooster Rock pinnacle at a small pullout. Walk to the railroad tracks then east to the icefall (15 minutes). This 2 pitch climb is usually ascended on the left side where the least amount of water drips. Prepare to get soaked anyway unless the conditions are premium. The 2nd pitch eases to a large amphitheatre. Two options: Rappel or continue up the easy gully to the scenic highway and Vista Overlook. Then descend down an easy dirt gully west of the Vista House parking lot.

3. **Latourrell Falls**
   35' I WI 2
   It is possible to do some minor, but limited, ice bouldering left of the main waterfall.

4. **Shepperds Dell area**
   This wind sheltered area offers several excellent options for leading. Drive west on the scenic highway (U.S. 30) from The Bridal Veil exit for approx. 2 miles. The climbs here are quite popular and will often remain climbable days after the other falls have collapsed. They are as follows from left to right.

A. **Original Route**
   60' I WI 2
   FA Jan. 1974 Phil Jones, Tim Carpenter
   A short ice climb leading to easy slopes above. Rappel from vine maples.

B. **Salamander**
   140' I WI 2+
   FA Feb. 1979 Jeff Thomas, Ed Newville
   Located approx. 100 yds. west of the Original Route.

C. **Water Heater**
   140' I WI 2+
   FA Jan. 1979 Jeff Thomas, Dave Jay
   Located approx. 50 yds. west of the Original Route.

D. **Unnamed**
   150' I WI ?
   A partially formed curtain of ice that has been top-roped.

E. **Bent Screw**
   150' I WI 3
   FA Feb. 1979 Ed Newville, Jeff Thomas
   One of the first to form and last to fall apart because the water source is from seeps and not stream flow. Usually wet and muddy near top. Rappel from a convenient tree at the summit. Good climb.

F. **The Column**
   100' I WI ?
   FA Jan. 1979 Alan Kearney, Sheri Nelson
   Short but steep climb with a larger volume of water. Needs an extended cold spell to freeze this climb.

5. **Bridal Suite**
   150' I WI ?
   FA Dec. 1985 Jeff and Bill Thomas
   A good one pitch climb nestled in a bowl high above the road and below the trail leading to Angel's Rest. Long approach but other potential does exist nearby.

6. **Slippery Dolphin**
   160' I WI ?
   FA Dec. 1983 Mark Cartier, Monty Mayko
   A steep and sustained lead located at the same pullout as the Gathering Storm. There is a good alternative climb located 100 yards west leading up a low angle corner.

7. **Gathering Storm**
   400' III WI 4 FA Feb. 1979 Jeff Thomas, Alan Kearney
   Approximately 1 3/4 miles east of the tiny community of Bridal Veil (U.S. 30) you will find the staggering Thomas-Kearney route. Park at a dirt pullout near a steep 160' bluff of rock. The waterfall immediately south of the road is the Slippery Dolphin. Hike the upper plateau south uphill to the next large cliff. Ascend the obvious major frozen waterfall. A short, steep first pitch leads to a huge bowl. The last is the longest and hardest.

8. **Mist Falls**
   200' I WI 2
   A relatively easy 1 to 1 1/2 pitch climb directly beneath the wind-whipped falls. Either climb up into the alcove and rappel or exit right to rappel from the trees. Expect a crackly suit of armor!   Park at a large signpost just before Wahkeena Falls and hike directly up the stream bed to the cliff.

9. **Chandelier Amphitheatre** - Ice Pillar
   Located just left and uphill from Mist Falls you will find an ice chandelier curtain of staggering proportions. Slightly to the right is a beautiful one pitch ice pillar leading into a large alcove. The pillar in the upper alcove does not connect and it is easier to traverse left along slopes to exit. The pillar is spectacular, but is virtually impossible to see from the road.

10. **The Chandelier Curtain**
    An impressive 300' massive curtain of hanging ice worth visiting. It is remarkable. Sorry, but it doesn't appear climbable even though it does connect from top to bottom. There are several possible ice gullies left and uphill from the curtain.

11. **Smooth Operator**
    100' I WI 3
    FRA Dec. 1990 Wayne Wallace and Tim Olson
    Park at Wahkeena Falls and take the right side trail. After a zig zag scramble directly uphill a distance towards two ice gullies. The right one has not seen an ascent (100') while the left is Smooth Operator. Both climbs fade into dirt and rock gullies. Rappel from nearby trees. Worth the hike.

12. **Wahkeena Falls**
    This area is generally good for photographing only. Too many tourists.

13. **Benson Lake Icefall**
    165' I WI 2-3
    Quite possibly the most frequently climbed chunk of ice in the Gorge. Often has 3-4 groups attacking the wall at the same time. Located approximately 1/2 mile west of Multnomah Falls and immediately across from Benson Lake. Expect liberal amounts of dripping water. Nonetheless, it is here that most climbers stop and check into the sport. There are easy slabs on the right and left with numerous trees for belays. Summitting out can be quite technical depending on the thickness of the ice.

14. **Dressed To Kill**
    160' II WI 3+ FA 1993 Tim and Cindy Olson

134

Approximately 150' left of Benson Icefall proper are two vertical smears that ease back at 35'. Dressed to kill is the right and longer variation that continues up on ice steps ending with a vertical, hollow chandelier that fades to dirt slopes at the top.

15. **Variation I**
100' I WI 2

16. **Area Classic**
100' I WI 2
Further left is an excellent low angle problem. Starts wide and becomes narrow higher up. Liberally protected with trees and bushes for anchors. The last section is usually too wet but the lower half is very popular.

17. **Pleasure Cruise**
40' I WI 2+
Deep in the trees 150' left of Area Classic you can find a fun, quality route that ascends past a small tree and abruptly ends on dirt slopes above.

18. **Shady Creek**
200' II WI 3
FA 1979 Ken Currens and Monty Mayko
Located up and right behind the lodge at Multnomah Falls. Although the area is crowded with tourists the climb is quite secluded. Involves two short leads of steep ice with one near vertical ice bulge to finish. Rappel from nearby trees.

19. **Multnomah Falls** (Right Side)
Always terrific to see, especially when the falls are encased in ghostly curtains of ice. The whole wall is not feasible to ascend due to lack of ice, but in Jan. 1979 Jeff Thomas and Ed Newville climbed the right side approximately 200'. They called it "The Once and Future King". Perhaps it could be climbed someday.

20. **Fame and Fortune**
200' II WI 3
Premium quality climb and readily accessible. There are no trees or rocks to rappel from. It's best to top out to the woods above, then hike down to the east. The crux is the first and last sections. Best if done in two short pitches. Great route but seldom sees a complete ascent.

21. **Blackjack**
500'+ IV WI 3
FA Dec. 1990 Wayne Wallace, Tim Olson
Located at mile post 21 on U.S. 30. A very exciting and challenging route with many pitches of moderate climbing. Park to the east of m.p. 21 at a large pullout, then hike up west on Gorge trail #400 and directly up to the base of a detached pillar (will be connected only after a mega-freeze). To begin the "moss variation" walk right 100' until you can angle up to a mossy arete on the right side of another gully system. No pro. Belay at a small fir tree. Move up easy gully then traverse directly left under a cliff band. Poor belay. Down step 100' to a lone fir tree and rappel into the Blackjack drainage. Ascend 3 main ice tiers, the last being a little wet near the top. Exit right to trees and rappel. Note: the first three pitches are poorly protected; may desire pitons or bolts.

22. **Black Diamond**
500'+ Potential
Located 1/4 mile east of mile post 21 at the dirt pullout next to a small bridge. Here is a supreme potential route that has never been attempted. It maintains outstanding exposure from start to finish and is vertical for over half its distance (with ice umbrellas) before easing back gently to 60°+. The only logical start is via steep mossy slabs on the lower right, for the first 20 ft. of the main icefall is detached. There are several other options for climbing in the area, some more realistic than others. This area is fairly well protected in a large amphitheatre.

23. Unknown
500' approx. IV potential
An excellent and beautiful (one of the prettiest I've seen) climb with many tiers. Has yet to see an ascent beyond 80'. Park to the west of Oneonta Gorge at the trailhead. Hike up westward to the base (20 min.) of this remarkable climb. The first pitch is gentle 65° ice followed by a vertical ice pillar to a wooded bench on the second pitch. The upper tiers can only be seen from the highway. Possible to exit left at 80' to rappel from bushes.

24. Oneonta Gorge
A good photographic stop but unless the stream freezes thick enough, exploration in the narrow gorge is limited.

25. Post Nasal Drip
200' II WI 3
A terrific, enjoyable route. Located east of Oneonta Gorge 1/2 mile at a small dirt pullout. Easily visible just uphill through the trees. The right and larger icefall is 20' wide, and is separated into two vertical sections. Both are sustained, while the second pitch fades near the top. Possible to exit left after the first pitch and rappel from trees (95').

26. Thick Enough to Screw
95' I WI 4
FA Dec. 1990 Tim Olson
To the left of the previous ice climb is a fabulous and desperate vertical ice smear. A classic testpiece, one of the best ice leads put up recently.

27. Horsetail Falls
200' III WI 5   FA Jan. 1993 Bill Price and Tim Olson
This is living proof that any ice can be climbed. A modern testpiece of phenomenal proportion, ascending the right side via the angels wings. A route that breaks with tradition and climbs on sacred ground.

28. Pencil Pusher
200' II WI 3
FA Dec. 1990 Wayne Wallace, Tim Olson
Uphill and to the right of Horsetail Falls are several exciting ice problems. Pencil Pusher is the central ice smear with a pillar at the second vertical step. The first pitch is a beautiful 70° ice smear. Finish up the right side of the pillar. An excellent option and not at all very difficult. Other potential lines exist to the left as well. To rappel, move right and down to near the edge of the cliff to a tree with a rappel sling. Perfect 80' rappel.

29. Peter Piper
90' I WI 2+
FA Dec. 1990 Tim Olson, Jay Green
To the right of Pencil Pusher is a short, fun ice climb. An easy lead on mostly slabby ice. Fades into the brushy hillside near top. Angle left to the rappel tree.

30. Ponytail
80' I WI 2+
A good, 70° ice climb that sees numerous ascents, particularly the first 80'. Located approx. 150' left of Horsetail Falls and offers easy access. Oh, yes, there is a second pitch (WI 4) on the upper right. The left smear looks terrible, but the right one can be climbed (no pro available).

31. Ainsworth Left
700'+ IV WI 5 (to high point)
This is THE ultimate Columbia Gorge classic ice route. Yes, it has been seriously attempted numerous times by very strong parties of climbers. All were humbled. Need I say more? To succeed an extended day will be necessary: from dawn to dusk.
Drive to the Ainsworth State Park overnight camp area and hike south via a trail and creek

drainage to the Ainsworth Creek amphitheatre. On the left face is the monster. This route does ice up with every major arctic cold snap, but may be wet if attempted too early. Someday this route will be conquered.

32. **Dodson**
700'+ IV WI 4+ (to high point) Feb. 1993 Bill Price, Tim Olson
South of the tiny community of Dodson and east of Katnai Rock is the huge vertical face of Yeon Mountain. The route is located near the left arete and can be seen from I-84. Much of it has been climbed (in 1993) except for the large hanging chandelier of ice referred to as the 'spitting dagger' on the last pitch.

33. **Tanner Creek Ice**
50' I WI 2
At the Bonneville Dam exit, turn south onto a graveled road that soon ends. Just beyond you will find several good easy to moderately angled ice climbs protected from the wind. Fun climbs.

34. **Starvation Creek**
200' II WI 3 FRA Dec. 1985 Scott Woolums, Terry Yates
One mile before Viento State Park (in the eastbound lane of I-84) you will find a rest stop at Starvation Creek. The icefall is climbable and there are several other possibilities nearby as well. A little exploration is all that is needed.

The following ice climbs are situated along the Washington State side of the Columbia River. To gain access to these drive east from Camas-Washougal on State Route 14.

35. **Cape Horn Area**
Easily one of the most impressive sights to see from across the river, these ice routes will readily capture the imagination. Of the nearly limitless possibilities, many are desperate WI 3 ice leads (or harder) and often 200'+ in length.
There are three tiers. The lowest tier is available by hiking along the railroad tracks westward 15 minutes from an access road to the east. Little is known of the ascents here.
The central tier can be accessed from the railroad tracks also, or via rappel from near Hwy. 14. The upper tier lies above the highway and just east of the steel chain-link protection nets. The ice routes at Cape Horn are highly technical, unrelenting and often long.

The known routes for the upper tier are as follows:

A. **Hanging Curtain**
80' I WI 3+
FA Winter 1979 Ian Wade and Scott Woolums

B. **Pillar I**
80' I WI 3
TR Winter 1979 Scott Woolums, Ian Wade

C. **Pillar II**
80' I WI 3+
FA 1979 Ian Wade, Scott Woolums

D. **Phantom Gully**
300' II WI 3
FA 1979 Monty Mayko, Robert McGown

E. **Silver Streak**
300' II WI 3+
FA 1979 Monty Mayko, Robert McGown

F. **Salmon Run**
   300' II WI 4+
   FA Dec. 1980 Jim Olson, Robert McGown

   The above technical waterfalls require one rope rappel descents. The Phantom Gully and Silver Streak are shaded the most and are reasonably protected from objective dangers.

36. **Hamilton Mountain**
    700'+ IV potential
    The Hamilton Mountain complex is located NE of Beacon Rock and may be accessed via a rough road leading up to an old gravel quarry. The road starts next to Hamilton Creek. The cliff band is approximately 45 min. uphill from the quarry.
    There are three main icefalls that collect on the vertical south face. One route has seen several attempts.

Bill Price leading Salmon Run on Columbia Gorge Ice

Mystery Climb

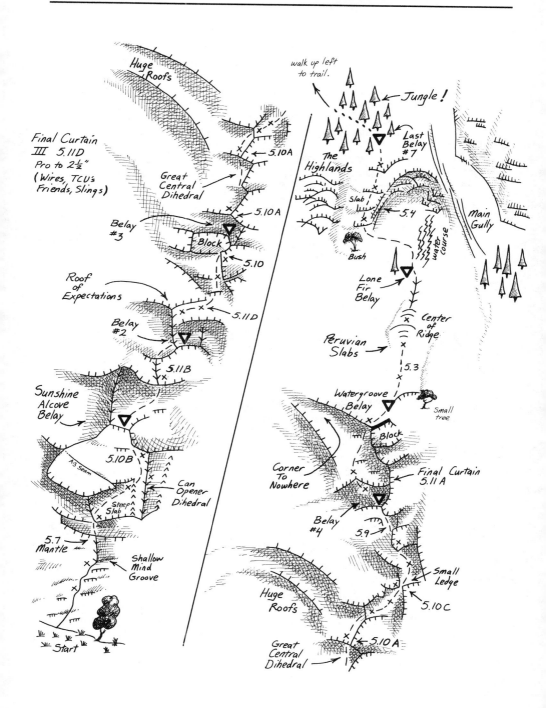

Huge Roofs

walk up left to trail.

Jungle !

5.10A

Last Belay #7

Final Curtain
III 5.11D
Pro to 2½"
(Wires, TCU's
Friends, Slings)

The Highlands

Great Central Dihedral

5.10A

Slab

5.4

Main Gully

Belay #3

Block

5.10

Bush

water course

Roof of Expectations

Lone Fir Belay

Belay #2

5.11D

Center of Ridge

Peruvian Slabs

5.3

5.11B

Sunshine Alcove Belay

Watergroove Belay

Small tree

Block

5.10B

A-3 Seam

Can Opener Dihedral

Corner To Nowhere

Final Curtain 5.11A

Steep Slab

5.7 Mantle

Belay #4

5.9

Shallow Mind Groove

Small Ledge

5.10C

Huge Roofs

5.10A

Start

Great Central Dihedral

139

Cragging Options

The next chapter contains a rich selection of alternative options for your climbing repertoire. Several are lowland cliffs near Portland, while most are either in the Columbia Gorge, at higher altitudes along the Mt. Hood scenic corridor or south towards Eugene.

I have included this article in the hope that you may find it an interest to seek a greater challenge: to explore beyond the urbanized confines of Portland. Generally, the crags are easily accessible by road and/or trail (1 minute for the shortest, 3-4 hrs. for the longest), and all of these are unique in special ways. These cragging options are excellent one day destination stops from Portland.

For example, Horsethief Butte offers many short bouldering and top-rope problems, while other places like Illumination Rock or Razorblade Pinnacle are true summits of unusual stature. The crags to the east of the Cascade Divide tend to be drier and warmer than the cliffs in Western Oregon, while the high altitude crags are especially suitable for climbing when the summertime temperatures soar into the 80's.

When exploring these places, remember to climb safely and dress according to the season (windbreakers, sweaters, bug repellant). Most of all, look around and enjoy the sights and sounds of an ever changing Oregon scenic wonderland.

Waterboard City Park

This secluded and undeveloped city park in Oregon City offers several minor cliffs. There are a few TR's and short lead routes available. The cliff band is quite short, yet fairly extensive and does offer some future route potential. There are several steep sections surrounded by cavernous gaping holes around large boulders, so be careful when exploring.

Approach by driving south on 99E to Tumwater Road (south of Oregon City) leading to South 2nd Street. Stop. Continue straight to the next stop. Turn right (SW) then immediately turn left onto John Adams Street and wander up this poor road grade to a dead end on the right. Walk uphill on the old paved road until you can see the minor crags. Most of the area spreads out to the right and south of the road. Routes range in difficulty from 5.4 to 5.10.

Elk Rock

Unusual, pocketed face climbs along the Willamette River, Much of the crag is quite dirty and vegetated, but is a potential area for further development provided you have a boat to gain access. At present the routes range in difficulty from 5.10 to 5.11. Elk Rock is located south of Sellwood Bridge halfway to Lake Oswego on U.S. 43 (a.k.a. Macadam Avenue). To approach the crag, either boat downstream from the city park in Lake Oswego (longest) or from across the river near Milwaukie (shortest) or upriver from the Sellwood Bridge.

Neahkahnie Mountain

Located several miles south of Cannon Beach along the Oregon Coast, this unique seacliff offers the air of exposure above the pounding surf. Several routes (mostly top-ropes) are available; some are leadable but the fixed gear quickly deteriorates over the years due to the ocean salts and should be considered dubious. Climb with care for even the solid appearing holds may break off; it is often better just top-roping most of the time. The beautiful and rugged Oregon coastline offers innumerable cliffs and sea pinnacles to explore; more than could ever be justifiably mentioned in this guide. For those of you with the interest, here are several areas worth a visit. Tillamook Head just north of Cannon Beach, Fogarty Creek State Park south of Lincoln City,

Sunset Bay near Coos Bay, and Bandon. Some cliffs are quite sound while others are virtual sand hills. Be wary of all loose hand holds when climbing.

Drive west on U.S. 26 to Cannon Beach Jct., then proceed south on U.S. 101 to Neahkahnie Mountain (just north of Manzanita). Drive to the parking area at Neahkahnie Viewpoint.

Chimney Rocks

An isolated, inspiring cluster of pinnacles scattered along a sub-ridge extending down from Silver Star Mountain. If the crag were situated in Portland, it would surely have been a very attractive climbing area. As it stands, though, the winds of spring are bone-chilling, while winter snows softly mantle the surrounding hills. The outcrop is beautifully situated, though, with breathtaking views of nearby mountains and the Columbia Gorge basin.

The needles are composed of andesite-mantled diorite and are quite sound, providing a fair number of crack routes as well as potential face routes. At present, climbs from 5.6 to 5.10 are available.

Approach via State Route 14 to Washougal. Take State Route 149 for 6.5 miles to County Road 11. Follow this road 3.9 miles to the Larch Mountain Road. Portions of the final 2 mile road along the ridge are heavily rutted, necessitating a 4-wheel drive vehicle or a good pair of hiking shoes. This crag is on private land.

Crown Point Area

The most popular minor pinnacle in the Columbia Gorge (frequently used by the Mazamas) would have to be Rooster Rock. The standard South Face route is reasonably stable and is roughly 120 ft. high, offering interesting but easy fifth class rock climbing (5.4).

Another fine option would be Pillars of Hercules, approximately 3 miles east of Rooster Rock on the south side of the freeway. The routes are somewhat loose but once a top-rope is set, they can be quite enjoyable. The easiest route is about 5.4 but poorly protected. Need 2 ropes for rappel. Last but not least is Crown Point, with the historical and panoramic Vista House situated upon its summit. Though there are two climbs available on the great north face, the rock is steep, vegetated, and of generally poor quality. The two climbs are the Zucchini Route (NE Face, 5.6 A2) and the West Chimney (5.5). Hard hats are recommended for safety.

Ozone

Drive east along State Highway 14 (Washington) through Washougal until the road rises to a high point above the Columbia River (17.5 miles from I-205) called Mount Pleasant. Park at a pullout 1/4 mile downhill and west from the high point. Descend via a drainage on the east side of the crag or by a well hidden but easy descent at the west end of the crag. The best potential climbs here are the aretes, for they are steep, clean and quite difficult. Some of the rock appears junky, yet with some cleaning most of it should be climbable. Only minor exploratory climbing at present to 5.10. It is a south facing crag and well protected from most of the nuke winds of the Gorge. Private land.

Wind Mountain

Located approximately 10 miles east of Cascade Locks (Bridge of the Gods) on the north side of the Columbia River along State Route 14, this mountain offers some exploratory cragging and several huge walls with good potential. The approaches will leave you short of breath, though, especially with a pack on. You will also find a small 40 ft. slab with good options on the south side just east of the "Keep Skamania County Clean" sign. Minor exploratory route climbing to date. This portion of the Gorge is known for ferocious wind gusts as well as that tiny creature called the tick.

Wooly Columns

This area was explored by renowned Alaskan Guide Scott Woolums and has good promise for future development. Of the few climbs available, these are 5.10 and approx. 120' in length. Bolts and pitons suggested. The crag is 2 1/2 miles east of Hood River (from the Toll Bridge) on the south side of I-84 adjacent to a small land-locked body of water.

Wankers Column

This crag offers steep 80° dihedral and thin crack climbing or face problems. A few leads exists, but most are generally top-ropes. Approximately 200+ ft. long and 60 ft. high. An excellent mid-winter option except for two drawbacks. There is a fairly thick ground cover of poison oak, and when the season is right, ticks abound. To approach, drive east from White Salmon - Bingen on State Route 14 (Washington side). Just east of Locke Lake, you will see a huge basaltic rim dipping downward into the Columbia River. Continue east and exit left onto a paved road at Rowland Lake. Park here and walk up a deer trail leading up and away from the lake. The crag faces westerly and is not visible until you hike 15+ minutes. Walk through secluded oak tree hollows, northwest from the car. An obvious stream drainage lies just to the west of the crag. Located on private land.

Horsethief Butte

A very popular, traditional place for teaching novices, Horsethief Butte has attracted many mid-winter enthusiasts escaping the bleak Portland rains. The crag offers limited lead routes and is best suited for bouldering and top-roping.

The longest climbs are situated on the outside of this fortress-like crag. Before the 20th century, local Indians frequented here for shelter, and today the place is under the protective jurisdiction of the State Parks of Washington. When the weather is showery in Portland, you can often find excellent if windy conditions at the Butte. The crag is roughly 30 ft. high on the inner walls. Beware of ticks in season.

Take I-84 east to Exit 87 just east of The Dalles. Cross the bridge over the Columbia River and drive about 3 miles north to State Route 14. Turn right (east) and drive 2 1/2 miles passing Horsethief Lake State Park. Park near a state park sanctuary sign just beyond a small bridge. Walk south and enter via a hidden entrance leading to the inner corridors. Overnight camping is not allowed.

Pete's Pile (a.k.a. Sunshine Dihedrals)

Near the Cooper Spur Road turnoff lies this amazing wonderland of basalt columns. The rimrock is very extensive and steep, 200 ft. at the highest point and perhaps 1000 ft. in length. The rock has much to offer in terms of limitless future potential, yet only a smattering of climbs have been established so far, from 5.6 to 5.10. Route cleaning here is a fairly involved, time consuming process, but the rewards are pure quality. Certainly 5.12 potential.

Drive south from Hood River on the East Fork Hood River Highway (35) for a total of 23.3 miles. Park at a dirt pullout on east side of the highway (the pullout is 3/4 mile south of the Cooper Spur Road and 1/3 mile north of the East Fork Trail #650).

An easy 10 minute approach trail angles leftward uphill toward the crag from the pullout. Pete's Pile is an excellent warm multi-season climbing area generally free of snow from April through October.

French's Dome

This unique and very accessible dome of rock lies amongst a canopy of evergreen trees on the lower west side of Mt. Hood. There are at least 10 routes available ranging from 5.6 to 5.12.

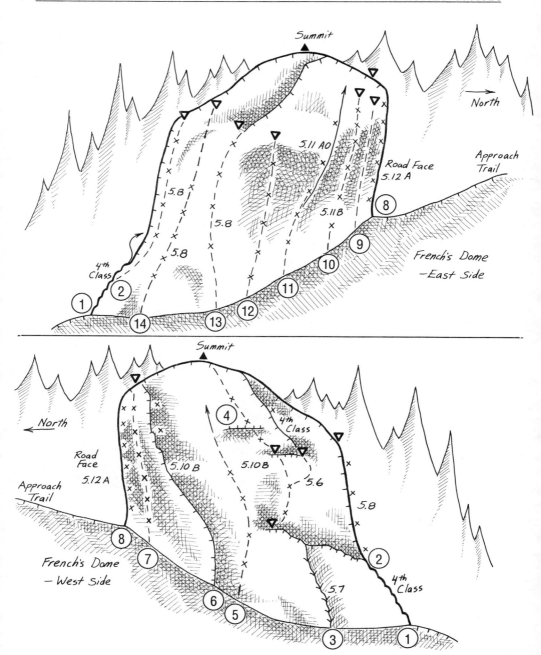

Most are fixed with pitons or bolts requiring only occasional natural pro placement, and are quite fun to lead. The overall height is 200 ft. from the longest side and 80 ft. on the road face.

The crag is located 6.2 miles up the Lolo Pass Road (F.S. 18) from its junction with U.S. 26 at Zig Zag. Look for a dirt pullout on the right. The tip of the Dome is barely visible above the trees.

Descend the trail (1 minute) to the crag and explore this interesting geological wonder of the woods. French's Dome is a peaceful climb area away from the hustle and bustle of real world politics. Misty Slab is the sloping buttress located 30 min. uphill from the Dome. An easily visible crag, yet because of the brushy approach ascents there have been kept to a minimum.

For the sake of popularity, the routes at French's Dome will be described clockwise, beginning with the all-time favorite, Giant's Staircase.

1. **Giant's Staircase** 5.6 ★★★
   QD's and runout

2. **Tin Tangle** 5.8 ★★
   QD's and runout

3. **Variation** start at
   Giant's Staircase 5.7
   No pro

4. **Static Cling** 5.10 B
   QD's

5. **Unknown** 5.11
   QD's

6. **Yellow Brick Road** 5.10 B
   Pro to 3" and runout

7. **Unknown** 5.12 A
   QD's

8. **Road Face** 5.12 A
   QD's

9. **Top-Rope** 5.12

10. **China Man** 5.11 B ★★
    QD's

11. **Nebula Wind** 5.11 A-3

12. **Unknown** 5.11 C

13. **Straw Man** 5.8 ★
    QD's and runout

14. **Alpha Centauri** 5.8 ★★
    QD's and good pro to 1"

Wayne Wallace on crux pitch, Razorblade Pinnacle (5.10 B)

Ramona Falls Crag

Minor climbing has been done here recently, but the area holds excellent potential for the future. The cliff is approx. 150' high and is southwesterly facing.

From the small community of Zig Zag drive north on F.S. Rd. 18 and turn right onto F.S. 1825. Continue on this narrow paved road past McNeil Campground then take a left onto F.S. 100. This quickly turns to a (very) rough gravel road. Either walk the 1 mile or drive slowly to the start of the Ramona Falls Trailhead. Cross the river on the foot bridge and take trail 797 to the left. At the next junction hike east on 797 toward Ramona Falls. The crag is on the north side of the trail approximately 1 1/2 miles from the foot bridge.

Razorblade Pinnacle 5,800 ft. elevation

Here is a true hidden alpine experience. One of the finest I've personally explored on Mt. Hood. It is a superb, isolated jewel of the hills, with a remarkable summit all its own. Approach via the Lolo Pass Road (F.S.18). Take F.S. 1828 near the McNiel-Riley campgrounds. It winds uphill to a gravelled side road leading to Top Spur trailhead.

Hike Top-Spur trail and then follow the Bald Mountain (Round the Mtn.) Trail south into the vast Sandy River basin. Take the southernmost drainage of the Muddy North Fork Sandy River. Follow its bank upward until the canyon steepens and appears forboding. Angle leftward up the steep hillside to the SW base of the Razorblade Pinnacle. The Gillette Arete, (5.10 or 5.9 A0) is an excellent quality multi-pitch climb.

Rappel via an easy tree to tree descent on the south face of the crag (can be done with a single rope). Need pro to 2" including cams. The potential for other new routes is good on the sunny south face while the overhung 350 ft. north face is simply mindboggling.

One long day is usually needed to hike the trail (3 hour approach) and ascend the pinnacle.

Salmon River Slab

Drive south from Zig Zag on F.S. 2618 for approximately 3.8 miles. At a pullout next to a good fishing hole on the Salmon River you will find a 75° black slab 80 ft. high and 50 ft. wide. There are several old aid routes, but as of yet it has not been developed for free climbing. Could yield six routes from 5.8 to 5.11. There are numerous other hidden crags in and around the Zig Zag area, and all that is needed is a little energy and interest.

Mirror Mountain (a.k.a. Ski Bowl) and Multorpor Slabs

Located south of U.S. 26 at Government Camp. Multorpor Mountain is the hill on the left, which yields several low angle slabs, while on the right is Mirror Mountain. Park and hike up the ski run 20 minutes to the obvious rocky outcrops. A fair number of the routes have been ascended but no records are available. During the summer the Multorpor Ski Area offers mountain bike courses and an alpine slide. Ice climbing can be found here during the coldest winter months as well.

It is worth note that just below the summit of Tom, Dick, Harry Mountain (overlooking Mirror Lake) there exists a fairly large wall of rock. The cliff is 100+ ft. high and several hundred wide and should yield a good selection of quality dihedral or thin crack problems from 5.9 to 5.11.

Illumination Rock

This challenging sharp profiled alpine peak is situated at the 9500 ft. level on the SW slopes of Mt. Hood. The approach generally takes 3-4 hrs. from Timberline Lodge, and while the regular routes (mentioned in Oregon High by J. Thomas) are available for summiting, they are often desperately poor in quality. Better options do exist on the vertical SE face and on several other outcrops near the South Chamber.

The rock offers smooth faces and many steep dihedral crack climbs. A few routes have been top-roped or established to date from 5.6 to 5.11. Future route potential usually requires ground-up climbing (hardhat suggested), an ice axe for the approach, as well as bolts and pitons for anchors. This is bold climbing! Look hard and you will find technically amazing routes, but please beware of all unstable rock.

During the winter months, excellent and extreme alpine ice climbing can also be found on this summit.

Newton Pinnacles

These surprising and secluded rock pinnacles are easily visible from the Hood River Meadows parking lot. Of the three separate pinnacles, the middle crag is the best. Park at the gate and walk to the ski run, then angle rightward and uphill directly toward the main pinnacle. A minor thrash up through a dense growth of trees brings you to the west face. A 30 minute hike total. The west face is approx. 80 ft. high and 165 ft. long and slightly overhung. The crag is liberally blessed with large holds and numerous cracks. To date there is an old aid route and several top-rope problems. Potential exists from 5.9 to 5.11.

Pig Iron Wall

Loose

Approach

Lamberson Butte - Gnarl Ridge Complex

Casually referred to as the "Leavenworth of Oregon," this extensive mega wall lies within the wooded Newton Creek drainage on the lower SE side of Mt. Hood. The area is remarkably photogenic. Roaring mountain streams, sheer rock faces, Mt. Hood towering above. Twisted whitebark pine trees and deep wooded slopes of mountain hemlock combine to make this a captivating destination.

The crag is 200 ft. at the highest and separated into large buttressed sections of granite-like quality rock along the slopes of this majestically scenic sub-alpine valley. The climbs at present range from 5.8 to 5.12, but virtually limitless route possibilities exist on this basalt crag.

Perhaps the ultimate route of simply staggering proportion at Lamberson is The Great Pig Iron Dihedral (5.10 A2+). This prominent 200 ft. long undulating dihedral glimmers in the sunlight from great distance. Another super classic is Bag of Tricks (5.10 C). This route ascends up next to a huge axe of rock via ledges, thin cracks and a technical face slab for 200 ft. before topping out to a wonderful view of the surrounding area.

There are routes here of every make and color: smooth-as-glass dihedrals, lightning bolt cracks, aretes, flake cracks, high-angle face routes and even roof problems. Only your climb rack and your ability will determine the route of ascent.

Ground-up climbing, though, is often the method used. It is quite bold, requiring thin pitons and bolts to succeed, with great rewards. Most routes are free climbed afterwards and make excellent leads. Please beware of unstable rock while grounding-up.

146

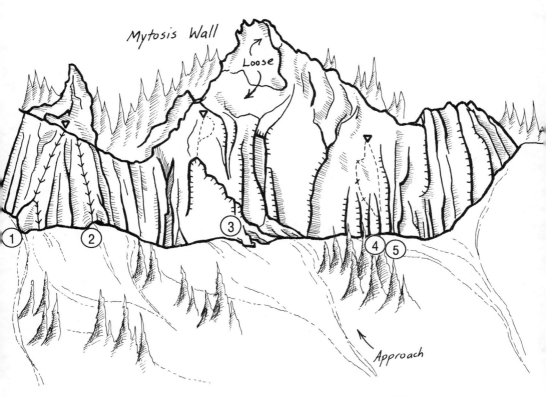

Park at the Hood River Meadows trailhead and hike NE (1 mile) toward Elk Meadows on trail #645. Take trail #646 that follows Newton Creek uphill to the Round-the-Mountain trail #600. Note: an excellent shortcut can be made by hiking along the creek through light brush for the last 1/2 mile of the approach. Ford the stream and angle up toward one of the crags.

The Lamberson Butte complex lies partway uphill on the southwest facing side of the Newton Creek drainage. The hike is an easy 1 1/2 hr. 3 mile approach.

Pig Iron Wall

1. _____
2. **Pig Newton** 5.10 D ★★
   120' Pro to 2" Needs pitons
3. **The Great Pig Iron Dihedral** 5.10 A2 ★★★
   150' Many KB, LA, TCU's and pro to 1"
4. **Headhunters** 5.11 B (PG-13) ★★★
   150' TCU's, RP's and pro to 1 1/2"
5. _____
6. **Panorama** 5.8
   165' Pro to 3"

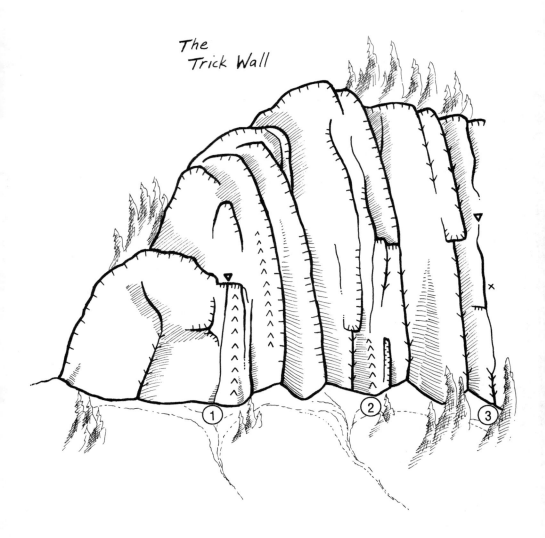

*The
Trick Wall*

Mytosis Wall

1. **Trafficosis** 5.8
   150' Pro to 2"

2. _____

3. **Mytosis** 5.10 C ★
   Multi-pitch Pro to 2" Cams recommended

4. **Thirty Six Light Years** 5.11+ or 5.9 A2 ★★★
   155' Pro to 2" TCU's suggested

5. **Catch Me If You Fall** 5.11 ★
   165' Pro to 2 1/2" Needs bolts and pitons

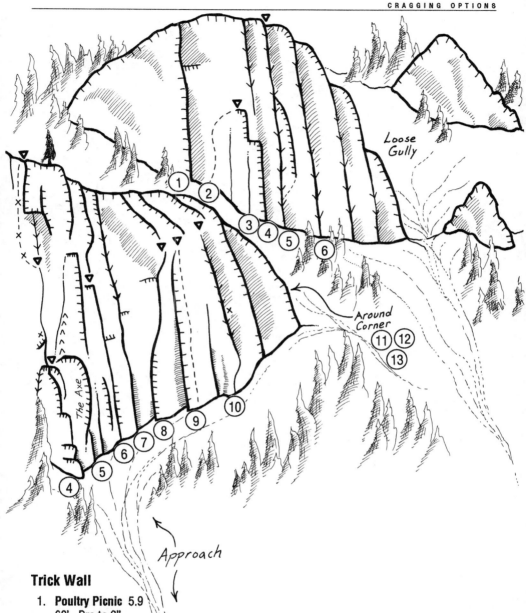

Trick Wall

1. **Poultry Picnic** 5.9
   60' Pro to 3"

2. **Pencil Arete**

3. **Crash of the Titans** 5.10 C ★★★
   100' Pro to 2 1/2" Cams recommended

4. **Bag of Tricks** 5.10 C (PG-13) ★★★
   Multi-pitch TCU's, RP's and pro to 3"

5. **Variation Start** 5.10 A
   60' Pro to 1 1/2" Needs pitons

6. **Top-Rope** 5.12
   80' Needs bolts

7. _____

8. **Trafalgar** 5.10 C ★
   80' TCU's, Friends to 3"
   required

9. **Top-Rope Arete** 5.11 B
   80'

10. **The Test Tube** 5.10 A A0 (R)
    80' Pitons and pro to 2"

11. **Quantum Gravity** 5.8 ★
    60' Pro to 3"

12. **Pushover** 5.10 C ★★
    60' Minor pro to 2"

13. **Sunset Bowl** 5.9
    80' Pro to 3"

Upper Trick Wall

1. _____

2. **Papa Tule** 5.10 A1
   80' Pitons and pro to 2"

3. **Lightning Bolt Crack** 5.12+
   Top-rope

4. **Mama Bo Jamma** 5.10 C
   ★★★
   80' Pro to 3" including cams

5. **The World is Collapsing**
   5.10 C ★
   150' Pro to 3" including cams

6. **Sacrisanctimonium** 5.10+ ★★
   165' Pro to 3" including cams

Climber leading Mama Bo Jamma (5.10C)

Harlen Roadside Quarry

Would a little bit of steep, quarried basalt out in sheep country seem inviting? It may be worth the visit. All the routes here are totally bolted considering the nature of the rock (somewhat loose and dirty). The wall extends for roughly 250 ft.; 40 ft. high on the left and 120 ft. on the right. The crag is quite steep at nearly 80°, with a total of seven free routes available as of this writing. Some future potential up to 5.12. The routes range in difficulty from 5.6 to 5.11 and face south to receive the warming effects of the sun.

Drive south to Corvallis, then west on U.S. 20 to the small community of Burnt Woods. Turn south on the paved road for 10 miles to the tiny cluster of houses called Harlen. Turn right (west) onto a gravel road for several miles, passing an overnight camping area. Approximately 1/2 mile beyond is the crag on the right.

The Menagerie

Here is a fascinating and protected wilderness area situated along the wooded south facing slopes of a small winding river. The rock pinnacles near Rooster Rock are quite solid and fun to climb, while the texture and approaches for the upper pinnacles (such as The Arch) are often contorted and brushy. Yet the favorites here are aplenty. The great Turkey Monster is absolutely staggering and has probably seen a bare handful of ascents since Eugene Dodd, Dave Jensen and

Bill Pratt completed it in 1966. The most frequented crags are Rabbit Ears, The Arch, Turkey Monster of course, Panorama Point, Rooster Rock, and Hen Rock.

Please inquire about the laws and ethics *before* visiting here!

Wolf Rock

This remarkable 900 ft. monolith of basalt casts a dark and forboding appearance down upon all who draw near. Even the easiest route involves a long and tenuous fourth class scramble. Yet Wolf Rock is an absolute must on everyone's list. It is well worth it.

One of the most incredible Oregon FA's took place here in 1972 when Wayne Arrington and Mike Seely ascended the gargantuan south face headwall through the dark and awe-inspiring roofs. They called it Barad-Dûr (Dark Tower) IV 5.9 A3. This seemingly improbable route presently goes free via a 5.11 A variation at the roof. The rock offers numerous other routes. Nearly all of the climbs were done ground-up, so expect lengthy runouts between bolts.

Drive SE from Albany on U.S. 20 through Sweet Home until you approach Iron Mtn. Take the F.S. Road 15 south for approximately 10 1/2 miles to the Meadows. Turn west on the same road (15) and park at one of several pullouts near the rock. A minor 15 minute approach brings you to the base of the wall. Be prepared for seemingly big-wall climbing if you intend to summit out.

Skinner Butte Columns

Located in Eugene, Oregon, The Columns offer a wealth of quality thin crack dihedrals for leading or top-roping. Though quite small in size, this crag is a fun place to develop your technique for crack climbing. Drive to Eugene on I-5 and take I-105 west. Follow this to its end at 7th Avenue. Turn left and go east for 3 blocks then take another left (north) onto Lincoln. Approximately 6 blocks later, on the right at a dirt pullout, you will find The Columns, below the west side of Skinner Butte.

Flagstone

Sardine Butte (5200') is located east of Eugene in the McKenzie River basin. Referred to as "Flagstone" by the locals, this area offers a good selection of bolted face climbs ranging from 5.8 to 5.11. The crag is approximately 150' in height. You can approach the crag by proceeding east of Eugene on U.S. 126 to a bridge at Fin Rock (approximately 2 miles west of the community of Blue River).

Continue southeast on graveled F.S. Road 2618 along Quartz Creek for roughly 10 miles to the junction of F.S. Road 350. Drive along this til you can see the crags. Easy access. Please be vigilant to local ethics.

The Hardman List

Broughton Bluff

1. **Gandalf's Grip** (complete) 5.9+
2. **Demian** 5.10 D
3. **Sheer Stress** (complete) 5.10 A
4. **Physical Graffiti** 5.10 D
5. **Dracula** 5.12 A
6. **Superstition** (complete) 5.11 A
7. **Lost Boys** 5.10 D

Rocky Butte

8. **Phylynx** 5.11 B

Madrone Wall

9. **Where the Wild Things Roam** 5.11 D
10. **Beam Me Up Mr. Scott** 5.11 C
11. **Catharsis** 5.11 C
12. **Mr. Noodle Arm** 5.11 B
13. **Nouveau Riche** 5.10 C

Carver Bridge Cliff

14. **Uncola** 5.11 C
15. **Smerk** (complete) 5.11 A

Beacon Rock

16. **Fear of Flying** 5.10 B
17. **Fire and Ice** 5.11 B
18. **Tennessee Walker** 5.10 D
19. **Blownout** 5.10 A
20. **Borderline** (complete) 5.11 B
21. **Flying Swallow** (complete) 5.10 D
22. **Blood, Sweat, and Smears** 5.10 C
23. **Steppenwolf** (to Big Ledge) 5.10 C
24. **Free For Some** (complete) 5.11 A
25. **Pipeline** 5.11 B

Climbing History
Author's note: This appendix lists FA data for virtually all of the climbs in this book. A special thanks to all of you who freely shared your part of this history. The occasional blank space simply indicates information that was unavailable at the time of publishing. There are bound to be errors in this guide. I hope that the mistakes found will be minor.

The following definitions will help readers to interpret the first ascent data:

FA (First Ascent): Aid ascent and/or attempted free ascent.

FFA (First Free Ascent): Free ascent with NO tension, weighting of pro or falls.

FRA (First Recorded Ascent): It is likely that the climb was done previously, but no record exists as to who did it.

TR (Top-rope): Climbing a route with a safety line that is anchored from above. Often done before a free ascent.

GFA (Ground-up First Ascent): Without pre-inspection.

BROUGHTON BLUFF

North Face
1. **Traffic Court** FFA (before) 8-87 Wayne Wallace, Robert McGown
      (ascent after collapse) 8-22-92 Tim Olson
2. **Variation**
3. **Gandalf's Grip** GFA (regular route) 1968 Steve Strauch, Jim O'Connell
      FFA (by variation) 9-28-69 Steve Strauch, John Hack
4. **New Wave** FFA 1st pitch 7-87 R. McGown, W. Wallace
5. **Peach Cling** GFA 1972 Jim Mayers, Gail Van Hoorn
      FFA summer 1978 Doug Bower and partner
6. _____
7. **Risky Business** FA 7-87 W. Wallace, R. McGown
8. **Reckless Driver** FFA 1st and 2nd pitch 2-7-87 T. Olson
      FFA Complete (1,2,3) 7-15-87 W. Wallace, R. McGown
9. **Sweet Emotion** FA 8-87 W. Wallace, R. McGown
10. **American Graffiti** FA 10-87 W. Wallace

Hanging Gardens Wall - Left Half
1. **Giants Staircase** FA Unknown
2. **Edges and Ledges** FFA 8-92 Greg Murray
3. **The Sickle** FRA 1972 Ancil Nance
4. **The Hammer** FA Unknown
5. **Prometheus Slab** FA 1965 Bob Waring, John Wells, Bruce Holcomb
6. **Spud** FA Unknown
7. **Tip City** FA 1979 Jim Olson, Jay Kerr
8. **Lean Years** FA Unknown
9. **Hangover** (TR) 1979 J. Kerr, J. Olson
10. **Chockstone Chimney** GFA 1965 B. Waring, J. Wells, B. Holcomb
11. **Milestone** FA Unknown

Hanging Gardens Wall - Right Half
12. **Loose Block Overhang** Probable FFA 1975 Monty Mayko, Jim Garrett
13. **Grace and Danger** FFA 6-30-91 Dave Sowerby
14. **Slapfest** FFA 1-12-92 T. Olson, Cindy Long
15. **Least Resistance** FRA 1971 T. Bielefeldt, Tim Carpenter, Bruce Weideman
      FFA Fall 1975 Roger Baker
16. **Dynamic Resistance** FFA 7-9-88 W. Wallace, R. McGown

17. **Sandy's Direct** FFA 1977 R. McGown, Mike Smelsar, Sandy Regan
18. **Face Not Friction** GFA 1975 Alan Campbell and partner
    FFA 5-30-81 Mark Cartier
19. **Hanging Gardens** GFA 1965 B. Waring, J. Wells, B. Holcomb
    FRFA 1974 Rick Borich
20. **BFD** FFA 1975 Bruce Casey, M. Mayko
21. **Mr. Potato** GFA 1973 A. Campbell and partner
    FFA 7-18-81 B. Casey, Jeff Thomas
22. **From Something to Nothing** FFA 10-11-87 W. Wallace, T. Olson
23. **Fun in the Mud** FA 1977 R. McGown, Terry Yates
24. **Circus Act** FFA 9-19-87 W. Wallace, T. Olson
25. **Shining Star** FA 1977 Mike Smelsar, R. McGown
    FFA complete 3-16-87 R. McGown, W. Wallace
26. **Hung Jury** FFA 5-87 R. McGown, W. Wallace
27. **Hang 'Em High** FFA 9-7-87 R. McGown, W. Wallace
28. **Main Vein** FFA 8-91 Chuck Buzzard, Steve Mrazek
29. **Sesame Street** GFA 1972 A. Campbell, Gail Van Hoorn
    FFA 7-8-73 Dean Fry and partner
30. **Demian** GFA Fall 1976 R. McGown, M. Smelsar
    FFA Unknown
31. **Endless Sleep** GFA Spring 1977 R. McGown, M. Smelsar
32. **Peer Pressure** GFA 1972 or 73 J. Mayers, A. Campbell
    FFA Spring 1977 M. Smelsar, R. McGown
33. **Scorpion Seams** GFA 1980 R. McGown, Steve Hillanger, Mike Corning
    FFA
34. **Black Prow** FA 1979 R. McGown, M. Simpson

Red Wall

1. **Arch De Triumph** FA 1987 W. Wallace
2. **Arcturas** (TR) 12-86 T. Olson
3. **Anastasia** (TR) 12-86 T. Olson
4. **Dead Bones** (TR)
5. **On The Loose** FFA 1978 R. McGown
6.   (TR) Greg Lyon
7. **Classic Crack** FA and FFA Unknown
    TR Free in 1972 by J. Mayers. Led Free in 1975 by Doug Bower
8. **Thai Stick** FA 1979 R. McGown
9. **Mr. Bentley** TR 1981 Ed Welter, Jack Goble
10. **Sheer Stress** GFA 1974 A. Campbell and partner
    FFA complete 1975 Charlie Priest, Charlie Martin
11. **Physical Graffiti** FA Summer 1977 R. McGown, M. Smelsar
    FFA Summer 1977 D. Bower and partner
12. **Habitual Ritual** FFA 2-5-92 Gary Rall
13. **Physical Direct** FFA 11-18-90 T. Olson, Cecil Colley
14. **Hit the Highway** FA 1977 B. Casey, M. Mayko
15. **Kashmir** FFA (via Classic Crack) 11-18-90 G. Rall
16. **Red Eye** FFA 1st pitch 1976 M. Mayko, B. Casey
    FA complete 1978 M. Cartier and partner
    FFA 10-3-78 J. Thomas, Paul Gleeson
17. **Critical Mass** FFA Summer 1981 R. McGown, Scott Woolums
    Retro bolt ascent on 9-5-90 by G. Rall
18. **E. Pluribus Pinhead** FFA 8-91 S. Mrazek, C. Buzzard

19. **Opus (Direct Start)** FFA 2-5-92 D. Sowerby
20. **Sheer Energy** GFA Fall 1979 Jim Olson or Alan Kearney
21. (TR)
22. **Hard Body** FFA 5-5-91 T. Olson, W. Wallace
23. **Shoot from the Hip** FFA 4-7-91 T. Olson
24. **Balls Not Friction** FA 7-88 W. Wallace
25. **That's the Way** FA 7-88 W. Wallace

Bridge Cliff
1. **Under Your Belt** FA 4-24-87 W. Wallace, Scott Tracy
2. **Walk on the Wild Side** GFA 1977 Jay Kerr, David Howe
3. **Edge of Eternity** FFA 2-25-88 W. Wallace, R. McGown, T. Olson
4. **Spidermonkey** GFA 1977 R. McGown, M. Simpson
5. **Fruit Bat** GFA 1977 R. McGown, D. Bower
6. **Seventh Sojourn** FA 1977 R. McGown, M. Simpson, Roger Baker
7. **Shandor** FA 1-8-88 W. Wallace

Spring Rock
1. **Toe Cleavage** FFA 11-6-87 W. Wallace
2. **Velcro Fly** FFA 4-9-89 T. Olson, W. Wallace
3. **Free Bird** FFA 11-8-87 W. Wallace
4. **Ground Effects** FFA Summer 1989 G. Lyon
5. **Jumping Jack Thrash** (TR) 10-86 J. Goble, E. Welter, M. Cartier
     FFA 9-5-90 G. Rall
6. **The Spring** GFA 1977 R. McGown, B. Casey
7. **Short Fuse** FFA 6-28-92 T. and C. Olson
8. **Dyno-Mite** FFA 11-27-87 W. Wallace

Bat Wall
1. **Hanging Tree** FA 6-2-77 R. McGown, J. Thomas
2. **Go Back to the Gym** GFA 10-28-90 W. Wallace, T. Olson
3. **Dracula** FA Unknown
     FFA 5-20-90 G. Rall, T. Olson
4. **Bela Lugosi** FFA 9-16-90 G. Rall
5. **Fright Night** FFA 7-12-91 Matthias Pausch
6. **The Haunting** GFA 1977 B. Casey, M. Mayko
     FFA 1-2-92 G. Rall
7. **Bad Omen** (got the horse for my saddle) FFA 12-16-90 T. Olson
8. **Danse Macabre** FFA 8-19-92 D. Sowerby
9. **Bloodsucker** GFA Summer 1977 R. McGown, M. Smelsar
     FFA 1-20-93 Jay Green
10. **Bloodline** GFA 2-91 W. Wallace, R. McGown
     FFA 1-19-92 D. Sowerby
11. (TR)
12. **Superstition** GFA 1977 R. McGown, S. Woolums, J. Olson
     FFA 7-11-81 J. Thomas, M. Cartier
13. **Lost Boys** FA Unknown
     FFA complete 12-2-90 W. Wallace, T. Olson, Jay Green, Mike Cartier
14. **Mystic Pizza** FFA 12-9-90 W. Wallace, T. Olson
15. **Mystic Void** FA 1977 R. McGown, S. Woolums
16. **Well Hung** GFA 1977 R. McGown, M. Simpson
     FFA Unknown
17. **Gold Arch** GFA 1978 R. McGown, D. Bower, T. Yates

18. **The Hunger** FFA 8-29-92 D. Sowerby
19. **Dark Shadows** GFA 1979 R. McGown, J. Olson, M. Simpson
    FFA 11-2-90 D. Sowerby, Mike Sessions
20.
21. **Manson Family Reunion** FA Unknown
    FFA 9-7-92 S. Mrazek
22.
23.
24.
25.

Trinity Wall
1. **Bust A Move** FFA 6-2-91 W. Wallace, T. Olson
2. **Father** FA 3-6-88 W. Wallace
    FFA 11-11-90 W. Wallace, T. Olson
3.
4.
Berlin Wall
1. **Closet Nazi** FFA 9-90 J. Green
2.
3. **Twist and Crawl** FA Spring 1991 W. Wallace, T. Olson
    FFA 7-91 M. Carter
4.
5. **Pride and Joy** FFA 11-11-90 T. Olson, W. Wallace

Jungle Cliff
1. **Zimbabwe** GFA 9-29-91 D. Sowerby, Greg Carmichael
2. **Slash and Burn** GFA 3-23-91 W. Wallace, T. Olson
            FFA 11-92 G. Sowerby
3. **Under the Yum-Yum Tree** GFA 2-7-88 W. Wallace, G. Lyon
4. **Tarzan** FFA 3-13-92 D. Sowerby
5. **Crime Wave** FFA 6-13-92 T. and C. Olson
6. **Gorilla Love Affair** FFA 2-9-92 C. Long and T. Olson
7. **Out of Africa** GFA 7-79 S. Woolums, R. McGown
8. **Heart of Darkness** FFA 4-27-91 D. Sowerby
9. **Mowgli's Revenge** FFA 2-2-92 D. Sowerby
10. **Amazon Woman** GFA Fall 1991 W. Wallace, T. Olson
    FFA 1-17-92 Heather Macdonald, C. Long
11. **Amazon Man** GFA 7-79 R. McGown, Levi grey, M. Simpson
12. **Killer Pygmy** GFA (to Skull Ledge) 11-30-91 W. Wallace, T. Olson
    GFA 2nd pitch 12-10-91 W. Wallace, R. McGown
13. **Mujahideen** GFA 11-27-87 W. Wallace

New Frontier Wall
1.
2. **Alma Mater** FFA 6-2-91 W. Wallace, T. Olson
3. **Happy Trails** FFA 1-2-91 D. Sowerby, Mike Smith
4. **Wild, Wild West** GFFA 2-23-91 D. Sowerby, Ric Weaver, T. Olson
5. **Pioneer Spirit** FFA 8-18-91 D. Sowerby
6. **Promised Land** FFA 9-7-91 D. Sowerby
7.

Rocky Butte

Poodle Pinnacle
1. **Poodle with a Mohawk** FFA 6-87 Gary Rall

Trivial Pinnacle
1. **Harlequin** FFA 8-9-87 T. Olson, R. McGown
2. **Trivial Pursuit** FA 8-9-87 R. McGown, T. Olson
3. **The Joker** FA Unknown

Silver Bullet Bluff
1. **Unknown**
2. **Captain She's Breaking Up** FA 8-87 R. McGown, Jim Mohel, T. Olson
3. **Unknown**
4. **Sundance Kid** FA Unknown
    FRFA 7-87 Greg Lyon, R. McGown, Chris McMullin
5. **Panama Red** FFA 7-87 G. Lyon, C. McMullin, R. McGown
6. **Miss Kitty** FA 7-87 R. McGown, Eric Simmons
7. **Gunsmoke** FFA 7-20-87 T. Olson, R. McGown
8. **Bite the Bullet** FFA 7-20-87 R. McGown, Wayne Wallace, T. Olson
9. **Jack of Hearts** FFA 7-15-87 W. Wallace, R. McGown, T. Olson
10. **Silver Bullet** FFA 7-20-87 R. McGown, T. Olson, Steve Wong
11. **Urban Cowboy** FFA 7-20-87 R. McGown, T. Olson, S. Wong
12. **Last Tango** FFA 7-87 R. McGown, T. Olson
13. **Fandango** FFA 7-13-87 T. Olson, R. McGown
14. **Midnight Warrior** FFA 7-13-87 T. Olson, R. McGown
15. **Superman Crack** FFA 7-25-87 T. Olson, R. McGown
16. **Centurion** FA 7-15-87 R. McGown, T. Olson
    FFA 7-87 W. Wallace, R. McGown
20. **Invisible Man** GFA 7-87 R. McGown, J. Mohel
21. **Temporary Arete** FFA 9-88 Ed and Vern Welter

Video Bluff
1. **Body Language** FFA 6-11-87 R. McGown, T. Olson
2. **Body Bionics** FFA 6-11-87 R. McGown, T. Olson
3. **AC / DC** FFA 6-6-87 Dan Wright, T. Olson
4. **Eve of Destruction** FFA 6-5-87 R. McGown, T. Olson, Jim Wright, Eve McDermitt
5. **Live Wire** FFA 6-5-87 R. McGown, T. Olson
6. **Damaged Circuit** FFA 6-5-87 T. Olson, R. McGown
7. **Robotics** FFA 6-6-87 T. Olson, D. Wright
8. **Edge of Might** FFA 8-87 Mike Pajunas, G. Rall
9. **Hard Contact** FFA 6-88 G. Lyon
10. **Lever or Leaver** FFA 8-87 M. Pajunas, G. Rall, John Sprecher
11. **Persistence of Time** FA Summer 1991 Chad Franklin
12. **Zivas Book** FFA 8-20-82 T. Olson, D. Wright
13. **Flakey Old Man** FFA 5-29-87 T. Olson, R. McGown
14. **MTV**
15. **Stranger Than Friction** FFA 5-29-87 T. Olson, R. McGown
16. **Panes of Reality** FFA 5-29-87 R. McGown, T. Olson
17. **Stained Glass** FFA 5-29-87 T. Olson, R. McGown
18. **Toxic Waltz** FA 11-91 C. Franklin
19. **E-Z Corner** FA Unknown

New Era
1. **Point of No Return** (TR) 9-10-87 T. Olson

2. **Simba** FFA 8-20-87 T. Olson
3. **Love on the Rocks** (TR) 8-87 D. Wright
4. **Fiddler on the Roof** FFA 8-87 T. Olson
5. **Cuts Like a Knife** FFA 8-87 R. McGown, Bob Scarborough

Dream Weaver Wall

1. **Dream Weaver** FFA 4-86 M. Pajunas, R. Moody
2. **Head Bangers Ball** FFA 10-9-88 W. Wallace
3. **Tiger Pause** FFA 10-85 M. Pajunas, Joe Parsley

Wizard Wall

1. **Kleen Korner** FA Unknown
2. **Naked Savage** FFA 6-4-87 R. McGown, T. Olson
3. **Lord of the Jungle** FFA 6-2-87 R. McGown, T. Olson
4. **Slavemaker** FFA 6-4-87 R. McGown, T. Olson
5. **Godmonster** FFA 5-24-87 R. McGown, T. Olson
6. **Eye in the Sky** FFA 6-2-87 R. McGown, T. Olson
7. **Phylynx (**TR) 1987 Mike Craig
    FFA 5-87 R. McGown, Larry Jennings
8. **Walk on Water** FA 6-87 R. McGown, W. Wallace
9. **Mind Games** FFA 5-26-87 R. McGown, T. Olson
10. **Wizard** FA 5-26-87 R. McGown, T. Olson, D. Wright

Far East Wall

1. **Great Wall of China** GFA 4-87 R. McGown and partner
2. **High Road to China** FFA 4-87 R. McGown, W. Wallace
3. **Chinese Finger Torture** GFA 4-87 R. McGown, T. Simms
4. **The Wanderer** FFA 9-87 D. Wright
5. **Ghost Rider** FFA 6-87 R. McGown, T. Olson, D. Wright
6. **(Flight of the) Seventh Moon** FFA 5-87 M. Pajunas
7. **Orient Express** FFA 5-87 M. Pajunas, Rita Hansen, Charlie Martin, G. Rall
8. **Secret Maze** FFA 6-87 M. Pajunas, R. McGown, D. Wright
9. **Tigers Eye** FFA 4-9-88 T. Olson, G. Lyon, Matt Papolski, Mike Larsen

Warrior Wall

1. **Smears For Fears** FFA 8-85 M. Pajunas, J. Parsley
2.
3. **Crack Warrior** FFA 8-85 M. Pajunas, J. Parsley
4. **You'll Dance to Anything** (TR) 7-88 G. Lyon
5. **Shear Madness** FFA 7-87 M. Pajunas, J. McCracken
6. **Quarry Cracker** FA 1986 M. Pajunas
7. **Lathe of Heaven** FA 1989 R. McGown and partner
8. **Arch Nemesis** FFA 8-85 R. McGown, D. Nakahira
9. **Boy Sage** FA 5-87 R. McGown, Roger Baker
10. **Jealous Rage** FA 5-87 R. McGown, R. Baker
11. **Emotional Rescue** GFFA 9-85 M. Pajunas, J. Parsley

Freeway Wall

1. **Simple Twist** GFA 4-87 R. McGown, C. McMullin, J. Fredericks
2. **Hyper Twist** FFA 5-87 D. Wright
3. **Passing Lane** GFA 5-87 M. Pajunas
4. **Speeding Down South** FA 5-87 M. Pajunas
5. **Ranger Danger** FFA 5-22-87 R. McGown, T. Olson

6. **Telegraph Road** (TR) 5-87 D. Wright
7. **Highway Star** GFA 7-77 Doug Bower, Shari Kearney, R. McGown
8. **Dead Mans Curve** FFA 5-87 R. McGown, T. Olson

Mean Street
1. **Thunder Road** GFFA 4-87 R. McGown, Jim Opdycke
2. **Lethal Ethics** FFA 6-87 W. Wallace, Dave Bloom
3. **Spiritual Journey** FFA 4-87 W. Wallace, R. McGown
4. **Little Arete** FFA 6-87 R. McGown, W. Wallace
5. **Seamingly Endless** FFA 4-87 R. McGown, W. Wallace
6. **Holy Bubbles** GFA 1983 G. Rall
    FFA
7. **Pluto** FA Summer 1990 C. Franklin
8. **No Leverage** FA 4-87 Mark Kerns
9. **Be Bold Or Not To Be** = True Blue Water Course
10. **Claymation** FFA 4-87 R. McGown, W. Wallace

Easy Street
xx Short Climbs

Toothpick Wall
1. **Reach For The Sky** GFA 4-87 M. Pajunas, G. Rall
2. **Zenith** (TR) 7-88 G. Lyon, Matt Pixler
3. **Blueberry Jam** FA 1977 R. McGown, Mike Smelsar
4. **Leading Edge** FA 4-87 R. McGown, W. Wallace
5. **Close To The Edge** FA (FFA?) 7-77 R. McGown, Doug Bower
6. **Toothpick** FA 1978 R. McGown, J. Sprecher
7. **Far From The Edge** (TR)
8. **Rob's Ravine** FA 1978 Bill Antel, R. McGown
9. **Competitive Edge** GFA 4-87 R. McGown, W. Wallace, D. Nakahira, C. Carlson
10. **Vertical Therapy** FA 1986 J. Parsley, Dennis Hemminger
11. **Power Surge** FFA 4-87 W. Wallace, R. McGown
12. **Stiff Fingers** FA 1986 D. Hemminger

Boulders In The Woods
xx

Breakfast Cracks
1. **"D" and Rising** FA 8-87 R. McGown, J. Mohel
2. **The Arete** FA Summer 1991 C. Franklin
3. **Blackberry Jam** FRA 1974 Jim Davis, T. Crossman
    FFA 1977 R. McGown, M. Smelsar
4. **Hot Tang** FA 1978 Ted Johnson, R. McGown, F. Ziel
5. **Expresso** FA 1977 Mark Simpson, Rich Warren, Scott Woolums
6. **Red Zinger** FA 7-87 R. McGown, D. Wright
7. **Orange Spice** FA 5-87 R. McGown, T. Olson, Dave Sagient
8. **Lemon Twist** FFA 5-87 R. McGown, T. Olson, D. Sagient
9. **Lunge and Plunge** (TR) Bill Coe, Mike Kruger
10. **White Rabbit** FRA 1977 R. McGown, M. Smelsar
11. **White Rabbit Buttress** (TR) 1984 D. Nakahira, B. Casey
    FFA Unknown
12.
13.

14. **Birds of Paradise** FA 1979 D. Bower, R. McGown, R. Baker
15.
16. **Wisdom Tooth** FA 1978 R. McGown, T. Yates, J. Alzner
17.
18. **Trix are for Kids** (TR)
19. **Time of Your Life** (TR)
20. **Swiss Miss** FA Unknown

Wall of Shadows
1. **Shadows in Space** FA 1986 R. McGown, M. Simpson
2. **Face Disgrace** (variation) FA 1986 R. McGown, M. Simpson
3. **Skywalker** GFA 1986 R. McGown, M. Simpson
4. **Mystic Traveler** FA 7-85 M. Pajunas
     FFA (?) R. McGown, M. Simpson
5. **Spiderline** GFA 1986 R. McGown, M. Simpson
6. **Foot Loose** FA 5-85 M. Pajunas, J. Parsley
7. **Joe's Garden** FA 6-85 J. Parsley, M. Pajunas
8. **Hang Loose** FFA 10-15-88 W. Wallace
9. **Seventh Wave** FA (?) M. Pajunas

MADRONE WALL

Left Corner Wall
1. **Jackson's Daring Deeds** FFA 9-88 John Jackson, Patrick Jackson
2. **Patrick's Dihedral** FFA 9-88 P. Jackson, J. Jackson
3. **Sheesh** FFA 9-88 J. Jackson, P. Jackson
4. **Identity Crisis** FFA 4-15-89 T. Olson, Cecil Colley
5. **Mental Crisis** FFA 2-28-89 G. Lyon
6. **Into The Black** FFA 4-15-89 T. Olson, C. Colley
7. **Talk, Talk, Talk** FFA 3-90 G. Lyon

Orange Wall
1. **Wild Blue Yonder** FFA 4-23-89 W. Wallace, R. McGown
2. **Where the Wild Things Roam** FFA 5-30-89 W. Wallace, R. McGown
3. **Tangerine Dream** FFA 3-13-89 R. McGown, K. Jackson
4. **Direct Start** 7-89 R. McGown, Keith Jackson
5. **Agent Orange** FFA 3-20-89 W. Wallace, R. McGown
6. **Subarachnoid Space** (TR)
7. **Midget Madness** FFA 9-88 Chuck Buzzard, J. Jackson, P. Jackson
8. **Graduation** FFA 6-88 J. Jackson and partner
9. **Chop the Monkey** FFA Spring 1989 Andy and Ellen Hatfield
10. **Route Crafters** FFA 6-88 C. Buzzard, Jeff Turner
11. **Cornick's Dihedral** FFA 6-88 Curt Cornick, C. Buzzard
12. **Surfing with the Alien** FFA 10-30-88 W. Wallace, T. Olson
13. **Wicked Little Nasty** FFA 3-16-90 T. Olson, R. McGown
14. **Variations** FA Unknown

Fourth Class Wall
1. **Cut and Dried** GFFA 4-29-89 W. Wallace, T. Olson
2. **Severed Heads** Spring 1991 Greg Lyon
3. **Short But Sweet** FFA 9-87 C. Buzzard, John Long
4. **Cult of Personality** FFA 4-12-89 W. Wallace, Jim Wright, Eve McDermitt
5. **Wolf of the Steps** FFA 3-89 R. McGown and partner

6. **Slippery Sage** FFA 3-89 R. McGown and partner

Madrone Wall
1. **Save the Whales** FFA 3-89 R. McGown, Keith Jackson
2. **Hungry For Duress** FFA 7-86 Scott Smith, C. Buzzard
3. **Beam Me Up Mr. Scott** FFA 6-87 C. Buzzard
4. **Scott Free** FFA 4-89 Darryl Nakahira, Bruce Casey
5. **Rising Desperation** FFA 9-86 C. Buzzard, S. Smith
6. **Direct Finish** FFA 9-86 C. Buzzard, S. Smith
7. **Dr. Opus Goes Power Lunging** FFA 10-88 C. Buzzard, D. Pihlija
8. **Spectrum** FFA 10-29-88 W. Wallace, T. Olson
9. **Aerial Display** FFA 8-88 C. Buzzard, J. Jackson
10. **Mixing it Up** FFA 8-86 C. Buzzard, J. Jackson
11. **Catharsis** FFA 8-88 C. Buzzard, C. Cornick
12. **Superstrings** FFA 1-10-89 W. Wallace, R. McGown
13. **Lost in the Delta Neighborhood** FFA 6-86 C. Buzzard, J. Frank
14. **Sultans of Swing** FFA 12-88 R. McGown, Ricardo Suito
15. **Scotty Hits The Warp Drive** FFA 8-87 S. Smith, C. Buzzard
16. **Double Dutch Left** FA Unknown
     FRA 6-86 Chuck and Patty Buzzard
17. **Subway to Venus** FFA 2-26-91 Gary Rall
18. **Trauma Center** FFA 1st pitch C. Buzzard
     FFA 2nd pitch C. Buzzard, J. Turney
19. **Double Dutch Right** FA 35' Unknown
     FRA 6-87 Chuck and Patty Buzzard
20. **Primary Gobbler** FA 6-87 C. Buzzard, J. Turney
21. **Whatever Blows Your Skirt Up** FFA 6-87 C. Buzzard, John Long
22. **Pillow Talk** FFA 12-25-88 W. Wallace, Mark Egge
23. **Ant Abuse** FFA 6-87 C. Buzzard, J. Jackson, C. Cornick
24. (TR)
25. **Mr. Noodle Arms** FFA Fall 1986 C. Buzzard and partner
26. **Sisters of the Road** FFA Fall 1986 C. Buzzard, Jerry Radant
27. **Full Spank Mode** FA 10-88 C. Buzzard
28. (TR)
29. **Arm Forces** FFA 6-88 C. Buzzard
31. **Cold Hand of Technology** FFA 12-27-88 T. Olson, G. Rall

Shining Wall
1. **Arm forces** FFA 6-88 C. Buzzard
2. **Cold Hand of Technology** FFA 12-27-88 T. Olson, G. Rall
3. **Red Scare** GFFA 12-29-88 W. Wallace, T. Olson
4. **Domino Effect** GFFA 10-30-88 W. Wallace, T. Olson
5. **Dirty Dancing** FRA 9-86 C. Buzzard, J. Frank
6. **Firing Line** FFA 12-10-88 W. Wallace, T. Olson, R. McGown
7. **Lord of the Rings** FA Unknown
8. **The Gift of Time** FA 12-88 R. McGown
     FFA Unknown
9. **Dancing in the Lion's Jaw** FA 35' Unknown
     FFA complete 6-9-89 W. Wallace, R. McGown
10. **Paleontologist** FFA 1st pitch 2-12-89 W. Wallace, R. McGown
     FFA 2nd pitch 3-89 R. McGown, D. Nakahira
11. **Rainman** FFA 2-15-89 W. Wallace, T. Olson
12. **Playing With Fire** FFA 11-8-88 W. Wallace, T. Olson, R. McGown

13. **Shining Wall** FFA 1-28-89 W. Wallace
14. **Cloudwalker** FFA 1-29-89 W. Wallace, T. Olson, R. McGown, Bill Dykstra
15. **Banana Belt** FFA 2-15-89 W. Wallace, R. McGown
16. **Fits and Starts** FFA 9-86 C. Buzzard, Jeff Frank
17. **Beginners Luck** FFA 9-86 C. Buzzard, J. Frank
18. **Gym Rats From Hell** FFA 4-6-89 W. Wallace, R. McGown
19. **Plywood Jungle** FFA 3-17-89 R. McGown, W. Wallace, K. Jackson
20. **Dihedral of Despair** FA Unknown
21. **Shattered Dreams** FFA 3-18-89 R. McGown, K. Jackson

Hardscrabble Wall
1. **Sacrifice** FFA 9-26-92 T. and C. Olson
2. **Inner Vision** FFA 6-89 C. Buzzard, Chris Surville
3. **Mind Games** FFA 4-7-89 T. Olson, W. Wallace
4. **Chicken** FFA 4-6-89 T. Olson, G. Lyon
5. **Gym Droid** FFA 1-21-90 T. Olson
6. **Life As We Know It** GFFA 4-7-89 W. Wallace
7. **Red Sun Rising** FFA 1-16-90 T. Olson, R. McGown
8. **It Takes a Thief** FFA 1-16-90 R. McGown, T. Olson
9. **American Girl** FFA 1-10-90 D. Sowerby, Mike Smith
10. **Miss Adventure** FFA 1-10-90 D. Sowerby, Jay green
11. **Primordial Soup** FA 10-89 R. McGown, Keith Jackson
12. **Crystal Hunter** FA 10-89 R. McGown, K. Jackson
13. **Winds of War** FFA 3-24-90 T. Olson, R. McGown
14. **Mountaineers Route** FA Unknown
15. **Punters in Paradise** FFA winter 1990 Josh Baker
16. **Red Fox** FFA 3-30-90 D. Sowerhy, R. McGown
17. **Windows of Your Mind** FFA 2-14-89 T. Olson, Greg Lyon
18. _____ (TR) 1989 Greg Lyon
19. _____ FFA 1989 Mike Sessions and partner
20. **Electric Everything** FFA 1989 Josh Baker and partner
21. **Cast of Characters** GFFA 1-28-89 W. Wallace, R. McGown
22. **Nouveau Riche** FFA 1-19-89 W. Wallace and partner
23. **Stud** FA Unknown
24. **Reinholds Dihedral** FA 3-89 R. McGown, Reinhold ?
25. **Eye of the Tiger** FA 3-89 R. McGown
26. **Fisticuffs** (TR)
27. **Goldfingers** FA 1-26-89 Victor Goldman, Thomas Miller
     FFA 2-1-89 T. Miller, Jeff Staley
28. **Girl Crazy** FFA (Before) 1989 C. Buzzard, C. Surville
     (ascent after bolts) 1-22-90 W. Wallace
29. **Unknown** FA 6-89 C. Buzzard, C. Surville
30. **Marginal Virgin** FFA 2-28-90 T. Olson
31. **The Arete** (TR)
32. **Exodus** FFA 2-27-89 R. McGown, T. Olson
33. **Divine Wind** FFA 4-5-89 T. Olson
34. **Tapestry** FFA 2-27-89 R. McGown, T. Olson
35. **Direct Start** FFA on-sight 4-8-89 C. Buzzard
36. **Sisters of Mercury** FFA 2-26-89 T. Olson, W. Wallace
37. **Chromesister** FFA 2-27-89 T. Olson, G. Lyon
38.
39. **Stampede** FFA 3-19-90 T. Olson, D. Sowerby, G. Lyon
40. **Logjam** FFA 3-19-90 T. Olson, D. Sowerby, G. Lyon

41. **Dangerous Breed** FFA 5-6-90 T. Olson, C. Colley, Gary Gallagher
42. **What's Your Motive?** FFA 2-15-89 T. Olson, W. Wallace, G. Lyon, R. McGown

CARVER BRIDGE CLIFF

Rockgarden Wall
1. **Crack in the Mirror** FFA 9-21-87 Mike Pajunas
2. **Unknown** FA Unknown
3. **Notorious** FA 9-22-87 M. Pajunas, R. McGown, Gary Rall
   FFA 10-87 M. Pajunas, Darryl Nakahira
4. **Margueritaville** GFFA Fall 1987 R. McGown, D. Nakahira
5. **Cherry Cola** FFA 8-89 G. Rall
6. **Uncola** FA 9-30-87 Tim Olson, R. McGown
   FFA Unknown
7. **Neptune** FA 9-87 T. Olson, R. McGown
8. **Smooth Torquer** FFA 5-89 Greg Lyon
9. **Smerk** FA 1st pitch 9-7-87 T. Olson, R. McGown
   FFA complete 10-15-88 T. Olson, Cecil Colley
10. **New Generation** FFA 1st pitch 8-23-87 Chris McMullin, T. Olson
    FFA complete 2-88 T. Olson, R. McGown, G. Lyon
11. **Free Ride** FFA 6-89 G. Lyon
12. **Scotch and Soda** FFA 9-7-87 T. Olson, R. McGown
13. **Tequila Sunrise** FFA 1st pitch 9-87 R. McGown, T. Olson
    FFA complete 2-88 T. Olson, G. Lyon
14. **Red Dihedral** FA Unknown
    FFA 6-11-88 T. Olson, Matt Pixler
15. **Unknown** (TR)
16. **Jungle Safari** FFA (complete) 3-88 W. Wallace, T. Olson
17. **Night Vision** FA 11-8-87 T. Olson, G. Lyon
    FFA complete 2-88 T. Olson, W. Wallace
18. **Sanity Assassin** FFA 11-87 G. Lyon, T. Olson
19. **Sea of Holes** FA 10-11-87 T. Olson, G. Lyon
    FFA complete 7-21-89 W. Wallace, T. Olson
    Note: Sport Court FFA Spring 1990 G. Lyon
20. **Shadow Fox** FFA 10-11-87 T. Olson, G. Lyon
21. **Battleship Arete** FFA 8-89 Virgil Morresette, T. Olson
22. **Night Life** FFA 8-89 T. Olson, V. Morresette
23. **Holiday in Cambodia** (TR) 3-88 W. Wallace
24. **Wally Street** FA 6-21-88 Bruce Casey
25. **Wally Wedding** FFA 10-25-88 D. Nakahira
26. **Sweat and the Flies** FFA 9-18-88 T. Olson

Wall In Between
1. **Passport to Insanity** FFA 3-88 T. Olson, G. Lyon, W. Wallace
2. **Burning From The Inside** FFA 5-88 G. Lyon
3. **Hinge of Fate** FFA 3-88 T. Olson, G. Lyon, R. McGown
4. **Eyes of a Stranger** FFA 4-16-88 T. Olson
5. **Shady Personality** FFA 3-88 T. Olson, G. Lyon, W. Wallace
6. **Rats in the Jungle** FFA 6-26-88 T. Olson, Matt Papolski

Yellow Wall
1. **Call to Greatness** GFA and FFA 2-88 W. Wallace, T. Olson
2. **Plastic Monkey** FFA 11-89 G. Rall

3. **Rites of Passage** FFA 1-88 T. Olson, R. McGown
  FFA complete D. Nakahira and partner
4. **Digital** FFA 5-25-89 G. Lyon
5. **Angular Motion** GFA 1975 Jeff Alzner, Terry Jenkins
  FFA 4-27-88 G. Lyon
6. **Out on a Limb** FFA 12-87 T. Olson, R. McGown, G. Lyon
7. **Smooth Operator** FA Unknown
8. **Talent Show** FA Unknown
9. **Blue Monday** FA Unknown
10. **Crimson Tide** FRA Summer 1976 Mark Simpson, Doug McMillan
11. **Spearfishing in Bermuda** FRA Summer 1976 M. Simpson, D. McMillan
12. **Leaning Uncertainty** FA Unknown
13. **King Rat** FFA 7-7-88 T. Olson, Mike Larson
14. **Chariots of Fire** GFA 2-88 W. Wallace, R. McGown
  FFA 7-6-89 W. Wallace

Ivy League Buttress
1. **Dreamscape** GFFA Winter 1988 R. McGown, G. Lyon, T. Olson
2. **Rip Grip** FFA 6-13-88 G. Lyon
3. **Rubicon** FFA 2-88 T. Olson, G. Lyon
4. **Edge of the Reef** FFA complete 3-14-89 T. Olson, G. Lyon
5. **Great Barrier Reef** FA 1-88 W. Wallace
6. **Challenger** FFA 4-88 W. Wallace, G. Lyon
7. **Last of the Mohicans** FFA 8-19-88 T. Olson
8. **Riders of the Purple Sage** FFA 1st pitch 8-21-88 T. Olson, Cecil Colley
  FA 2nd pitch 8-88 T. Olson, R. McGown
9. **Penguins in Heat** FFA 5-2-90 Jay Green and partner
10. **Hexelerator** FA complete 11-15-89 G. Lyon, T. Olson
11. **House of Cards** FFA 3-16-90 T. Olson, R. McGown
12. **Aphid-City-O** FFA 3-1-90 T. Olson, G, Lyon

BEACON ROCK

1. **Pacific Rim** FFA 9-10-89 Wayne Wallace, Tim Olson
2. **Boardwalk** FFA Fall 1985 Bill Coe, Bob McMahon
3. **East Buttress**
4.
5. **Obnoxious Cubbyhole** GFA 1977 Dick Morse, Chet Sutterlin
6. **Stone Rodeo** FA 5-87 W. Wallace, Robert McGown
  FFA 6-87 R. McGown, Dan Wright
7. **Rock Police** FFA 9-11-89 W. Wallace, R. McGown
8. **Return to the Sky** GFA 7-84 R. McGown, Mark Simpson
9. **Sky Pilot** GFA 4-85 R. McGown, Scott Woolums
10. **Couchmaster** GFA 1985 Bill Coe, Gary Rall, Jim Opdycke
11. **Jingus Jam** FA 4-85 S. Woolums, R. McGown
12. **Cruisin' Direct Finish** FA 1-6-87 R. McGown, W. Wallace
13. **Cosmic Dust** FA 1985 R. McGown, S. Woolums
  FFA ? Darryl Nakahira
14. **Cruisin'** FA 1985 Dennis Hemminger, J. Opdycke
15. **Stardust** FA 1985 Scott Tracy, J. Opdycke
16. **Rock Master** FA 1985 B. Coe, J. Opdycke, Gini Hornbecker
  FFA 1985 Bruce Casey and partner
17. **Rookie Nookie** FA 1985 S. Woolums, R. McGown

FFA 1986 S. Tracy, J. Opdycke
18. **Icy Treats** FFA 12-84 Mark Cartier, D. Nakahira
19. **Switchblade** GFA 3-85 R. McGown, Guigi Regis
20. **Bladerunner** GFA 3-85 R. McGown, G. Regis
FFA 7-14-86 Jeff Thomas
21. **Fire and Ice** FFA 6-30-90 T. Olson, Jim Yoder
22. **More Balls Than Nuts** FFA Spring 1985 M. Cartier, D. Nakahira
23. **No Balls No Falls** FFA Spring 1986 S. Tracy, J. Opdycke
24. **Levitation Blues** GFA 1985 J. Yoder, R. McGown, J. Opdycke
25. **Repo Man** FA Summer 1985 (?) R. McGown, M. Simpson
26. **Cigarette** FFA 3-1-87 T. Olson
27. **Lethal Ejection** FA 1985 Ron Allen, J. Opdycke
28. **South East Face** GFA 4-29-54 John Ohrenschall, Gene Todd
29. **Variation** FA 1974 Steve Lyford and partner
30. **Desdichado (var.)** FFA 10-89 W. Wallace, T. Olson
31. **Dyna Flux** FA 10-89 R. McGown and partner
32.
33. **Jill's Thrill** GFA 1985 R. McGown, J. Opdycke, Jill Green
34. **Tooth Faerie** FFA 7-26-92 T. and Cindy Olson
35. **To The Edge And Beyond** FFA 8-88 W. Wallace, Reinhold Buche
36. **Fear of Flying** GFA 1985 R. McGown, Guigi Regis
37. **Desperado** FA 1975 R. McGown, J. Opdycke
38. **Right Gull** GFA 1965 Dean Caldwell, Chuck Brown
FFA 10-72 Dean Fry
39. **Vulcans Variation** FFA 9-86 T. Olson
40. **Muriel's Memoir** FFA 7-77 Muriel Lodder (Sharp), R. McGown
41. **Synapse** FFA 8-90 R. McGown, W. Wallace
42. **Death and Taxes** FFA 8-2-90 W. Wallace
43. **Lost Variation** GFA 5-10-58 Charlie Carpenter, Paul Resta
44. **Elusive Element** FFA 6-22-90 R. McGown, W. Wallace
45. **Cloud Nine** FFA 10-24-87 W. Wallace, T. Olson
46. **High and Mighty** FA 6-5-89 W. Wallace, T. Olson
47. **Sacrilege** FFA 9-18-90 T. Olson
48.
49. **Diagonal Desperation** FA 1978 R. McGown, S. Woolums
50.
51. **Riverside** FA 10-13-77 J. Thomas, Jim Dunavant
52.
53.
54. **Little Wing** FFA 1985 J. Opdycke, R. McGown, M. Cartier
FA 2nd-3rd pitch R. McGown, S. Tracy
55. **Broken Arrow** FA 1975 R. McGown, J. Green
56. **Idiot** FA 1985 R. McGown
FFA Summer 1985 M. Cartier
57. **Magic Fingers** FA 1985 J. Yoder, R. McGown, J. Opdycke
58. **Wrong Gull** FA 1977 (?) Avery Tichner
FFA 8-31-77 J. Thomas, Shari Kearney, Jack Holmgren
59. **Sorceror's Apprentice** FA 1980 R. McGown, Jim Olson
60. **Old Warriors Never Die** FFA 1990 Jim Yoder
61. **Seagull** GFA 1st pitch 9-3-77 R. McGown, J. Thomas
FA complete 10-4-77 J. Thomas, J. Dunavant
62. **Tennessee Walker** FFA 1979 (?) J. Walker or A. Tichner
63. **Too Close for Comfort** FFA 8-27-88 W. Wallace, R. Buche

64. **Left Gull** GFA 1965 D. Caldwell, C. Erwin
FRFA 7-6-73 J. Thomas, Steve Lyford
65. **Summer Daze** GFA 1975 (?) A. Tichner, R. McGown
FFA Spring 1985 M. Cartier, D. Nakahira
66.
67. **Bluebird Direct** FA 10-16-77 J. Thomas, B. Casey
68. **Spring Fever** FA Spring 1986 S. Tracy, J. Opdycke
69. **Winter Delight** FFA 1988 R. Allen, Mike Jackson
70. **Sufficiently Breathless** FA Summer 1977 S. Woolums, Terry Yates, R. McGown
71. **Fall Guy** FFA Fall 1990 R. Allen, S. Tracy
72. **Aging Fags** FFA Summer 1985 A. Tichner
73. **Blownout Direct** FFA Fall 1990 S. Tracy, J. Opdycke
74. **Tombstone Territory** FA Fall 1990 J. Opdycke, M. Simpson
75. **Bluebird** GFA 1972 Jeff Elphinston, Dave Mention
FFA 9-11-76 J. Thomas, Monty Mayko, Ed Newville
76. **Variation** FA (original finish) 1972 J. Elphinston, D. Mention
77. **Bridge of the Gods** GFA 1987 R. McGown, W. Wallace, S. Woolums
FFA
78. **Pirates** FA R. McGown
FFA July 1985 M. Cartier, D. Nakahira
79. **Blownout** GFA 1-19/20-69 Steve Strauch, Danny Gates
FFA 10-16-76 J. Thomas, Ken Currens
80. **Second Wind** FA Fall 1981 Ted Johnson, Bill Strayer
81. **Borderline** FFA 1st pitch 6-1-89 T. Olson, Tim Wolfe, Neal Olson
FFA 2nd pitch 6-4-89 T. Olson, W. Wallace
82. **Grunge Book** GFA 5-70 Wayne Haack, Steve Strauch
83. **Excalibur** FFA 7-8-90 T. Olson, W. Wallace
84. **Crankenstein**
85. **Wild Turkeys** FA Summer 1970 Brian Holcomb, Neal Olson, Glen Kirkpatrick
86.
87. **Psychic Wound** FFA Spring 1985 S. Tracy, J. Opdycke
88. **Flying Dutchman** GFA Fall 1984 Bob McMahon, J. Opdycke, B. Coe
FFA Fall 1984 M. Cartier
89. **Bears in Heat** FFA Summer 1985 M. Cartier, D. Nakahira
90. **Smooth Dancer** GFA Summer 1974 Alan Kearney, Les Nugent, Malcolm Ulrich
91. **Dirty Double Overhang** GFA 7-73 A. Kearney, Dave Henry, M. Ulrich
92.
93. **Takes Fist** GFA Spring 1981 T. Johnson, Mike Pajunas
FFA 6-29-81 M. Cartier, J. Thomas
94.
95. **Ground Zero** GFA Summer 1984 J. Opdycke, B. Coe, Jay Bergren
FFA 1985 D. Nakahira, M. Cartier
96. **Nuke-U-Later** FFA 1987 (?) R. Allen, and partner
97. **Iron Maiden** GFA 3-85 R. McGown, Jeff Alzner
98. **Flying Swallow** GFA 1965 Kim Schmitz, Earl Levin, D. Caldwell
FFA 8-10-77 J. Thomas, Del Young
99. **Variation** FA 8-10-77 J. Thomas, M. Cartier
100. **Direct Start (to Flying Swallow)** TR
101. **Local Access Only** FFA 8-89 Nathan Charleton, Eric Freden
102. **Reasonable Richard** FFA 9-89 T. Olson, N. Olson, Jim Davis
103. **Black Maria** FFA 9-23-89 T. Olson, E. Freden, N. Charleton, Tim Doyle
104. **Flight Time** FA 1st pitch 7-77 J. Thomas, M. Cartier
FFA 1st pitch 8-1-81 J. Thomas, M. Cartier

FFA 2nd pitch 1984 J. Olson
FA 3rd pitch 1977 R. McGown, B. Antel
105.
106. **Flying Circus** FA 1st pitch 6-18-77 J. Thomas, N. Olson
FA complete J. Thomas, Mike Smelsar
107. **Blood, Sweat and Smears** FA 7-20-77 J. Thomas, R. McGown
108. **True Grunt** FA 7-77 J. Thomas, M. Cartier
109. **Steppenwolf** GFA 5-71 Les Nugent, Bill Herman, Bill Nickle
FFA (to Big Ledge) 5-77 R. McGown, Levi Grey
FA (above Big Ledge) 7-78 R. McGown, Doug Bower
FFA (above Big Ledge for 80') 1982 or 83 Alan Lester, M. Cartier
110. **Dod's Jam** GFA (to Big Ledge) Summer 1961 Eugene Dod, Bob Martin, E. Levin
FA complete 5-72 J. Thomas, Dean Fry
FFA Summer 1972 Wayne Arrington, Jack Barrar
111. **Dod's Deviation** FA 6-12-77 R. McGown, M. Smelsar
112. **Journey to the East** GFA Spring 1983 R. McGown
113. **Devil's Backbone** FA 1989 N. Charleton, R. Allen
114. **The Norseman** FFA 7-14-88 M. Cartier
115. **Dastardly Crack** FA 1965 B. Martin, K. Schmitz, Gerald Bjorkman
FFA 7-6-73 J. Thomas, Steve Lyford
116. **Squeeze Box** FA 7-20-77 R. McGown, J. Thomas
117. **Edge of Fear** GFA 6-89 R. McGown, Steve Hillinger
118. **Free For All** FA 8-73 D. Fry, S. Lyford
119. **Free For Some** FA Unknown
FRA Summer 1977 R. McGown, M. Smelsar
120. **Windsurfer** FA 9-86 R. McGown, S. Woolums
121. **Fresh Squeeze** FA Summer 1989 N. Charleton, E. Freden
122.
123. **Pipeline** GFA Summer 1977 R. McGown
FFA 8-2-81 T. Johnson, Charlie Priest
124. **Pipe Dream** GFA 5-84 R. McGown, B. Antel
FFA 7-84 J. Olson, M. Dennuci
125. **Pipeline Headwall** FFA 5-85 R. McGown, B. Antel
126. **Silver Crow** GFA 5-82 R. McGown, M. Simpson
127. **Axe of Karma** GFA 4-86 R. McGown, Bob Scarborough
128. **Red Ice** GFFA 2-86 R. McGown, S. Woolums
129. **Doubting Thomas** FA Unknown
130. **Boys of Summer** FFA 5-86 R. McGown, M. Simpson
131. **Fingers of a Fisherman** GFFA 5-86 R. McGown, R. Krukowski
132. **Crack of Dawn** GFA 1986 R. McGown, R, Krukowski
133. **Jensen's Ridge** GFA 1968 B. Martin, D. Jensen
FFA 4-13-74 J. Thomas
134. **Updraft to Heaven** GFA 6-77 R. McGown, L. Grey
135. **Mostly Air** GFA Summer 1981 R. McGown, M. Simpson
136. **Lay Lady Lay** FA 6-77 R. McGown, M. Simpson
137. **Rip City** FA 7-9-77 J. Thomas, M. Smelsar
138. **Hard Times** FA 7-3-77 J. Thomas
139. **Ragtime** FA 11-12-76 J. Thomas, Willis Krause
FFA 1981 T. Johnson, D. Young
140. **Synchronicity** FA Summer 1982 R. McGown, J. Olson
141. **Boulder Problem in the Sky** FA 4-7-74 J. Thomas, Tim Miller
FFA 11-11-76 J. Thomas, C. Sutterlin
142. **Iron Cross** GFA 7-8-77 R. McGown, M. Lodder
143. **Variation** FA 10-22-76 D. Young, J. Thomas

Appendix II

Climbs by Grade

Broughton Bluff

5.4
- [ ] Prometheus Slab

5.5

5.6
- [ ] Giant's Staircase

5.7
- [ ] The Hammer ★
- [ ] Arch De Triumph

5.8
- [ ] The Sickle ★★★
- [ ] That's the Way
- [ ] Edges and Ledges ★

5.8+
- [ ] American Graffiti
- [ ] Balls Not Friction
- [ ] Toe Cleavage

5.9
- [ ] Spud
- [ ] Chockstone Chimney
- [ ] Loose Block Overhang ★★★
- [ ] BFD ★
- [ ] Annastasia
- [ ] Physical Direct
- [ ] Spidermonkey ★
- [ ] Seventh Sojourn
- [ ] Shandor
- [ ] Traffic Court ★

5.9+
- [ ] Variation
- [ ] Sesame Street ★★
- [ ] Classic Crack ★★★
- [ ] Under Your Belt
- [ ] Gandalf's Grip ★★★

5.10 A
- [ ] Variation I
- [ ] Risky Business ★
- [ ] Tip City ★★
- [ ] Least Resistance
- [ ] Hanging Gardens ★★
- [ ] Sheer Stress ★★★
- [ ] Sheer Energy
- [ ] The Spring ★
- [ ] Mystic Void
- [ ] Pride and Joy
- [ ] Zimbabwe
- [ ] Happy Trails

5.10 B
- [ ] Sweet Emotion
- [ ] Hang 'Em High
- [ ] Walk on the Wildside ★★
- [ ] Fruit Bat ★
- [ ] Dyno-Mite
- [ ] Well Hung ★★

5.10 C
- [ ] Reckless Driver ★
- [ ] Lean Years ★
- [ ] Sandy's Direct ★★
- [ ] From Something to Nothing
- [ ] Fun in the Mud
- [ ] Shining Star ★
- [ ] Peer Pressure
- [ ] Red Eye ★★
- [ ] Shoot From the Hip ★
- [ ] Wild, Wild West
- [ ] Crime Wave

5.10 D
- [ ] Dynamic Resistance
- [ ] Hung Jury
- [ ] Demian ★★★
- [ ] Arcturus
- [ ] Thai Stick ★★
- [ ] Physical Graffiti ★★★
- [ ] Velcro Fly
- [ ] Hanging Tree
- [ ] Lost Boys ★★
- [ ] Mystic Pizza
- [ ] Under the Yum Yum Tree
- [ ] Amazon Woman
- [ ] Alma Mater ★★
- [ ] Gorilla Love Affair ★★
- [ ] Short Fuse ★
- [ ] Dead Bones

5.11 A
- [ ] Hangover

- [ ] Mr. Potato
- [ ] Main Vein
- [ ] Endless Steep
- [ ] On the Loose ★★
- [ ] Hit the Highway
- [ ] Free Bird ★★
- [ ] Superstition ★★★
- [ ] Gold Arch
- [ ] Dark Shadows ★
- [ ] Father ★
- [ ] Habitual Ritual

5.11 B
- [ ] Peach Cling ★★
- [ ] Grace & Danger
- [ ] Black Prow
- [ ] Hard Body ★★
- [ ] Bust A Move ★
- [ ] Mowgli's Revenge
- [ ] Pioneer Spirit ★

5.11 C
- [ ] Critical Mass ★★★
- [ ] Promised Land ★★
- [ ] New Wave

5.11 D
- [ ] Face Not Friction ★★
- [ ] Gallows Pole
- [ ] E. Pluribus Pinhead ★★★
- [ ] Edge of Eternity ★
- [ ] Jumping Jack Thrash ★★
- [ ] Bloodsucker
- [ ] The Hunger
- [ ] Twist and Crawl
- [ ] Amazon Man
- [ ] Slash and Burn

5.11+
- [ ] Mr. Bentley ★★
- [ ] Opus

5.12A
- [ ] Dracula ★★★
- [ ] Closet Nazi ★★
- [ ] Danse Macabre

5.12B
- [ ] Slapfest ★★
- [ ] Kashmir ★★

- ☐ Ground Effects ★★
- ☐ Bela Lugosi ★★
- ☐ The Haunting ★
- ☐ Bad Omen ★★★
- ☐ Bloodline ★★★
- ☐ Heart of Darkness ★

5.12 C
- ☐ Tarzan

5.12 D
- ☐ Scorpion Seams ★

5.13 A

5.13 B

5.13 C
- ☐ Fright Night

Aid Routes
- ☐ Out of Africa II 5.9 A3
- ☐ Killer Pygmy III 5.10+ A4
- ☐ Go Back To The Gym II 5.7 A4

Rocky Butte
5.4
- ☐ E-Z Corner

5.5

5.6
- ☐ Quarry Cracker
- ☐ Passing Lane
- ☐ Joes Garden

5.7
- ☐ Miss Kitty
- ☐ Flakey Old Man ★★

5.8
- ☐ The Joker
- ☐ Captain She's Breaking Up
- ☐ Urban Cowboy ★★
- ☐ Midnight Warrior
- ☐ Superman Crack ★
- ☐ AC / DC
- ☐ Robotics
- ☐ Simba ★
- ☐ Fiddler on the Roof
- ☐ Orient Express ★
- ☐ Speeding Down South

5.8+
- ☐ Eve of Destruction

5.9
- ☐ Gunsmoke ★★
- ☐ Silverbullet ★
- ☐ Stained Glass ★
- ☐ Dead Man's Curve
- ☐ Little Arete
- ☐ Blueberry Jam ★★★
- ☐ Rob's Ravine
- ☐ Vertical Therapy ★★
- ☐ Stiff Fingers
- ☐ Expresso ★★
- ☐ Foot Loose

5.9+
- ☐ Panama Red
- ☐ Jack of Hearts ★
- ☐ Invisible Man
- ☐ Lord of the Jungle
- ☐ Ranger Danger

5.10 A
- ☐ Harlequin ★
- ☐ Sundance Kid
- ☐ Last Tango
- ☐ MTV
- ☐ Panes of Reality
- ☐ Cuts Like a Knife
- ☐ Naked Savage
- ☐ Mind Games
- ☐ Ghost Rider
- ☐ Smears for Fears
- ☐ Sheer Madness
- ☐ Thunder Road
- ☐ Reach for the Sky ★
- ☐ Power Surge
- ☐ Temporary Arete

5.10 B
- ☐ Trivial Pursuit
- ☐ Ziva's Book ★★
- ☐ Stranger Than Friction ★★★
- ☐ Slavemaker
- ☐ Great Wall of China ★
- ☐ Tiger's Eye
- ☐ Emotional Rescue ★★★
- ☐ "D" and Rising
- ☐ Blackberry Jam ★★★
- ☐ Lemon Twist
- ☐ White Rabbit ★★★

- ☐ Shadows in Space

5.10 C
- ☐ Fandango ★★★
- ☐ Body Language
- ☐ Lever or Leaver
- ☐ Godmonster
- ☐ Eye in the Sky ★
- ☐ Highway Star ★
- ☐ Claymation
- ☐ Hot Tang ★

5.10 D
- ☐ Centurion ★★
- ☐ Live Wire ★★
- ☐ Chinese Finger Torture ★
- ☐ The Wanderer ★
- ☐ Lethal Ethics
- ☐ Spiritual Journey
- ☐ Leading Edge
- ☐ Birds of Paradise ★★★
- ☐ Skywalker

5.10+
- ☐ Boy Sage

5.11 A
- ☐ Poodle with a Mohawk
- ☐ Bite the Bullet ★★★
- ☐ Damaged Circuit ★★
- ☐ Wizard ★★★
- ☐ Flight of the Seventh Moon ★★
- ☐ Arch Nemesis ★
- ☐ Simple Twist
- ☐ Hyper Twist
- ☐ Telegraph Road
- ☐ Competitive Edge
- ☐ Lunge and Plunge
- ☐ Mystic Traveler
- ☐ Lathe of Heaven

5.11 B
- ☐ Body Bionics
- ☐ Edge of Might ★★
- ☐ Phylynx ★★★
- ☐ High Road to China
- ☐ Secret Maze ★
- ☐ Crack Warrior ★★★
- ☐ Seamingly Endless ★
- ☐ Holy Bubbles ★
- ☐ Orange Spice ★
- ☐ Wisdom Tooth

5.11 C
- ☐ Point of No Return ★
- ☐ You'll Dance to Anything ★★
- ☐ Jealous Rage
- ☐ No Leverage
- ☐ Be Bold or Not To Be
- ☐ Toothpick ★★★
- ☐ Red Zinger ★★
- ☐ Persistence of Time

5.11 D
- ☐ Walk on Water ★

5.11+
- ☐ Love on the Rocks
- ☐ Stump the Jock
- ☐ White Rabbit Buttress ★★
- ☐ Face Disgrace
- ☐ Spider Line
- ☐ Hang Loose

5.12 A
- ☐ Zenith
- ☐ Close to the Edge ★★★
- ☐ Seventh Wave
- ☐ The Arete
- ☐ Toxic Waltz

5.12 B
- ☐ Pluto

5.12 C
- ☐ Hard Contact

Madrone Wall
5.5
- ☐ Beginner's Luck

5.6
- ☐ Sisters of Mercury ★
- ☐ Double Dutch Right ★

5.7
- ☒ Double Dutch Left ★★
- ☐ Dirty Dancing
- ☐ Chicken
- ☐ Electric Everything ★
- ☐ Stud

5.8
- ☐ Route Crafters ★★

- ☐ Slippery Sage
- ☐ Life as We Know It
- ☐ Exodus

5.8+
- ☐ Chop the Monkey

5.9
- ☐ Patrick's Dihedral ★
- ☐ Into The Black ★
- ☐ Graduation
- ☐ Cornick's Dihedral ★★
- ☐ Wolf of the Steps
- ☐ Sultans of Swing
- ☐ Domino Effect
- ☐ Lord of the Rings
- ☐ Plywood Jungle ★
- ☐ Gym Droid
- ☐ American Girl
- ☐ Cast of Characters
- ☐ The Arete
- ☐ Tapestry
- ☐ Stampede
- ☐ Primordial Soup

5.9+
- ☐ Punters in Paradise

5.10 A
- ☐ Jackson's Daring Deeds
- ☐ Tangerine Dream ★
- ☐ Save the Whales
- ☐ Hungry For Duress
- ☐ Rising Desperation ★★
- ☐ Lost in the Delta Neighborhood
- ☐ Ant Abuse ★★
- ☐ Fits and Starts
- ☐ Sacrifice
- ☐ Miss Adventure
- ☐ Windows of Your Mind★★
- ☐ Reinholds Dihedral
- ☐ Goldfingers ★★
- ☐ Girl Crazy
- ☐ Logjam ★
- ☐ What's Your Motive? ★★
- ☐ Direct Finish (Rising Desperation)

5.10 B
- ☐ Identity Crisis ★★
- ☐ Wicked Little Nasty
- ☐ Spectrum ★★

- ☐ Mixing It Up
- ☐ Pillow Talk ★★
- ☐ Paleontologist ★★
- ☐ Red Sun Rising ★★
- ☐ Chromesister
- ☐ Dangerous Breed ★
- ☐ Whatever Blows Your Skirt Up ★
- ☐ Crystal Hunter

5.10 C
- ☐ Sheesh ★★★
- ☐ Wild Blue Yonder ★★
- ☐ Cut and Dried
- ☐ Scotty Hits the Warp Drive
- ☐ Cold Hand of Technology
- ☐ Red Scare
- ☐ Banana Belt
- ☐ Gym Rats from Hell ★★
- ☐ Shattered Dreams
- ☐ Nouveau Riche ★★★
- ☐ Eye of the Tiger
- ☐ Marginal Virgin
- ☐ Primary Gobbler

5.10 D
- ☐ Direct Start (Tangerine Dream) ★
- ☐ Midget Madness
- ☐ Surfin' with the Alien ★
- ☐ Short but Sweet ★
- ☐ Cult of Personality ★
- ☐ Sisters of the Road ★★
- ☐ It Takes a Thief ★★

5.11 A
- ☐ Superstrings
- ☐ The Gift of Time
- ☐ Inner Vision
- ☐ Winds of War ★★
- ☐ Red Fox

5.11 B
- ☐ Aerial Display ★★
- ☐ Trauma Center ★
- ☐ Mr. Noodle Arms ★★★
- ☐ Arm Forces ★★★
- ☐ Rain Man ★★
- ☐ Playing With Fire
- ☐ Mind Games ★★★

5.11 C
- [ ] Beam Me Up Mr. Scott ★★★
- [ ] Dr. Opus Goes Power Lunging ★
- [ ] Catharsis ★★★
- [ ] Firing Line
- [ ] Dancing in the Lion's Jaw ★★
- [ ] Cloudwalker ★
- [ ] Fisticuffs ★
- [ ] Divine Wind ★★★
- [ ] Direct Start (To Divine Wind)

5.11 D
- [ ] Mental Crisis ★
- [ ] Where The Wild Things Roam ★★★
- [ ] Agent Orange ★★
- [ ] Full Spank Mode ★★★
- [ ] Shining Wall ★★★

5.12 A
- [ ] Talk, Talk, Talk ★★
- [ ] Subway to Venus ★★

5.12 B
- [ ] Sub-Arachnoid Space
- [ ] Severed Heads
- [ ] Scott Free ★★★

Carver Bridge Cliff
5.4
- [ ] Smooth Operator ★
- [ ] Spearfishing in Bermuda

5.5
- [ ] Talent Show ★

5.6

5.7
- [ ] Sanity Assassin
- [ ] Leaning Uncertainty
- [ ] Great Barrier Reef

5.8
- [ ] Shadowfox ★
- [ ] Passport to Insanity

5.9
- [ ] Crack in the Mirror ★★
- [ ] Neptune ★
- [ ] Battleship Arete
- [ ] Crimson Tide ★
- [ ] Rubicon ★★
- [ ] Last of the Mohicans ★

5.9+
- [ ] New Generation ★★★
- [ ] Blue Monday

5.10 A
- [ ] Red Dihedral ★★
- [ ] Jungle Safari ★★
- [ ] Holiday in Cambodia
- [ ] Eyes of a Stranger
- [ ] Rats in the Jungle
- [ ] Out on a Limb ★

5.10 B
- [ ] Night Life
- [ ] Shady Personality
- [ ] Edge of the Reef ★★
- [ ] Aphid City-O

5.10 C
- [ ] Tequila Sunrise
- [ ] Hinge of Fate ★★
- [ ] Call to Greatness ★★
- [ ] King Rat

5.10 D
- [ ] Margueritaville
- [ ] Scotch and Soda ★★★
- [ ] Sweat and the Flies ★

5.11 A
- [ ] Smerk ★★★
- [ ] House of Cards

5.11 B
- [ ] Notorious ★★★
- [ ] Night Vision ★★
- [ ] Dreamscape ★★
- [ ] Riders of the Purple Sage ★★

5.11 C
- [ ] Uncola ★★★
- [ ] Rites of Passage ★★★
- [ ] Chariots of Fire ★★★

- [ ] Challenger ★★
- [ ] Hexelerator

5.11 D
- [ ] Cherry Cola ★★
- [ ] Burning From the Inside ★★

5.12 A
- [ ] Free Ride
- [ ] Sea of Holes ★★★
- [ ] Wally Street ★★★
- [ ] Angular Motion ★★★
- [ ] Penguins in Heat

5.12 B
- [ ] Wally Wedding

5.12 C
- [ ] Smooth Torquer ★★
- [ ] Rip Grip ★

5.12 D
- [ ] Digital ★★

5.13 A
- [ ] Plastic Monkey

Beacon Rock
5.6
- [ ] Boardwalk

5.7
- [ ] Cruisin' ★★★
- [ ] Southeast Face ★★★
- [ ] Tombstone Territory

5.8
- [ ] Stardust ★★
- [ ] Lost Variation
- [ ] Little Wing ★★
- [ ] Free For All ★★★
- [ ] Vulcans Variation

5.9
- [ ] Couchmaster
- [ ] Jingus Jam
- [ ] Variation
- [ ] Jill's Thrill
- [ ] Cloud Nine ★
- [ ] Blownout Direct
- [ ] Variation

☐ Reasonable Richard ★★
☐ Black Maria
☐ Dods Deviation ★
☐ Dastardly Crack ★★
☐ Crack of Dawn
☐ Variation
☐ Muriel's Memoir

5.10 A
☐ Return to the Sky
☐ Cigarette
☐ Right Gull ★★★
☐ Left Gull
☐ Spring Fever ★★
☐ Sufficiently Breathless ★★
☐ Bluebird ★
☐ Blownout ★★★
☐ Local Access Only
☐ Fingers of a Fisherman
☐ Rip City ★★
☐ Broken Arrow
☐ Tooth Faerie

5.10B
☐ Cosmic Dust
☐ Fear of Flying ★★★
☐ Riverside
☐ Winter Delight ★★★
☐ Psychic Wound
☐ Flying Dutchman ★★
☐ Variation ★
☐ Squeezebox ★
☐ Mostly Air
☐ Lay Lady Lay ★★★
☐ Windsurfer ★★★

5.10 C
☐ Pacific Rim ★★
☐ Rock Police ★
☐ Desdichado
☐ Wrong Gull ★★
☐ Seagull ★★
☐ Nuke-U-Later
☐ Flying Circus
☐ Blood, Sweat and Smears ★★
☐ Steppenwolf ★★★
☐ Dod's Jam ★★★
☐ Doubting Thomas
☐ Hard Times
☐ Rag Time

☐ Rookie Nookie ★★
☐ Bladerunner ★★
☐ Repo Man
☐ Synapse

5.10 D
☐ Icy Treats ★
☐ Elusive Element ★
☐ Sacrilege ★★★
☐ Diagonal Desperation
☐ Sorcerer's Apprentice
☐ Tennessee Walker ★★
☐ Bluebird Direct ★
☐ Fall Guy ★★
☐ Aging Fags ★
☐ Takes Fist ★
☐ Flying Swallow ★★★
☐ Red Ice ★
☐ Boulder Problem in the Sky ★★
☐ Levitation Blues
☐ Desperado

5.11 A
☐ Sky Pilot
☐ Crankenstein
☐ Direct Start (To Flying Swallow) (TR)
☐ True Grunt ★
☐ Free For Some ★★★
☐ Jensen's Ridge ★
☐ Switchblade
☐ No Balls No Falls
☐ Crankenstein (TR)

5.11 B
☐ Fire and Ice ★★★
☐ Dynaflux
☐ To The Edge and Beyond
☐ High and Mighty ★★
☐ Borderline ★★★
☐ Bears in Heat ★★
☐ Pipeline ★★★
☐ Iron Cross
☐ More Balls Than Nuts
☐ Pipeline Headwall

5.11 C
☐ Direct Finish (to Cruisin')
☐ Rock Master ★★
☐ Summer Daze ★★
☐ Flight Time ★★

5.11 D
☐ Second Wind ★
☐ Ground Zero ★★★
☐ Freshsqueeze ★

5.12 A
☐ Stone Rodeo ★★★
☐ Idiot ★
☐ Pirates
☐ Pipe Dream
☐ Too Close for Comfort
☐ Devil's Backbone ★★

5.12 B
☐ Old Warriors Never Die ★★
☐ Bridge of the Gods ★
☐ Excalibur ★★★
☐ The Norseman ★★

5.12 C
☐ Death and Taxes ★★
☐ Magic Fingers ★

Aid Routes
☐ Obnoxious Cubbyhole 5.7 A2
☐ Grunge Book III 5.10 A A2
☐ Wild Turkeys III 5.10C A3
☐ Smooth Dancer III 5.9 A2
☐ Dirty Double Overhang III 5.7 A3
☐ Diagonal Desperation 5.10D AO
☐ Updraft to Heaven II 5.10 D AI
☐ Journey to the East IV 5.11 A4
☐ Edge of Fear IV 5.11 A4
☐ Silver Crow IV 5.10 D A3
☐ Axe of Karma IV 5.10 C A3

Darkness rides the branched,
Into the blue,
Twig the old, make
Room for the new.
Soup upon the pastures,
Waiters cater theory's call,
Moonlit bride, conspicuous eyed.
Blindmen grope the wall.
Check your luggage
Nearer comes the train.
Engine whistles blowing,
Only days remain,
Settled back on easy chair,
Breath in the evening, misted air,
Careless thoughts, restless as a mare.
On a long, long journey from
This land, here; To another land, there.

Index

CLIMBING NOTES

B R O K E N   R O C K

(Outcrop located between Bat Wall and Trident at Broughton Bluff)

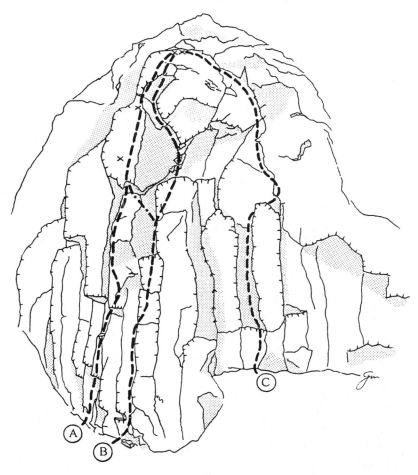

A. STATIC CLING 5.11a (height a factor moving past first bolt) nuts to 3/4", small TCU's
   VARIATION 5.10d — using Plan B start
B. PLAN B 5.10a pro to 2", (1 1/2 Friend, 0 TCU recommended)
C. LICKETY SPLIT 5.6 pro to 2", 3 1/2 Friend or 10 Hex

F.A. Greg Murray
   A. January 1993 **B.** December 1992 **C.** November 1992

Note: Beware of poison oak off the beaten path

PORTLAND ROCK GYM

(503) 232-8310
2034 SE 6th Ave
Portland, OR 97214
(Corner of SE 6th &
Lincoln)

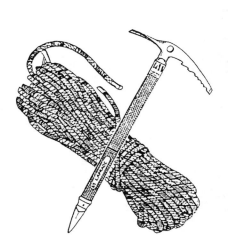
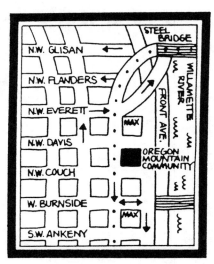

6775 SW 111TH AVENUE
BEAVERTON, OREGON 97005
PHONE: (503) 644-3517

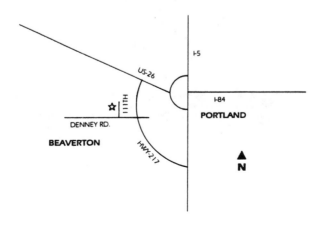